Josh

May all of your
adventures be blessed
by the Holy Spirit

Dennis

Philippians 4:6-10

No Mere Coincidences, a journey of faith

Printed in the United States of America

First Printing, 2014

ISBN-13: 978-1502560391

info@MinistryoftheSheep.org

Bible translations used, unless otherwise marked are from the
English Standard Version (ESV)
others may be
KJV~King James Version
MKJV~Modern King James Version

No Mere Coincidences, a journey of faith

# CONTENTS

## Preface

In October, 2008 I returned to the United States from Honduras, after six months of working at Fundación amor y Esperanza (Foundation Love and Hope), an orphanage operated by Impact Ministries International.

I was praying about what direction my life should take, when God led me to form Ministry of the Sheep International; A Bible based organization to meet spiritual, physical and emotional needs.

By March 2009 I had organized the ministry the best I knew how and I prayed about what I should do to get people to recognize it.

As I prayed, I felt the Holy Spirit ask, "Are you willing to walk for it?" I said that I would do anything.

The following day I found out about the National Missionary Convention, which was to be held in Peoria, IL in Mid-November and I thought "So, in November, I walk to Peoria IL?"

The very next day, I learned of the Christians United for Israel Summit, which was taking place in Washington, DC in July. Though I didn't have the funds to attend the summit, I felt that I was to make my way there.

I thought "There's a lot of time between July and mid-November and, immediately remembered The Reyes family, whom I had met in Honduras. They lived in Naples, FL and had invited me to visit them when I returned to the United States.

God made it clear to me that the journey was not so much about Ministry of the Sheep, but to reach out and care for others; to minister to the people God put in my path during the journey.

The journey was to be done on faith, relying on God for everything. I was not to ask for anything but water and a place to set my tent up. I wasn't to ask for rides but I knew that, if offered a ride, I could accept it; as it would be a chance to minister.

I wanted the journey to begin on a weekend and decided on May 30, 2009. I set my goal to average 25 miles a day and, when I finished planning the journey, I would walk into Washington, DC the day the Summit started and Peoria, IL the day the convention started.

While sharing about the journey with friends on *agapejesus.com* (now *christkorner.com*), it was recommended that I do a nightly, live video update while on the journey. We prayed about it and, within a few days, God had provided a netbook computer and wireless internet service.

It was also recommended that I keep a journal during the journey. The following is from my journal, and is about how God has every moment of our lives in his care.

I pray that the events that I lived will inspire and encourage you, the reader, to seek a closer relationship with our Father in Heaven, and open the eyes of Christians to the needs around them.

Dennis Mixer

Dedicated to Christians around the world who face ridicule, persecution, torture and even death on a daily basis to live and spread the good news of Jesus Christ.

Therefore I say to you, Do not be anxious for your life, what you shall eat, or what you shall drink; nor for your body, what you shall put on. Is not life more than food, and the body more than clothing? (Mat 6:25 MKJV)

No Mere Coincidences, a journey of faith

# THE JOURNEY BEGINS

I left Emmanuel Christian Center in Spring Lake Park, Minnesota without any fanfare. I wasn't expecting any. Although Emmanuel is a big church, not many knew about my journey. I had shared it with few outside of family, and had only shared it with Pastor Denyes and the Men's group at church.

My sister, Lois and her son, Derrick, stopped by to say goodbye on Thursday; my younger brother, Joe, and his family came over Friday to say goodbye; giving me a gift card to start my journey. Before leaving, I said farewell to my mother, then my sister, Dolores, dropped me off at the church before heading to work.

I planned to travel thirty-four miles today –in order to get out of Minneapolis –so I had my backpack on and was heading South on University Ave. by 7:30am.

It was a beautiful morning, clear and about 60 degrees; I reached the outskirts of Minneapolis in about two hours. Stopping at a Convenience store just inside the city limits, the clerk asked where I was headed. When I told her that I had just started a 4,000 mile journey she asked if I was doing it by train hopping. I told her "No, I'm walking." Her response was, "Are you crazy?" I assured her that there had never been any question that I was; but I wondered, which would be crazier, walking with an 80 pound backpack or trying to jump onto a moving train with one.

I thought I was prepared for the trip. I had walked several hundred miles, in full pack, in the past two months. While I knew that I would be getting into some good size hills, I believed it would be a few days and, they would *gradually* get bigger and steeper.

I was *wrong*! I knew I was wrong the second I saw the hill with the ski slope, southwest of Minneapolis. I remembered seeing the hill as a child, when we traveled south of the city on Highway 100. I guess I had assumed that I would be passing the hill on the highway, like we did years earlier. In those days Highway 100 was more a country highway. Now it was a limited access, multiple lane –and the route to bypass it on foot was right up the hill.

I had already carried my backpack for 8 hours. To top it off, I had finished the last of my water and had been looking for a place to refill my bottles. As I climbed the hill I had thoughts of just giving up. I know –sounds wimpy. I was tired, hot, thirsty, and my body was starting to feel like rubber; The straps of the backpack were cutting into my shoulders, and I just wanted to quit.

I don't know what made me think about it. A book came to mind; *Pilgrims' Progress* by John Bunyan; a description of how, even though he had many temptations to deal with and all this weight on his shoulders, Pilgrim kept pressing forward.

I did, of course, make it to the top of the hill, and, after what seemed like another 10 miles (though it was only about 1½), found Bush Lake Park, complete with a water faucet. I took a long break, and, had it not been that I still had several miles to go, would have considered spending the night there.

One of the hardest things I think I've ever done was to put the backpack on to continue that evening. But I did, and hiked a few more miles, finding a Burger King just in time to make the first video update, which was scheduled online.

After the update I hiked another mile or so and, after crossing the river into Shakopee, found a place to pitch my tent beside the Minnesota River. I was still a few miles short of my goal. My intent was to sleep for a couple of hours, then continue walking in order to make Lonsdale, MN for evening service at my brother's church the next night.

## Sunday-May 31, 2009

I woke up at about 1:30am. I thought about getting up and continuing, but my body just wouldn't do it. I could tell that the temperature had dropped quite a bit too.

For the past two weeks, the temperature had stayed above

60 degrees at night. I chose a lightweight sleeping bag –good to 50 degrees– to conserve space. I put a small towel over my head, but it was little help. When I awoke again, it was about 4:00, and I was shivering uncontrollably. I later discovered that the temperature had dropped into the 30's that night.

I forced myself to get up. With my sleeping bag wrapped around my shoulders, I packed everything and stepped out of the tent. The dew was so heavy that you would have thought it had just rained; and the fog covering the low areas was *thick*. Once everything else was packed, I put on a second T-shirt and rolled up the sleeping bag.

Although it was cold and damp, I couldn't escape noticing the beauty of the fog hanging over a meadow. I took a couple photos before starting on the day's trek; somewhat disappointed in myself for not having the discipline to get started earlier.

I was hoping to make it to the evening service at Triumphant Life Church in Lonsdale, MN, a church my older brother, Ron, pastored. When I confirmed with Ron that he would be home on Sunday night, he let me know that Tom Stammon would be at the church that day. Tom is the founder of *Impact Ministries International* and had helped me get started in ministry by flying me to Honduras to work at the orphanage and farm his ministry operates there.

The trail I was on ended and turned into a road, which passed under U.S. Highway 169 and paralleled County Rd 101 for a mile, *then* connected with CR101. Unfortunately, I wanted to go the other way on CR101, which meant that I had to backtrack. It would have been a relatively easy climb up the embankment to it.

But, as I was starting to learn, in *all* things, God had a plan. As soon as I started walking back, a car pulled over and a young Latino man offered me a ride. He drove me about 4 miles, which gave me a chance to talk to him about Jesus. Had I taken the shortcut, I would have missed the opportunity to witness to him. When he dropped me off, he turned around and went back the way we had come. I continued on my way, sad that I hadn't asked his name.

I pressed on, going South on Highway 13 towards Prior Lake, my body and feet still aching from the day before. After about an hour and a half I decided to stop at a convenience store to take a break.

As I was walking through the parking lot, a van pulled up and the driver asked where he could take me. I thought it was a weird way of offering a ride, but I told him that I was headed for Lonsdale. When he looked somewhat disappointed I quickly added that, any distance would be appreciated. He replied, "No, I'm supposed to take you where you need to get to today." As I climbed into the van, I gave him a ministry card. He looked at my card and exclaimed, "That explains it."

Eric, as I learned was his name, was on his way to church when he passed me, going the opposite direction, and felt that he needed to take me somewhere. He went to a gas station, got gas and two cups of coffee, and then returned to pick me up. Eric drove the remainder of the distance to Lonsdale; dropping me off just as the morning service started.

After the service Tom asked if I could share an experience from Honduras in the evening service, but said I needed to keep it to about 5 minutes. Take the most rewarding and fulfilling six months of your life, choose one experience and sum it up in five minutes. I decided to talk about how the language of God's love can change lives.

# JUNE

### Monday-June 1, 2009

It had rained during the night and the air was cool and clean. I got started at about 6:00am, walking east on Highway 19 from Lonsdale, towards Northfield, enjoying the country scenery.

About seven miles along I stopped at Highway 19 and the I-35 interchange to get something to eat. I had just gotten back on the road when a car pulled over in front of me. As I walked past the door the driver, a young man, was taking a Bible off of the passenger seat and moving it to the back seat. He then offered me a ride into Northfield.

His name was Tom and we had a good talk about teaching biblical truths without compromising the scriptures to appease men. I don't know how we happened upon that subject. Maybe he was planning on going into ministry and God wanted him to focus on teaching truth rather than worrying about the number of members his church had.

When we got into Northfield, the road I was to take was closed and Tom said that he would get me past the detour. By the time we were around the road work I was almost to Wastedo, MN, the spot I had planned on stopping for the night. Tom felt led to give me a Minnesota map, and we pray together before parting ways.

When I got to Wastedo, it was only 9:00am, so I continued walking, South on U.S. Highway 52. After about an hour, another vehicle stopped and offered me a ride. I was really surprised at the number of rides I was getting. When I planned the journey I thought that, maybe, once a week or so, someone might offer me a ride.

This man's name was also Dennis and we talked about missions and about the trip he and his son had taken the year before. Dennis was only going a few miles on Highway 52 so, after saying goodbyes and God Blesses, we parted ways and I continued walking.

I came to Zumbrota, MN –and, since I was already halfway to my next day's destination –I decided to spend the night there. After getting some lunch at a small cafe I headed to a park, searched out a pavilion and began writing my journal

It was an active park, young parents with their toddlers in the playground, groups of kids riding their bikes around, a group of teens playing volleyball, walkers and runners, softball and soccer. It was refreshing to see the small town atmosphere.

**Tuesday-June 2, 2009**

It was another cold night. I vowed that I would stop at the first store that had fleece blankets and buy one. Soon the sun was up and the air started to get warmer. I came to the town of Pine Island, not even realizing that I was supposed to go through there, and decided to take a break. Only after I looked at the directions did I discover that I was supposed to pick up the Douglas Trial at the other end of town.

Pine Island was one of those towns that time seemed to stand still for. Its Main Street was host to a church which, according to the date in one of the stained glass windows, had been built in 1900. The downtown area was nostalgic, lined with old-fashioned street lights which held hanging baskets full of blooming flowers. Occasionally, I would come upon a house that brought back memories of my grandparents' home; Houses that, in times past, might have been decorated with red, white and blue banners across their front porch for the fourth of July. Their yard filled with tables of food and folding chairs full of relatives and friends; sitting around drinking grandma's famous lemonade, while young kids ran around with sparklers. If the cars were older you would think you had entered a time warp and were actually *in* the 1960's.

At some point along my walk through the past, I missed my turn onto Douglas Trail. I did, however, come across County road 3, which went south, so I took it. After walking a while I thought I was seeing things; a quarter mile ahead, I saw a tractor, pulling a wagon, with two horses behind it. My first thought was, "this guy has the cart before the horses." I asked the man – whose name was Weiss –about the Douglas Trail. He told me that it would cross the road I was on a few miles ahead. Of course, before I left, I had to ask about his activities. Weiss, who was probably in his late 70's, was preparing the horses for a Wagon Train trip, later in the year.

I continued walking, following the directions Weiss had given me. I began wondering how much further I would travel before coming upon the Douglas Trail. Just about this time a car went past, the first one that I had seen on that road. The car stopped, backed up and the driver offered me a ride to Rochester.

I introduced myself to him, and he told me he went by "Lucky" –a name which, for some reason, I associate with an older, skinny white guy wearing a fishing hat. I don't know why, I just do. This Lucky however, was a young African-American, over 6' tall, and about 275 lbs. He seemed to me more like a football player nicknamed "Moose" or "Bear."

As it turned out, Lucky wasn't normally on this road; he had taken a friend to a nearby town and was on his way home. He took me to the edge of Rochester, which gave me about 15 minutes to share Christ with him. It also put me further ahead of schedule, which I really hadn't planned for; I had arranged to spend a night with my nephew, Andrew, and his new wife, Merica, when I got to Lewiston-- on Thursday.

I walked into downtown Rochester. There, I saw a man sitting on a bench outside the door of a business. As I walked by I heard him ask a lady if he could ask her a question. Curious now, I sat on a bench on the other side of the doors, and just watched and listened for a while.

Eventually, a young lady came out of the business and sat beside me to smoke a cigarette. About the same time, a man I had seen talking to the one sitting on the bench, came by. I asked him what the man was asking everyone and he said he was asking if they wanted a free ticket to heaven. The young lady sitting next to me laughed and said, "Yeah, today! Yesterday he was yelling at people that they were going to hell... One day he was right up in my face calling me a whore."

I thought about the time Jesus said "Many will come in my name, claiming that 'I am he', but will lead many astray." How many people had this man pushed away from God because he was claiming that Jesus was Lord, yet his actions didn't show Christ?

I talked to the young lady about what it truly means to be a Christian and, as her break ended, I gave her a card and asked her if she would go to the website and click on the "R U Saved" button. She said she would, and I pray that she did.

After walking out of Rochester a few miles, and not finding any churches, I set up camp beside the train tracks. I made a small fire, making a mental note to buy some marshmallows.

**Wednesday-June 3, 2009**

Another cold night! I regretted not taking time to buy a blanket in Rochester.

Breaking camp, I made my way East on Highway 14 towards St. Charles, MN. I came to the town of Dover a few hours later and opted for the grill part of a Bar & Grill for some lunch. There was one other customer inside; a young lady in Military BDUs.

I ordered a meal and, a few minutes later, the young lady asked me where I was headed. I told her, giving her a card, and answered her questions about my journey. The meal came and I ate, washing it down with a coke, then paid my tab and said my goodbyes. The young lady said that she lived in Lewiston, and, if she saw me along the road, she would give me a ride. I thanked her and explained that I didn't want to get there until the next night, then continued on my way.

About a mile outside of town I came to a creek that was flowing with clear, sparkling water. By now the sun was getting hot and the water –after not bathing for two days –was looking very inviting. I found a secluded place to put on a pair of shorts and took my first cold water bath since leaving Honduras.

After drying off, I walked to St. Charles, MN. That evening I found Faith Lutheran Church on the east outskirts of the city limit. Behind it was a large yard, with a nice cushion of thick grass. The night wasn't as cold as it had been and the ground was level and smooth, so I had a good night's sleep.

**Thursday-June 4, 2009**

I awoke this morning at about 5:00. Tonight I would be at my nephew's home in Lewiston. Andrew and Merica had just been married in December, and would be having their first child

14

–which was due Christmas Day.

As I walked, I noticed what appeared to be buggy-wheel tracks and hoof prints on the shoulder. I kept looking for road signs, like they had in Missouri, letting drivers know to watch for horse drawn vehicles, but I never saw any.

I came to County Road 37, where the map instructions told me to turn. Turning onto a gravel road, I soon noticed buggy tracks and hoof prints on this road as well.

After a short distance, I saw a sight I hadn't seen since leaving Missouri two years prior, Amish wagons and buggies. There were two barns and Holstein cows. I also noticed a refrigeration unit, like they use on semi-trailers. To me that meant one thing in an Amish area; Fresh milk!

I made my way to a barn. Above the door was a sign that named Allen & Mary Detweiler and family as the owners. I found Mr. Detweiler and his family busy milking the cows; there were the adults, a young man in his late teens and two young boys, their hats worn and faces dirty. The scene was something that, as a photographer, I found hard to resist. However, the Amish don't believe in having their pictures taken and I was respectful, leaving cameras in their cases.

One thing I have learned about the Amish is that, while they don't want outsiders polluting their children's minds with the things of this world, they are very non-judging of strangers. True to my expectations, I was greeted warmly and, after visiting with Mr. Detweiler for a few minutes, I asked if I might buy some milk from him. After surrendering a bottle of water to the parched ground, I had a bottle of fresh, non-pasteurized, non-homogenized whole milk. If you've never had 'real' milk, you don't understand the pleasure I had, savoring every drop. I left, regretting that I had no way to carry and keep a *gallon* of it.

As I continued along the gravel road, I thought about the vastness of the farm land. I remember, as a child, hearing stories of people whose neighbors were a mile away, and of waiting hours for a doctor to make it to their house when someone was ill. It really gave me a new respect for our parents and grandparents –though I *still* have a hard time believing the parts about walking 10 miles to and from school in 5 feet of snow…UPHILL both ways.

Ironically, the next hill I climbed seemed *impossibly* long. But, at the last mile, I was offered a ride into town, and finally made it to Lewiston. It was still early so I walked around to see what it had to offer, then sat at a roadside park writing.

About 2:15pm, I called Andrew, only to find out that he had been home until about a half hour before, and was now at work. Still, he gave me directions to his house and let me know that Merica would be home before long.

Finding the house was not so easy. I found the road, but it just went around to another one, so I went back to where I had turned and was trying to figure out what to do, as the other way appeared to go back into the downtown area.

About that time I heard my name being called and, when I looked around, I saw the young lady from the grill in Dover. It turned out that she lived on that corner. She asked if I had found my nephew and, when I told her the directions, told me that the road, though it looked as it went into town, actually curved back south, ending in a cul-de-sac.

That evening I enjoyed a home cooked meal with Andrew and Merica; and was entertained by Merica's story of how she almost killed her parents' dog; which began with the explanation of how, several years prior, she came to be in possession of the preserved organs of a deer and a cow.

### Friday-June 5, 2009

I woke up at 4:30. I had promised Andrew that I would wake him before leaving. I got my things packed, prayed and read my Bible until about 6:00 before waking him up. Before leaving Andrew and I prayed together, asking for safety and guidance.

I knew I was in for a long day. While plotting the day by day route I had, for some reason, planned on 32 miles for today. Don't ask me why –I could only trust that God had a purpose.

Walking mile after mile of deserted country road, I wasn't even finding a spot to take my backpack off and rest. Occasionally I would come to a spot where a sign indicated a town, but saw nothing but an occasional house. I came to a T-intersection with Interstate 90 paralleling it just a few hundred feet away.

I finally saw an exit, but when I reached the intersection, there was nothing but a big truck dealership/repair shop and a warehouse. I went to the truck shop and got permission to use their restroom and refill my water bottles, but as there was really no place to rest, I headed back on my way, walking another hour before coming to another spot I could stop.

Here, there was only a store with farming products. It did have a nice little hill with a large tree for shade so, I decided to stop there for lunch. With a sandwich and a bottle of water in me, I took a short nap under the tree before leaving.

I had walked another hour when I came upon a Llama ranch. As I approached, all the Llamas got up and, as I passed them, started to walk with me. A couple of the younger ones would run ahead, stop and stand there watching me, like they were saying, "Why so slow old man?" When I got up to them, they would run ahead again.

It was another half hour before I came to the next intersection. I was beginning to think I had missed a road somewhere, as, to me, it seemed that I should have gotten to my turn by then. Pulling out the map that Tom had given me on the third day, I tried to find the road I was supposed to turn on. About that time a car stopped and the driver wanted to know where I was headed. I told him and, though he didn't know where it was, he offered me a ride to a restaurant where I could get directions.

After dropping me off, he turned around and went back the way he had come. It really amazed that almost everyone who had given me rides to this point had gone out of their way and had to turn around to get where they were going.

There were only two things at this intersection, a mechanics garage and the restaurant. By this time it was about 4:00pm and I was getting hungry. When I got inside I ordered a sandwich and asked directions to Pine Creek. The waitress didn't know where it was but directed me to another customer whom, according to her, knew where everything was. As it turned out, the road I wanted was the intersection I was at. After hearing about my journey, the man gave me the names of some "good people along the way."

After eating, I headed down the road, coming to my turn a couple miles later. A short distance further the road started angling downward and kept going downward, and downward, and the sides of the road soon became cliffs. All I could think as I walked downhill was, eventually I'm going to have to walk uphill to get out of this.

The road finally stopped descending and began winding through a beautiful valley. At about 7:00pm I decided that I had better find someplace to spend the night. I came to a house where a lady was out front. Giving her my ministry card, I asked about pitching my tent beside their garage. After checking with her husband, who said it was no problem, she introduced herself as Denise, her husband, Dean, and her son, Paul.

I got my tent up just at 8:00pm and then tried to get online. No signal for the computer. So I tried to call on the phone to let someone know that I wouldn't be able to do the online update; nothing there either. Dean told me that they don't get cell phone signals there –but asked if I wanted supper, so I had a nice dinner. Afterward, we sat up until almost 10:00, chatting.

**Saturday-June 6, 2009**

I had a dream last night. In my dream all the kids from the home in Honduras were with me. As I played games with them, they thanked me for showing them God's love.

As they were thanking me they started to change, going from the happy kids they were, to scared, hurt and hungry kids. Then, they became *different* kids; kids that had never known love and never knew when they would eat again; Kids in clothes they had found or stolen –clothes that hadn't been washed in weeks.

These kids wanted to know why I hadn't visited *them*, to show them God's love. They wanted to know why I had never told them about Jesus; why I had never given them anything to eat or tended their wounds. They wanted to know why I had never comforted them on a stormy night. As the dream ended and I was waking, the kids I worked with were back. The last thing I heard them say was "*Te Quiero*". For a few minutes I could only lay there, crying and talking to God.

When I did get up, I emptied my backpack and did a little sewing on a seam that was ripping out, ate a banana and granola bar and, after thanking my host, I headed on through the valley.

Pine Creek, named after the creek that snaked its way through the valley, was truly beautiful. It was a mixture of produce farms, dairy farms, people who liked the simple life, and others whose homes were 10 acre showplaces. There was even one spot that reminded me of an old commune of hippies; about 20 acres of garden and green-houses, with several people out working it by hand.

There was the "Gator Golf Range" though I don't recall seeing any gators in Minnesota before. Then, there was the farm that had old shotguns welded on top of old wagon wheels and a sign that stated "NO TRESPASSING, INCLUDING PUBLIC OFFICIALS AND AGENTS THERE OF" –one of those things that make you go; "Hmmm".

As I had realized the night before, roads that go down must eventually go up. And it did. And it went up more, and about the time I didn't think I could take one more step upward, I got to the top and there was the city of La Crescent, MN. After resting a few minutes at a park, I headed through town, towards the bridge that would take me across the Mississippi River, into La Crosse, WI.

As I was making my to the bridge it started to drizzle and I could tell that it wasn't going to stop anytime soon. I hadn't gotten very far when a van pulled up beside me and a lady offered me a ride into La Crosse, which I gladly accepted. Once in town I continued South on U.S. 14/61 but, as I did, the drizzle turned into a sprinkle. It was at this point, as I passed a tattoo parlor, I heard someone yelling to me. The owner of the parlor wanted to know if I would like an umbrella.

An umbrella is one of the last things I would expect to find in a tattoo parlor. He gave me one, making me promise not to throw it out when I was done with it, but to give it to someone else. Shortly after that it started to *pour* rain. At first I tried to take refuge in a bus stop shelter, but as the water was being splashed up into it, I decided to make a break for an A&W restaurant across the street.

The restaurant was really nostalgic, complete with high stools and tables and a jukebox. There was a group of kids there from a Catholic school in St. Paul, MN. They were the school choir and were in La Crosse for a singing competition. A Priest went up to the jukebox, studied it for a minute, and put a coin in. "Stand by Me" starts playing and one of the kids begins to sing along, then another and another and soon everyone in the restaurant is singing. I almost felt like I was on a movie set or something.

The rain finally stopped and I was able to get on my way again. I was traveling a bit slower because the backpack had gotten wet and, while I had my things in plastic bags, the backpack itself held a good ten pounds of water.

I had pretty much decided that I wasn't going to make my goal of Coon Valley, WI that day, when a car pulled up. The two ladies in the car offered me a ride and I loaded everything into the back seat. It turned out that Gail and C.J., as they introduced themselves, had just decided to go for a drive that afternoon and, seeing me, decided that their drive would take them where ever I was going. We headed out and shortly came to a hill. We went uphill for what seemed like miles and, when we reached the top, there was Coon Valley. Gail and C.J. dropped me off and then turned around and went back the way we had come.

Coon Valley was a quaint little town. It had a Church, a convenience store, and a few shops. There was a Library that had a lion-shaped drinking fountain in front, and a bar that had a sign prohibiting snowmobile parking. Then there was the Rustic Valley Family Center.

Rustic Valley Family Center is a catchall. There's space for about six travel trailers to hook up, a Fitness Center and a pizza shop with an old fashioned ice cream parlor. I went inside and was warmly greeted by a man named Ken. He asked about my backpack and, when I told him about my journey, he offered me a place to pitch my tent behind one of the trailer spots. I asked him if the fitness center had a shower I might use, and he pointing me in the direction of the shower.

When I was done, I went back to the pizza shop. Although it sounded good, I had just eaten at the A&W. But, since it had been years since I'd had a good, Old-Fashioned malt, I did order a strawberry banana malt.

After sitting inside for a while, I went out to pitch my tent. As it happened, while I was pulling the tent poles out, the piece that supports the lip over the door went flying. In that area there were hundreds of square feet of ground covered in grass, a paved area big enough for a large RV and two 3" pipes –one for the water valve and the other for the sewer line. Guess where the poles went. Right down a pipe, and by now it was dark. I got the tent set up first, as it was starting to sprinkle again, then, with my flashlight, went to see about the pole. Thankfully, it had fallen into the pipe for the water line instead of the sewage and, with the help of my emergency fishing kit, I retrieved it.

## Sunday-June 7, 2009

Sunday morning! The rain had stopped and the sky was clear. A weather front had passed through during the night with dry air and a good breeze. The tent was dry except for the bottom. I quickly got everything packed and was soon on my way. There was a church in town, but, not wanting to wait half the day to attend it, thought I might find a country church along the way to attend.

Fifteen minutes after I started walking a car passed me,

turned around, and came back; the driver offering a ride. He introduced himself as Ed and asked where I was headed. I told him where the directions told me to turn and he asked where that was supposed to take me. When I answered Viola, WI., He said he would take me there. As it turned out, the only reason Ed was on the road at that time of morning was because his niece's fiance had asked him for a ride, to spend the day with her at a hospital.

Viola was a small town, which made claim to being the heart of Kickapoo Valley. It had a storefront which sported a wall made of deer antlers and a local newspaper; the Epitaph-News. The hours posted were Monday-Friday mornings *and*, 'per chance, Wednesday afternoon'.

I saw a church steeple and made my way to the United Methodist church. Going inside, I was greeted by a group of ladies. After setting my backpack down I introduced myself to the ladies and was taken to the office to meet the pastor.

Pastor Lavern was a joyful woman, who asked me about Ministry Of The Sheep and told me about working with a ministry in Northeastern Uganda. Later, during the service she introduced me and had me tell the congregation about my journey and ministry.

After the service, just about everyone came up to me and greeted me, wishing me well in the ministry and on the journey. One lady, whose name escaped me, came up and said that she felt led to offer me a ride to Richland Center. Although I hadn't told them which way I was headed, Richland Center was to be my next destination. She told me she would pick me up at the local convenience store in about an hour. After saying the last goodbyes, I collected all my gear and made my way to the store, where I got something to eat and then went outside to enjoy the weather.

While I was waiting, a car with a young couple pulled up and to get gas. The young man went inside and paid; when he came back out he asked about the backpack and we started talking. After a few minutes he asked me the question: "Where will you go when you die?" When I told him I planned on spending eternity in heaven, he asked why I thought I would go to heaven. I had to smile at this. My guess is that this young man, whom I learned was Casey, was a fan of Ray Comfort.

We had a great talk about how, 'being a good person' doesn't get you to heaven, nor does asking forgiveness one time, when you are 12 years old, and then living however you want the rest of your life. Casey had a very good grasp on repentance being a turning from the sin and grace being a chance for redemption, not a license to sin. It was very refreshing to find a young person so full of truth and on fire for God.

My ride showed up and I got to Richland Center within minutes instead of hours. I spent some time at a restaurant, using their WI-FI, then started looking for a church that had an evening service. I found a Church of the Nazarene that had an evening Bible Study that started at 6:00. I got there a few minutes early and Pastor Charles Hayes greeted me. Soon, a few more people showed up.

We had a nice, open discussion study on forgiveness, and afterward I got a chance to talk to some of the members about the journey. Some were wondering where I was going to spend the night and I told them the location.

Going back to the area with the restaurants, I went into one and got my computer set up just in time for the 8:00 update. As there were no churches around the restaurants, I found a place behind one of the businesses, that was somewhat secluded. As I got into the tent, it started sprinkling and I could tell that there was a storm headed my direction.

## Monday-June 8, 2009

What a night! The sprinkling turned into a downpour and I awakened a few minutes after midnight to discover that my pillow was wet. Then I rolled over, into a pool of water on the tent floor. The wind was whipping the cover of the tent around and, as it did, the water was coming in. I had tried to anchor the tent down when I set it up, but the spot that I had chosen had no soil, just gravel with grass growing through it.

I had considered moving the tent, but with the rain getting closer I figured that, between me and the backpack, I would be fine. I did my best to keep the water to one side of the tent. Failing in that, I then –spread eagle –tried to keep the corners of the tent down with my feet and hands.

I actually did manage to get a little more sleep, and finally got up at about 4:45. I had just about everything packed when one of the men from the church pulled up. He had been concerned about me, in the storm, throughout the night and wanted to check on me as soon as he got up. He also gave me a little money to get something to eat with. As we talked, he assured me that everything was downhill to Madison, WI. I thanked him and he headed on his way.

I got breakfast and then I found a store; buying a small fleece blanket and a sweatshirt before leaving town, heading for Spring Green WI. The walk to Spring Green was easy and uneventful. I made it there by 3:30 and, as I had been told, it was all downhill.

At first glance, I thought Spring Green was just a spot on the map. There didn't seem to be much there except a gas station and a lumber yard. However, as there was a chain restaurant behind the gas station, I decided there must be more than meets the eye. I found someone to ask about the location of a Laundromat –which by now I was in much need of –and found it without trouble.

*Be not forgetful to entertain strangers: for thereby some have entertained angels unawares. (Hebrews 13:2)*

The first thing I did was go into the bathroom, cleaning myself up and changing into a pair of shorts and T-shirt. That done, I soaped up all my clothes. I had gotten used to bar laundry soap in Honduras–and it was easier to carry and cheaper than buying little boxes at Laundromat.

I hadn't thought about it as I haven't used a Laundromat in years, but, I had no change. I had one $1.00 bill and a $10.00 bill. To top it off, the change machine wouldn't work. There was one other person in the Laundromat, a man of about 60, with unkempt hair and beard. He had a rough look to him and looked like he might be homeless.

He saw me trying to put the bill into the change machine and said, 'That machine doesn't take tens.' My first thought was that this man was watching me. He offered to take my $10.00 bill to the bank so I didn't have to put everything into my backpack wet and then tote it the four blocks to the bank. I wondered, if I give him the ten dollars, would I ever see the man or the money again. There were clothes in a dryer, but I had no way of knowing if they were his or not.

As I was thinking this, the Holy Spirit asked me why I was judging him because of his appearance. I gave the man the $10.00 and he left. He was back, within a few minutes in fact, and with a roll of quarters. I thanked him and proceeded to put change into the machines. I was planning to buy him something to drink once the washing machines were running, but, without me noticing, and in the few short seconds that it took me to put quarters in the washing machine, The man was gone. The clothes that had been in the dryer were gone as well. There had been no cars outside the Laundromat and there was no sign of him in the area. I have often wondered if the man might have been an angel, sent to test me.

I moved on once my laundry was done, and headed towards the downtown area. Like many small towns, they roll up the sidewalks at 5:00pm, and there isn't much open. I found a group of people, in what looked like a little park, between the buildings. Many of the people were dressed in bib overalls and straw hats. One was in dress pants, white shirt, black vest and a top hat which had a well worn look to it.

I approached the group and asked a man if it was a play, private function or what. He told me it was a private party, but invited me to stay. As I was taking a ministry card out for him, he offered me a beer, which I declined, and after looking at the card, he offered me a coke or lemonade. I accepted the lemonade and he went off to get it.

It turned out that it was a birthday party for a woman named Diane, who works at the bank. Diane came over with a small pet carrier; a piglet in it, which was her birthday present. I asked about getting a picture of her with it, and she and the piglet posed for the camera.

I found out that the 'park' was the patio of a restaurant so, wishing Diane a happy birthday and thanking the man for the lemonade, I went around the corner to the entrance. The restaurant was named The Shed. Inside, I found out from the waitress, Luanne, that Diane's party had been a surprise party. Her co-workers and members of her card club had arranged it and, as she apparently loves gardening, decided on a 'Green Acres' theme, hence the outfits. After enjoying a cup of soup, I left to the sounds of the group behind the restaurant singing the theme song from Green Acres.

Two blocks later I found the city park and what seemed to be the rest of the town that weren't at the birthday party. There were two softball games going on and it seemed like everyone was in attendance. Across the street was Christ Lutheran Church and, as there were people there, I went to see if I could find the pastor. I didn't, but I did find a very helpful man named Mike who obtained permission to set up for the night.

### Tuesday-June 9, 2009

LAZY! That's my only excuse. That and the fact that I had barely slept the previous night –I didn't get up until almost 6:30am.

I had been awakened sometime around 1:00am by the voices of what sounded like three teenage boys, cutting through the churchyard. I listened as they passed by to make sure they didn't have any mischief in mind. As I drifted back to sleep, I had to smile as I thought of the time my brother, Joe, and I had a sleep over with some of our friends.

I was about 12 or so. One of our friends had gotten hold of some fire crackers and we sneaked out in the early morning hours, lighting the firecrackers off in the city park. I don't remember seeing my dad run before, but, when I saw the dark figure trotting across the field, I knew we were busted.

I woke up again at 4:30 and decided to sleep for just a few more minutes. The few minutes turned into two hours. I quickly packed and headed down Highway 14 towards Cross Plains, WI.

A little way out of town was an old bridge, the kind with the metal works over the top of it. It looked like it was about half a mile long. In order to cross the river, I would have to walk across the bridge, with almost no shoulder.

As I crossed it, I could see the waters below me swirling and churning and I knew the last thing I wanted to do was get blown over when a semi truck went past me. With the backpack on, it not only sets me off balance a little, but it also acts as a wind catcher. Whenever a truck was passing by, I would stop and grab hold of a beam.

About a mile after I made it across the bridge there was a historical marker where I could get away from the road a bit. As I hadn't stopped for breakfast I thought I'd make a sandwich. As soon as I pulled my arm from one strap of the backpack, I felt the other strap give; one of the plastic fasteners had broken.

God had prepared me for this though, as a fastener had broken while training. I hadn't thought of equipment failure until then. When I went to get parts to fix it, I made sure I bought a few extra in case it happened again. Once it was fixed, I set upon my way –without eating. Another mile up the road, however, I came to Peck's Farm Market.

The sign said that Peck's Farm Market had been a family business since 1889. Besides the variety of fruits and vegetables, Amish made canned goods other country goodies, It had a petting zoo with different animals, including an alligator.

I made a sandwich with the last of my peanut butter and my last banana, washed it down with a bottle of local root beer and continued on my way. A short while later I was offered a ride by a man in a pickup truck. I asked his name, but he never did tell me. Instead, he asked where I was headed and I told him, along with talking about the ministry; He questioned the ministry name.

As I was telling him the meaning and the biblical significance of it, he changed the subject. He commented that I should get a car instead of walking. I got the feeling that, despite his kindness, he had no knowledge of God or Jesus –he actually seemed to be afraid of hearing about them.

When we came to the town Mazomanie he abruptly pulled over to the side of the road, making the excuse of having to take care of some business down a road we had just passed. I felt that there were forces at work to keep this man from hearing about God. I thanked him, he made a U-turn and was gone.

A couple of blocks later, I came to the edge of town and County Road KP, which was my next turn. Not far ahead, I came to Lake Marion; a small man-made lake with a park built around it. On top of a high hill across the street, 'Old Glory' flew High above the pine trees.

There was a mother with two daughters there trying to catch a frog with a minnow net, and two men, spending the early afternoon fishing. It was the type of park that I could sit in for hours, but that wouldn't get me where I needed to go.

I came to Cross Plains, WI. There wasn't much on the main road, but I did find a Subway, and, as it was getting late, went inside to get ready for the update. A couple of the young employees were curious about my adventure and I was able to witness to them for a few minutes.

As I left Subway my phone beeped, indicating that I had a message but, when I went to check it, I wasn't getting a signal. I figured I would check it the next day, when I got into an area with better phone service.

I walked out of town and came to an area that was neatly mowed, with the sign welcoming travelers to Cross plains and a grove of pine trees edging it. I found a spot in the pines and made camp for the night.

## Wednesday-June 10, 2009
*"Woe to you, scribes and Pharisees, hypocrites!..."*

No Mere Coincidences, a journey of faith

I was on my way early this morning.  I had about 30 miles to cover and the road was heavily traveled as it led into Madison. It also *did not* have a paved shoulder and the gravel shoulder was Steeply angled on both sides of the road.  I would walk along one side for a while, then, when my feet got sore, I would cross the road to the other side.  As I walked I could feel blisters forming on my heels, the sides of my feet and under my big toes.

There wasn't really much between Cross Plains and Middleton.  Once in Middleton I found a church, looking for a place to clean up.  I will refrain from naming any denomination, as I don't want to embarrass anyone.

At the church office, the door was locked, but there was a buzzer –so I rang it.  The door was answered by a lady and, after giving her my card and explaining my journey, I asked if there might be a restroom I could use brush my teeth and shave.  The lady kind of hem-hawed around, then asked someone further in the building about a shelter.  I let her know that I didn't need a shelter, just a sink.  She said that their pastor had just stepped out the back door and I could ask him.

When I approached, he was talking to a man, whom I believe was the caretaker.  I gave him my card and told him a little about myself, then asked if there might be somewhere I could shave.  He immediately said, "Not really."  I explained that I was representing my ministry and my Heavenly Father, and didn't want to be looked at as being a 'derelict'.

He stood, staring at the ministry card for a moment, then asked the caretaker if there was a restroom with an outlet near the sink.  I told him I didn't need an outlet, just a sink, and he finally told the caretaker to show me one of the restrooms.

I was shocked.  Isaiah 58 and Matthew 25 both talk about caring for others, yet it took this pastor, being told who I was and what I was about, nearly 10 minutes to decide to let me use a restroom.  What if I had led him to believe I *was* homeless?

For myself, had I not known God, I would have walked away very bitter towards 'Christians' because of the experience. As it was, I did leave wondering "If this is how the shepherd acts, what the sheep are like?" and the words of Jesus, speaking to the religious leaders of the day, came to mind; *"Woe to you, scribes and Pharisees, hypocrites! For you travel across sea and land to make a single proselyte, and when he becomes a proselyte, you make him twice as much a child of hell as yourselves."(Matthew 23:15 ESV)*

I went on, making my way south on University Avenue into Madison, and an hour or so later found a spot to take a break. I figured I would check out who had called me the night before. That was when I discovered that I had lost my phone. I remembered leaving it out of the backpack that morning, but, I didn't remember picking it up. When I hoisted my backpack onto my shoulders it probably went flying, and was now lying under the pine trees in Cross Plains.

As I continued on through Madison, a spry 50 year old, using a cane, walked up beside me. He started to talk to me about my backpack and I told him about my journey. I learned that his name was Michael and, having recently being released from prison, was in a transition house. He talked about getting his life straightened out as he had two children, one in his teens and another 20 year old, that he needed to make up for not being there for as they grew up. I told him that the best way to stay on the narrow path was to give his life to God and strive to become like Jesus. We walked and talked for a few blocks, then came to where Michael had to turn. Before parting ways we spent a moment praying on the sidewalk.

As I walked through Downtown Madison the street names changed, and soon, I wasn't sure I was on the right road; either I hadn't come to the intersection where I was supposed to turn or, I had missed it. I remembered that Highway 12 would take me to Highway 51 south, so I asked a store employee which direction Highway 12 was and headed that way.

The directions had me meet up with John Nolan Road, and follow it to the highway. John Noland Road made its way around Lake Mendota. It was a scenic walk, with people out jogging, walking, bicycling and fishing, and the afternoon traffic rushing around. I took some pictures of the skyline of Downtown Madison over the lake, and a couple of men fishing –one of whom looked like he could play the lead in the Old Man and the Sea, by Hemingway.

I finally came to Highway 12 and, as it looked like a busy highway, I watched for signs excluding pedestrians. Not seeing any, I continued walking onto the highway and walked for a good two miles. I was crossing a bridge just a short distance from Highway 51, when all of a sudden there was a Deputy Sheriff's truck behind me. The deputy got out, walked around the vehicle and, with deep concern in his voice said, "What are you doing, you can't walk out here, it's dangerous!" I told him that I had watched for signs as I entered the highway and saw none. He said there were signs at all the entrances. When I told him I entered on John Noland and he said, "That's the only one that's not posted." He said he was going to take me off the highway, and helped me put my backpack into his vehicle.

I gave him one of my cards and asked his name. He said his name was Bob. Deputy Bob drove me to Highway 51, then south a little to get me out of the main city traffic. He was talking about how dangerous it was, walking on a highway like I was. I involuntarily chuckled, and then apologized, telling him that I didn't mean to sound disrespectful, but, walking down the highway was safe compared to some situations I had been in during my life.

I think the biggest danger of me walking down the highway would be the driver, too busy watching the fat old man with the backpack, instead of the car in front of them.

Anyway, I made it through Madison, and continued walking south on Highway 51. After a couple hours, I came to a small bar & grill. By now I had finished most of my water, and wanted to see about getting more.

I asked the bartender about getting some water, and he said no problem; as I was taking my pack off to get my bottles, he put a large glass of ice water on the bar. Realizing I wanted the bottles filled, he asked if I wanted some ice in the bottles too.

I sat down next to a Native American lady, who had the most classic looking, round face and a smile that would give the sun competition. She asked where I was hiking to and I told her about the journey and the ministry, giving her, the bartender and a couple other customers each one of the ministry cards, telling them about the meaning of the ministry name. I find that is a good way to start talking about Jesus without people being turned off right away –somewhat of a gospel icebreaker.

Six miles later I reached Lake Kegosa. I came to a little bar & grill, and, as it was already 7:45pm, I went in. It wasn't the type of place I would take a family with children. I think that, on weekends, it would be reminiscent of "The Boar's Nest" from the Dukes of Hazard, complete with the waitress wearing 'Daisy Duke' shorts. Nonetheless, I ordered dinner and prepared for the update.

I didn't get done online until well after 9:00, then I set out to find a place to sleep, finding a clear area in the trees, although it was covered with vines. I set my tent up and, as I lay there, began to realize how sore my feet really were. Walking on the slanted shoulders had left large blisters on them and I wasn't able to lie on my back with my heels on the ground. I had to lay my feet onto their sides, and even then, I could still feel the blood pulsating through them.

Even with my throbbing feet, and lying on the vines, I managed to fall asleep.

**Thursday-June 11, 2009**
When I woke up the next morning I stepped out of the tent; only to find that there was a clearing, with soft soil and dry leaves not 5 feet away, on the other side of a large tree limb. I probably would have slept much better there, but I wasn't going to stay there all day to find out. I decided that, as I was a day ahead of schedule, and because my feet were blistered from the day before, I would take a couple of easy days and split my next destination up into a two day journey.

I got everything packed and headed down the road. Within

a quarter mile I came to a gas station, where I went in and got a cup of coffee. As it had been a few days since I had actually showered, I asked the cashier about a park or beach at the lake. I found out that there was only one public access, and it was on the other side of the lake. She did tell me there was a large church just inside of town.

I thanked her and headed on my way, walking close to two miles before I came to the road I had been told to take. I finally came to Lake View Church, a large Evangelical Free church. I found the office doors, but they didn't open until 8:00, so I waited for people to show up. One lady arrived a few minutes before 8:00, but not wanting to frighten her, I waited for another one to arrive. Then I went up and asked if there was a place I might clean up.

The ladies said that there was, and, if I would wait for one of the men to arrive, I could use it. They invited me in and asked if I had eaten yet that morning and offered me some oatmeal. Their names were Jeanne and Julie. Shortly, Pastor Graham arrived and they showed me a restroom, which had a shower in it.

This was a little bit of heaven. When people ask me what I missed the most in Honduras, the answer is 'Hot showers'. We did have running water some of the time, but there were no water heaters. When we didn't have running water, we'd have to carry a bucket upstairs from the cistern and then dump the cold water on ourselves a scoop at a time.

After shaving and taking a long shower, I went back to the office, where Pastor Graham offered me a cup of coffee. Julie said that she had stopped at the market that morning, and she offered me some fruit to take with me, which I accepted. I spent a couple hours after that catching up on my journal, and then told the ladies in the office that I would be leaving and thanked them for their kindness. Jeanne, Julie and another lady, Tara, gathered around, praying for me. I left feeling I had experienced the epitome of Christianity.

My intent was to leave town and make my way to Albion, WI. Instead, I ended up still being in Lake Kegosa two hours later. First, I found a store to replace my surge protector which I had left in Cross Plains, then I visited a couple Antique shops and spent time walking around enjoying the Scandinavian town. As I was about to leave, I heard my name and, looking, saw Julie, from the church, waving goodbye to me.

At last out of town, I walked most the way to Albion before getting a ride from an older man named Ed, who drove me to Albion and left me at the city park, where there was a pavilion where I could sit and write.

As I was sitting there typing and watching two men prepared a foundation form, a third man started talking to me. His name was Bob Venski, and he was one of the Township Directors. Bob was telling me about the Township and about the local baseball team, The Tigers, who played there every Sunday. Then he told me that if I needed to eat somewhere that night I should eat at Ray's Family Restaurant in Edgerton and told me how to get there.

As I continued typing a couple of men showed up at the ball field and soon were joined by a few more. I went over to them and asked if they were the local team that Bob had been so proud of. Learning that they were, and asked if I could get a photo of them. They said that I could, but if I waited a few minutes, more would show up.

As I waited, I talked with the leader, letting him know about the ministry, and its purpose and goals. And I told him about my journey of faith. He too told me that if I needed a place to eat, I should try Ray's Family Restaurant.

The rest the team got there and I took a photo, thanked them and left, with them wishing me the best with my journey. When I came to the intersection I thought Bob had told me to take to get to Edgerton, I asked a man laying some water lines if that was the right way to go to. He said it was, and then said if I waited a minute he was headed that way. I told him about the ministry and my journey, we talked about Jesus a bit and then he told me if I needed to eat someplace I should try Ray's.

I decided that if three people told me to try this restaurant, then maybe I should try it so, I asked him to drop me off as near there as he was going. He dropped me off in the parking lot, I thanked him and then he turned around and went the way we had just come from.

Ray's was a nostalgic restaurant; with a counter where you could sit, as well as tables and booths. The young waitress, Joanna, was friendly without being flirtatious and the service was quick. As I sat there enjoying a Gyro and soup, an older man came in and was seated behind me. A few minutes later, Joanna sat down by the man and went over all the items on the menu, explaining what it came with and how it was prepared. I assumed that the man must be experiencing Ray's for the first time as well, but later it was clear that this was a nightly routine with the gentleman and the waitresses.

I could have sat there for the rest of the night enjoying the friendly atmosphere, but as Ray's closed at 8:00 I had to leave and find a place to do my nightly update. After walking several blocks I found a city park that had a band playing oldies at the pavilion; which seemed to be the only place with an outlet.

Next to the city park was a VFW where I found an outlet on the back porch of the building. Hoping they wouldn't mind, I set up on the porch and had a good chat with several friends that night, then stayed on chatting with my brother, Joe until almost 10:00pm. As it was late and I was too tired to find another place to sleep, I set-up my tent on the porch.

**Friday-June 12, 2009**

Once again made it through the night without interruption. I and went to a convenience store, buying a couple donuts and coffee for breakfast. As I was still taking an easy day for my feet to recuperate, I returned to the VFW and sat working on my journal some more. At about 11:00 I decided that I had better move on towards Milton.

I walked the ten miles or so and, just as I came to the Milton city limit, I saw a church, about a block to the right –but in order to get there I had to go one block into town, one block right and then back.

You may have heard it said that God's timing is perfect. He is never early nor is He ever late. He is always right on time. I have found this to be so true during the Journey. For instance, had I left Rustic Valley Family Center in Coon Valley, WI a few minutes later, I would have missed a ride all the way to Viola, had I missed the ride to Viola, I would have missed a ride to Richland Center and so on and so on…

This was no exception. As I walked up to Hope Lutheran Church of Milton OH, a pickup pulled in and, it just happened to be the pastor. Had I been there five minutes sooner, I would have found the church locked, left, and, even if I had passed him on the road, probably would not have connected with him.

As it turned out the pastor, whose name was Matt Powell, was there to do a wedding rehearsal. I gave him my ministry card and asked if it would be Okay to spend the night on the grounds. He immediately said it would be fine, and then invited me inside to wash up. He also showed me where the kitchen was, telling me to help myself to anything that wasn't marked with someone's name. I found a few items, and after eating I went outside and set up my tent. The church had a few acres, and there was a garage with an overhang that had picnic tables set under it.

When I did the update that night I moved the computer around to show where I was. Everyone seemed to think that I was at a campground until I showed the church in the background.

Sometime during the night it started to rain. Not a pourdown, wind blowing the tent around storm, just a nice gentle soothing rain. The kind that just relaxes you.

### Saturday-June 13, 2009

*And we know that all things work together for good to those who love God, to those who are called according to His purpose. (Rom 8:28)*

When I woke up at 5:00 it was still raining. I put

everything under the pavilion, leaving the tent set up so it could dry. For about an hour and a half I prayed, read my Bible and worked on my journal. Then, with the rain having stopped, I packed, and made my way through the sleepy little town.

I came to a Laundromat but decided to wait and find one in Walworth, WI that night; however, at the other end of town there was another one. This time I felt that this was as good a time as any to wash my clothes. I wasn't inside for five minutes when the sky opened up and the rain started pouring down again. I read some more scriptures while the clothes washed and dried, and I waited for the rain to stop again.

When it finally stopped –around 11:00am, I decided that I would probably have another peanut butter sandwich for lunch, so I walked the couple blocks to the edge of town, and was half way across the highway, when I saw a Burger King a block away. Changing my mind, I got a meal and, as I was about to sit down, saw a mail carrier sitting there eating. I was fairly certain that I knew where I was going, but I felt led to ask the mailman to make sure.

I asked him if County Road M was just on the other side of the highway and he told me that it was, then he asked where I was headed to. As I was telling him, I handed him a card, which he looked at, then asked me to tell him the meaning behind the name Ministry of the Sheep. As it turned out, he knew the meaning but wanted to make sure I understood it. I told him the vision to fulfill the scripture in my everyday life and told him about the kids I was trying to take care of in India.

We talked for a while until he was finished eating. Telling me that he had to get back to work, he asked if he could pray for me. So, there in Burger King, Eddie Fisher of Milton, IL, servant of the Most High God and brother in Christ, laid a caring arm across my shoulder and ministered to me through prayer. As Eddie prayed, I felt that Jesus also had an arm across my shoulder saying "I know it's a long road to travel, but I'm right beside you."

With the late start I was getting I knew I wouldn't be able

to make it to Walworth by night unless God intervened.
I had been walking for about three hours when my right ankle
started to stiffen up and the bottom of my feet were feeling
'mushy'. I don't know of another name to call it. It felt as
though I had been walking on river rock in my bare feet all day.

Eventually I came to a town called Johnstown, but the only
business was a tractor dealer. I had been looking for a place to sit
and rest for at least an hour without success, when I came to a
farm that had a small containment wall that was just the right
height to sit on. I sat down, took my backpack off and began
massaging my ankle. Soon, an older man came out of the house
and walked towards me. He asked if I was alright and said that I
looked sick. I assured him that I was fine, other than my ankle
and feet hurting, and I gave him one of my cards, which he just
stuck in his pocket, apparently not caring who I might be.

He asked if I wanted some water and turned on the faucet
from a well that was right there, going on to tell me that people
had been drinking from that well for over 100 years and everyone
said it was the best water they had ever had. I filled my bottle,
drank some water and had to agree that it was the best, purist
tasting water I had ever drank from a well.

I found out that this man was Bill Morrison and he was 86
years young. Bill's father had bought the farm in 1919. Bill was
born there and never left.

Bill then gave me a history of Johnstown. It seems that at
one time, County Road M was called the Old Chicago Road. It
was used by the stage coaches and was the first stop west from
Milwaukee and the last stop east to Milwaukee. In its prime it
had two hotels and two saloons. But then, the railroad came and
there wasn't a need for the stop there anymore and the town died
away.

Bill asked if I was hungry and offered me something to eat.
As I had eaten an early lunch and wasn't sure where I would be at
dinner time, I accepted his offer and we went inside the house
where I met his wife. I forgot to write her name down, so I'll just
refer to her as Bill's wife.

No Mere Coincidences, a journey of faith

Bill's wife started making a grilled cheese sandwich for me as we talked about the ministry and the journey. Then, she found a chicken leg in the refrigerator, then some vegetarian spaghetti. Suddenly she stops talking, looks at me and says "You going to pray so you can start eating?" I did, asking God to bless the food as well as blessing my hosts. As I'm eating this buffet of food, she sets a big piece of cherry cheesecake in front of me.

During the meal I spoke more about the journey, mentioning that I wasn't going to make my goal for the day. She asked, "Can you take rides?" and I told her I could accept rides but couldn't solicit them. She looked at Bill and said "Well, ask him if he wants a ride Bill!" Bill, of course, asked "Would you like a ride?" and I accepted.

We got to Walworth and Bill dropped me off at the town square. Seeing a Mexican restaurant, I went in for a coke and then decided to walk into the Mexican store that was on the front of the building. I was immediately overcome by the smells. They brought back so many memories and thoughts of the kids in Honduras.

I have discovered over the last couple of years that, sometimes, God doesn't always lead you to what is for you, but for someone else's growth. I believe this was the case here. I finally got around to locating a church for the night and, felt led to try a Church on the south end of town. I made contact with a young, female Police Officer and asked if she knew how to contact the pastor of the church. She didn't seem to know that the church was in town; when she tried to pronounce the name she couldn't. I had the feeling that she may not have had much contact with Christians.

She found the number on her contact list, but, when she called it, she got voice mail. I heard her explain that I was a minister, on a journey, requesting to set up a tent on the church lawn for the night. When she finished leaving the message she said that she thought it would be OK to go ahead and set up there, as it was getting late.

The church sat on a good ten acres, most of which *wasn't*

sodded or seeded. I put my tent up where I wouldn't damage the new sod, and set up to do my broadcast. About 8:45 the officer came by; she seemed somewhat shocked. She said that she was sorry but, the pastor had called back and said a big "NO".

This somewhat shocked me too. I knew the denomination taught caring for people. But I thanked the officer and told her that I would be out in 10 minutes. After I repacked everything, I decided that I couldn't go without leaving a note. In effect it said:

*What saddens me more than finding a shepherd, of my Father's sheep, that has so little understanding of the ways of Christ, is that the young officer, who couldn't pronounce the name of your church, may have had her first look at people claiming to follow Jesus last night.*

I folded the note around my card, wedged it between the front doors. Walking about a quarter mile, I found a beautiful spot along the road, and in 20 minutes I was set up and asleep.

### Sunday-June 14, 2009

I'm not sure where I am, other than knowing I'm at the State Line. I hadn't plotted the next day's travels before leaving the church the night before, but knew that I had a long way to walk on 14 Highway, so I just started walking. There wasn't much south of Walworth, WI for quite a distance.

Eventually I came to the city of Harvard, IL and stopped at a gas station. From there I could see a church just up the road and I headed for it. It turned out to be a United Methodist. I got there just a few minutes before the service started, asking a greeter where I could shave and wash before the service. He pointed the way to the restroom and I quickly tried to make myself look presentable.

When I got back to the sanctuary, I was greeted by a lively lady named Janet Harlow. She was curious about my journey and Ministry of the Sheep. I also got to meet the pastor, Soon Sun Lee, for just a moment before the service started. She is a wonderful Korean lady from whom, when she was talking with the people, I could feel genuine concern and love for them.

The service started and Janet sang a solo, and then let everyone know who I was and about my journey. After the service everyone was asking me about the ministry and the journey. Janet found me again and I thanked her for letting everyone know about me. She and I talked for a couple more minutes and she slipped me a little money to "help me on my way."

As people started leaving Pastor Soon invited me to dinner with her family. I thanked her but declined, explaining that I still had 25 miles to cover, with it already close to noon. Not willing to be cheated out of her blessing, she gave me some money so I could eat something later.

Once again, God was watching out for me. I left the church and walked South on Highway 14. I decided to get a burger to eat as I walked, as the next town was several miles away. That only took a few minutes, so I was soon walking again.

Just as I was done with the hamburger, a car pulled into the last place it was safe to do so, and the driver offered me a ride to Woodstock, IL; about half the distance I needed to cover that day.
This man's name was Paul. He actually drove me about two miles further than he was going to turn, and deposited me on the south side of Woodstock, WI.

I started walking again and after about 4 hours reached Crystal Lake, IL. Stopping at a convenience store I did a quick online search and located a church I was sure would have a Sunday evening service. Looking at the map, I figured it was only a few blocks from where I was. Sure I could make it before services started, I headed that way. But, when I got to where I thought the church was there was no church.

I did see a man working in his yard, and asked if he knew where the church was. He didn't, but asked his wife –who didn't know either. She went into the house and returned with a phone book and a glass of ice water. I thought of the words of Jesus, *"And whoever shall give to one of these little ones a cup of cold*

41

*water to drink, only in the name of a disciple, truly I say to you, He shall in no way lose his reward." (Matthew 10:42)*

This couple's name was Steven and Lorraine. Lorraine reminded me so much of my niece, Merica. The genuine joy that flowed out of her affected everyone around her. After finding out where the church was, I was told that it was still over a mile away. Thankfully, Steven offered me a ride to it, and I arrived a few minutes before the service would start. He went in with me to make sure that I would be welcomed –if not he was going to help me find another church.

There were actually two church buildings on the premises. Only one was having service that evening. This was Luz De Betel, a Latino congregation. I asked a lady where the Pastor was, in the best Spanish I knew, and she indicated to a man on the platform, playing the guitar, preparing for worship. When he saw that I was waiting on him, he came down and introduced himself as Nick Torres.

I explained my journey and asked if I could remain on the church grounds that evening, to which he readily said yes. I also asked if they had an interpreter, as I didn't know much Spanish. He told me that he would interpret for me.

Pastor Nick asked more about my journey and the Ministry of the Sheep and, as we talked, he let me know that he had been doing a series on discipleship and that I was living the sermons.

We had a wonderful service, with Pastor Nick graciously doing it in both Spanish and English. After the service they had a time of fellowship with sandwiches and side dishes, which they invited me to partake in.

I had broadcast the service online and, since my computer was set up, I ran a slide show of the Honduras kids. Several of the members were watching it and I started telling them, through an interpreter, that they were the kids I had worked with the previous summer. One of them commented that they were surprised I remembered their names and I said "Of course I do, they are MI NIÑOS." I will never forget them or their stories.

I shared some of the stories of how the kids had come to

the home and, as I went on, I could see that some of them were starting to get emotional. I got a sense that some may have had similar stories before coming to the United States.

At the end of the evening, as people were preparing to leave, Pastor Nick called everyone together to surround me and the entire congregation of Luz De Betel Church covered me in their prayers. I spent the night in such a peace that I don't think an earthquake could have interrupted it.

## Monday-June 15, 2009

I knew I was getting closer to a major metropolitan area as I left Crystal Lake. Highway 14 was now four lanes, and, from the time I started walking on it, there was a steady line of vehicles headed into the Chicago area. There was also almost no shoulder, and the drivers didn't seem to like me walking the six inch strip between the white line and the edge of the road. Deputy Bob thought walking on Highway 12 in Madison was scary; he should have seen me there.

After walking for eight hours I was offered a ride by a city courtesy bus in Barrington, IL, and deposited in Palatine. Soon I was in Arlington Heights, IL and found a place to get something to eat and do the nightly broadcast. After that I set out trying to find a place to sleep.

I had seen neither parks nor churches as of yet, and was looking beside the rail system for a spot that was secluded and flat, when I suddenly felt led to go behind a business across the street. There I found a paved area that had some lawn chairs. The area was enclosed by a hedge of bushes on one side and privacy fences on the other two sides. I considered setting up the tent, but decided that, as it was a nice night, I would just sit in one of the chairs and use my blanket to cover myself. After I was settled in, I got the sense that I should move my backpack out of sight, so I put it behind the chair.

I had just started to doze off when I was pulled back to consciousness by the sounds of approaching footsteps. A second later a man came around the shrubs. I said "good evening" in a quiet voice, so not to overly startle him. He walked near, peering into the darkness to see me, as though trying to recognize me. I told him my name but didn't feel inspired to tell him any more than that.

He started out telling me that this was his place. There were others that came and went, but he had 'lived' there for close to year, including during the winter months. Then he set down the rules; no drinking, if you smoke pick up your butts, no women, if you have to go to the bathroom, go somewhere else.

This man's name was Lance. He had been out of work for over a year and unable to find a job. He made a point to let me know that he was Homeless, not a bum. He said he actively looked for work and when he needed help, like a pair of pants or some food, he would do something, like take out trash or clean the bathrooms at the shelter. He said that, when he did get some money, he would often use some to buy another homeless person some medicine or food if they needed it more than he did.

I started talking then, and asked if he was a Christian. When he said that he was, I asked what it was that made him a Christian. He started talking about caring for others, making God first in your life and others second, putting yourself last.

Out of curiosity, I asked him how he felt about being homeless and how God was treating him. He let me know that, at the worst that he had had it, he had met people who had it worse and, that if he hadn't lost his job and home, he would not have had the chance to meet the people that he had been witnessing to.

Lance and I had been talking for close to an hour when another man came in. He introduced the newcomer as Mark, and the two of them pulled sleeping bags and tarps out from under the bushes and laid them out on the ground.

I sat there for a while talking to God and afterward knew what I needed to do. God said it was time to leave. I pulled my backpack out and tucked the blanket into it. Then, I wrapped half the money I had been given the morning before around a ministry card. I told Lance that I needed to leave and said my goodbyes, handing him my card, asking him to look me up online someday.

Back out on the road, not sure where I would sleep, I kept going until I found the road that I was to turn on next. After just a few blocks I was out of the business district and into a residential area, where I found a church. Walking around it, I found an area that was blocked from the road by some bushes, with grass between the bushes and the building. I again considered setting up the tent, but suddenly felt that God was saying "I'll be your shelter tonight." So I unrolled my sleeping bag, lay on top of it and covered myself with my blanket. It was after midnight by then and I barely remember lying down.

## Tuesday-June 16, 2009

I awoke this morning after a good night's sleep. I hadn't even been pestered by a single insect during the night. It hadn't rained and in fact, there wasn't even any dew on the ground.

I rolled my sleeping bag up and headed for my goal of Willow springs, IL. Today I would be walking past O'Hare airport. The walk was as I expected it to be; a lot of industry and warehouses, no sidewalks and often, no shoulder.

I walked for a couple hours, then it started to rain. At first it was a light sprinkle, but soon became heavier. It was one of those scattered showers, lasting a few minutes, stopping, and then starting up again. I took shelter where I could find it to wait for the rain to let up and then continued on my way. This went on for the next few hours.

At 3:00 pm I was only in Hinsdale, IL; miles from my destination. Suddenly there was a cloud burst. I was about half a block from a park with a shelter and several ball fields. I trotted towards a shelter and, once there, I sat for almost an hour and a half, waiting for the rain to let up.

About 4:30 a man came by. He was in charge of the ball fields and was "checking to see if they could play on them if the rain stopped" I was thinking "Ah, pouring down rain for almost 2 hours, probably not!" But, as in so many other cases, God had sent him my way. I told him about the journey I was on, and the ministry, and he offered to transport me anywhere in town. I asked if he could take me to a church.

He dropped me off at Redeemer Evangelical Lutheran Church. As it was after 5:00pm, wondered if anyone would still be there; but was soon ashamed at my doubt that God would take care of me. There were, of course, people there.

The pastor, Michael Bradburn, welcomed me with open arms, said I could pitch my tent on the property. He apologized that they didn't have any food there to offer me but, did tell me where I could get a good meal at a good price. He then told me that there was a Bishop there from South Africa, whom they supported, that would be doing an open forum with the church council that evening and he invited me to join in.

Later I enjoyed an evening of listening to Bishop Ndanganeni Phaswana, of South Africa. Bishop Phaswana was caring for the A.I.D.S. victims and orphans of South Africa. His love and compassion for these people was so deep that you couldn't help but feel it as he spoke.

## Wednesday-June 17, 2009

I woke up early and quickly packed. It had stopped raining, and, as I had slept under a covered drive, the tent was dried out. My clothing, however, was a different story. As the temperature had dropped during the rain, I had put on my sweatshirt. It was still soaked, The backpack was wet and the clothes I had been wearing were damp. In all I think I was carrying an extra 15lbs. of weight. Nevertheless, I was on the road by 5:00am but, as I came to where I was to turn, it started to rain again.

It was always interesting how this worked. I had walked two hours without seeing any place to stop, use the restroom or get anything to eat or drink. Now, as it starts to rain, there was a gas station a block away. I took refuge inside and waited a good hour before the rain stopped. Once I was on my way again, I decided that I needed to find a Laundromat. I found one, started the clothes washing and re-plotted my route to Flossmoor, IL.

Once I plotted the route to Flossmoor I found a McDonald's

and spent the last of my cash on a meal. As I gave thanks to God for the meal I added, "and Lord, you told me to do this journey on faith, and I'm standing on that." I commenced eating and, before I was finished, an elderly lady, leaving the counter with her meal, walked up to me, handed me a $20.00 bill and said 'I was told to give this to you...and I think you know who told me!' In awe I said, "Yes ma'am, I do. Thank you for listening." and she smiled and walked off.

After eating I did the nightly update and shared this with everyone there, who were in even more awe than I was. With the update done, I set out to find a place to sleep. The road went from Business to residential and I had about decided that I was in for a long walk. Then I came to a large, open field with a little brush area in the center of it. I walked through the tall grass to the bushes and began setting up the tent while at the same time praying that there weren't Chiggers in the grass there. Once, while in the National Guard, I set up my shelter in tall grass and I was covered, head to toe, with chiggers. I think there are 500 home remedies for them and none of them work.

## Thursday-June 18, 2009

*"You can't ask God to lead and guide you and then, as soon as His guidance leads you a different direction, say "Sorry God, that's not in the plan."*

I woke up the next morning to the sound of rain hitting the tent and quickly packed and took the tent down before it got soaked. Afterward, I walked a few blocks to a gas station and waited for the rain to stop. Once it did I headed out and within a couple hours I was offered a ride by a man who introduced himself as St. Thomas.

A few minutes after he picked me up Thomas asked how long I had been in the military. Somewhat taken back by this, I told him, and then asked how he knew I had served. He said it was because I walked with authority. While Thomas was extremely nice and I could tell that he was acting from his heart,

47

he seemed to focus on me being a vet, and soon he was dropping me off at the War Memorial Park in Munster, Indiana instead of Flossmoor, Illinois. I had realized that we were headed in the wrong direction but felt that there was a reason for it. When asked later why I went so far off the route plan I simply said "You can't ask God to lead and guide you and then, as soon as His guidance leads you a different direction, say "Sorry God, that's not in the plan." You have to go where He leads. I don't know the purpose for it. It may be as simple as Thomas needed someone to talk to who would listen to him, or maybe I would meet someone else on the new route that I was supposed to minister to. Whatever the reason, I was now in Munster, IN; and I took the opportunity to tour the memorial.

I found that, if I got to Highway 41, it would get me back on route in a couple days, so I headed towards Cedar Lake, IN and came to a Catholic church in St. John, IN. On the grounds there was an old frontier style building, so I went to check it out. It turned out to be the first church built in the area in the 1830's. It had been restored, and it was open, so I went on inside, hoping not to offend anyone there –as I'm not Catholic and I don't observe their traditions, like kneeling/bowing towards the cross, crossing myself, etc.

The inside was beautiful compared to the rustic look of the outside. While the windows on the outside were rough-cut and plain looking, the inside was stained glass. The roof on the outside was peaked, but on the inside was a beautiful vaulted ceiling. While the walls of the outside were gray, rough-cut beams with mud filling the gaps, the inside was smooth with rich wood paneling and trim. I sat there for a few minutes, enjoying the quiet and meditated on the Lord.

As I left, I felt that there was something I was missing in the whole setting. I was almost a block away when it hit me; whether it was intended by man or not, this church with it's the plain –in some people's opinion 'ugly' exterior– represented the exterior of man, and the way God can transform you on the inside to be beautiful and full of his peace. When we let God work

48

inside of us, all though the same body, our spirit is renewed to something beautiful.

An hour or so later I came to a place that was called "A Journey of Christ's Passion", and decided it was a good time for another break, so I went in. It was a walk-through display; starting with "Last supper" and going to the resurrection.

I moved on, and was about a mile and a half from Cedar Lake, IN when I was picked up. The lady, who I believe said her name was Sandy, had passed me and then turned around. She took me into town, where there was a gas station and a restaurant. She also told me where a church was and, after a light dinner, I found the Community Bible Church. I got permission to set up my tent and got it up, then sewed on my backpack, which was ripping out again.

**Friday-June 19, 2009**

I made it through another storm last night. At least I was able to put the tent stakes in the ground this time. There were times I'm sure my tent looked more like a lean-to than a dome.

Going back to the restaurant for breakfast, I heard the News about straight line winds during the night. This morning, however, the sky was clear and the sun was evaporating the water on the ground. It was also making it extremely humid.

The heat index was worse than it had been so far this trip; and I kept needing to stop and get my bottles refilled every couple of hours. On one of these breaks I laid in the shade of a tree for a few minutes and, as I sat up, a pickup truck made a U-turn and pulled up beside me. Inside were three women, the type that you would expect to see on the back of a motorcycle. They asked where I was headed, and I said Fowler. They told me to get in the back and we were off, headed down the road.

We stopped at a gas station a short time later, and I got a chance to talk to two of the women for a few moments. Introducing myself and giving them my card, I discovering that these three were sisters were headed out to party. As the women dropped me off where Highway 41 and 52 separated I asked them to check out my website and to take a few minutes to read the page entitled R U Saved. They told me they would and I left, sorry that I didn't have more time to share Jesus with them. I prayed that, one day they would look the site up.

From where I was dropped off, it was about three miles to Fowler, and I had covered about two of them when a vehicle pulled up and the driver told me it was too hot to be out walking. He took me into town and dropped me off at a church. There was a man there mowing the lawn and I explained who I was and asked about pitching my tent there. He said it was no problem and, after thanking him, I walked a few blocks back to the highway to get something to eat.

Passing an American Legion I felt led to go inside. I gave them my card and talked to several of the people gathered there then asked if they had some place I could shave and clean up and they showed me the bathroom. After cleaning up I thanked them, and one of them told me about a breakfast there in the morning. I thanked him for the invitation and left.

As I walked through the downtown I decided that, before I left, I should get pictures. The town was very nostalgic, with a one screen movie theater and a six lane bowling alley. But, since I could hear the thunder closing in, I decided I should get to the church and set my tent up, finishing just as it started to rain and the wind began blowing.

As I was broadcasting my update, I heard a voice saying, "Excuse me, sir." When I opened the flap of the tent a man introduced himself as Ed Schroder. He verified that I had been at the American Legion earlier, and then invited me to the breakfast the next morning, saying that he would pay for it. I told him that I would be there and thanked him.

**Saturday-June 20, 2009**

It rained most of the night, but by morning it was clear and the sky was promising some sunshine. I got packed and made my way to the American Legion. When I walked in there was a man collecting money and, before I could say anything, he said

"You're that missionary fellow, go on in." As I thanked him I saw Ed, the man that had invited me the night before. Ed welcomed me and introduced me to the bunch there, then had me tell them a little about the journey.

I filled a plate of Southern style breakfast; scrambled eggs, sausage, biscuits –and then smothered it all in sausage gravy. I wasn't far enough south yet for Grits to be included in the menu.

I sat there eating and talking to the various groups of people. Some had served in Korea and Vietnam, some, like me, were Desert Storm veterans and a couple that had served in the current Gulf War. It was a room of People that believed in freedom, and had fought to make sure others had that freedom.

After eating and sharing about God for a while, I again thanked Ed for the breakfast. When he shook my hand, he slipped me an envelope and told me that it was from the Legion to help me along the way. I thanked him again, said goodbye to everyone and headed out.

While walking through the downtown section of Fowler I took time for a few photos. At the movie theater, a man asked if his car was in the way. I told him no and we started talking about the old theater. His name was Lloyd, the owner of Lloyd's Barber Shop. He said the theater had been built in 1935 and had been in operation all but 25 years of that time. It had been restored to look just like it did the day it opened. Lloyd and I talked for a few more minutes and I headed on down the road. I figured as late as it was getting, I would end up short of the day's goal, but, I was a day ahead of schedule anyway.

God had other plans though. After only walking about 3 miles, a pickup truck pulled over behind me, and I was offered a ride by what I thought was a couple. As it turned out, they were brother-in-law/sister-in-law whose families had gone to a campground the night before and they were joining them. Their names were Steve and Lori. Both of them were full of joy, as if nothing in the world was amiss.

Steve asked several questions about the ministry and India and told me that one of his friends was preparing for a missions trip to China.  He said that each member of the mission team was only allowed so many bibles and their names had to be clearly written inside of them so that if they were found in the hands of a Chinese citizen they would know who to arrest.

I thought about the freedom we, as Americans, take for granted.  We are able to own as many bibles as we want, and able to share them with whomever we want –and yet so many never read them *or* share them.  In other countries, people can be arrested, tortured and even killed for their faith and yet, these people go out every day to spread the word of God.

We quickly came to where Lori and Steve had to turn, so we said our goodbyes and I continued walking, going on for another two hours.  At that point, a car, coming from the opposite direction, turned around and then stopped beside me.  This was a young lady, about 25 years old.  She asked if I would like a ride, but said that she was only going about 5 miles up the road.  I gladly accepted.

Her name was Cynthia and she told me that she had gone past me a few minutes earlier.  Cynthia said that, when she saw me, she felt that she was supposed to pick me up, but, as she didn't pick up strangers, she ignored the feeling.  As she got further away, the feeling became stronger and she told God, 'Whatever happens, let it be in your will.' and she turned around. As we talked, and she learned more about me and the ministry, she told me that she was actually just stopping ahead to pick up her two daughters, then they would be going on to Lafayette; which was actually further than my day's goal.

We stopped at her house and she introduced me to her husband, Dan.  She had two daughters, the older being 7 years old, and when Cynthia introduced me to her, she came over and gave me a big hug.  Cynthia got the girls ready and we were back on the road.  We talked about God, the body of Christ, and the importance of true discipleship.  When we reached Lafayette, Cynthia took me to the far side as she was actually running early. When I thanked her, she thanked me, saying that I had been a real blessing to her.  I have found it interesting that, as I think I'm getting blessed by those who are helping me, they are thanking me for being such a blessing to them.

I now found myself in Lafayette, IN, at 11:15am, having to decide whether to continue on or stop for the day. I didn't really see any place to spend a day, as I was already basically out of town. There was a large convenience store and I considered getting something to eat, but as I had eaten a large breakfast just a few hours earlier –and, as there was no place to sit down –I decided to wait and get something at the next town, and so headed down the road.

The road was straight, flat and nearly desolate. I walked and walked, and the temperature rose. The only shade was trees in people's yards. I would walk for a while, stop under a tree and if I needed water, I would ask at the house. I did this for the next six hours. At one house I finished my water and lay in the shade. I told God that I needed his strength to go any further and, after laying there a few minutes went up to the house to ask about water.

No one was home there but, at this particular point, there were three houses in a row, and, two houses up was an elderly man out in front. Before I could even approach him, he was shouting out "Would you like some ice water?" I, of course, said yes and walked up the drive to him, asking if I might be able to fill my bottles too –he took them into the house to his wife, and then invited me to sit in the shade, and we began talking.

His name was Glen Platt and his wife was Martha. It turned out that their son had passed me on a motorcycle and told them about me walking up the road. They had been watching for me to make sure I had water, as it was so hot.

Martha appeared with two sandwiches, a large glass of Ice water and my filled bottles. She told Glen that their daughter and son-in-law wanted to know if they –Glen and Martha –wanted to meet them at the Dairy Queen in Thorntown. They then asked if they could take me there.

In Thorntown I tried to contact my second cousin, Dawn, who lives in Lebanon, IN to let her know that I was now two days ahead of schedule. Dawn and her husband, Dave, are the Directors of the Adolescent Girls Center for Indiana Teen Challenge in Indianapolis.

I did the nightly update, and was putting the computer away, when the phone rang; it was Dawn. She explained that both she and her husband had commitments the next day, but they had made a reservation at a hotel for me. After talking for a few minutes Dawn came to Thorntown, picked me up and took me into Lebanon. She showed me where the church was and then got me situated in the hotel across the street from the church.

On a day that I didn't think I would meet my goal, God had not only provided me with rides that covered two days of walking; but had me where I felt like I was in paradise compared to how I had been living the last three weeks.

Even though it was already well after 10:00pm, the first thing I did was sit in the hot-tub for almost an hour. Then I slept on a mattress for the first time since Lewiston, MN.

## Sunday-June 21, 2009

I really didn't feel like getting up this morning. I was lying in a large, comfortable bed, with no threat of being rained on. I knew the church service started at 10:00 and I would need to check out before going to it; so, I forced myself to get up and go down to the continental breakfast the hotel offered.
After a good meal and a long hot shower, I dressed, packed and headed for church.

The church was River of Life Assembly of God. It was a congregation that David, Dawn's husband, had pastored for several years before God called them to work with Teen Challenge full time. The pastor was now Matthew Eckart, who was a young man with a passion for God.

I often tell people that I am a minister, not a preacher. I minister to people's needs, I counsel people one on one, I do okay in a Bible study, but I have a hard time keeping on one subject. Once I talk for a few minutes I seem to find rabbit trails everywhere. Pastor Eckart, however, was anointed by God to preach. I don't think he was using any notes, but he preached with such passion, love and conviction that you just knew it was the Holy Spirit speaking through him.

As it was well into the afternoon by the time I was out of church, I decided to take the day off and, after getting lunch, found a Laundromat and washed my clothes. That done, I found a park pavilion and worked on my journal until it was time for the nightly update.

That night I slept in the park, totally amazed that, even there, in a city park, I was able to set up a tent and never be checked by the police.

**Monday-June 22, 2009**

More rain during the night. I woke about 4:45am and was walking a few minutes after 5:00. The road I walked on today paralleled the Interstate 65, from Lebanon to Indianapolis, and there was very little traffic on the road.

After about 2 hours I noticed the sky back towards Lebanon was getting dark as night and it seemed to be headed towards me. I headed for some buildings that were a quarter mile away. I got under the cover of building just as the sky opened up and the rain came in sheets. It ended as quickly; 15 minutes or so later. I continued walking, thinking that I had plotted a course that would take me around Indianapolis, but instead I found myself in the city, and within a heavy retail area.

Although I found a place to get something to eat, there was nowhere to settle in for the night, so I decided to walk for a couple more hours. I put my location in Google map and found the quickest and most direct way out of the city.

Two hours later I found myself in a rough part of town. As it was time for the update, I did a quick one; telling everyone that I was going to walk until I was out of the area. Walking another two hours, the area still looked rough, so I kept walking –and also kept in prayer –until I finally found a church.

It seemed to have nothing but parking lot around it, but I felt that I should walk around it. When I did, I found a spot where I would be isolated, and able to know if anyone was approaching, having just enough room to lay my sleeping bag down and lay on top of it.

I prayed that God would keep me safe and, though I didn't sleep well, I did get some sleep in between gunshots and sirens.

**Tuesday-June 23, 2009**

I actually slept a little later than usual. I think that, with the alertness I had kept throughout the night, as dawn approached, I let my defenses down a little –so I didn't get on the road until almost 6:30am. I followed the route I had plotted the night before, and was shortly outside Indianapolis, heading for my day's goal; Fountaintown, Indiana.

At about 3:00 a pickup truck stopped beside me and I was offered a ride. As I climbed into the truck I saw a Bible on the seat. It wasn't the kind of Bible I've seen in many vehicles – thrown in the dash or in the back window for so long that it's covered in dust. This one was a beautiful Bible. It was the type of Bible that had its cover and pages worn out from use.

The driver's name was Bill. Bill asked me where I was headed and I told him Fountaintown. We started talking and he was soon telling me his testimony about how he had started towards a promising career in music but that God had other plans for him. Caught up in talking, we passed right through Fountaintown and, by the time we realized it, were half way to Rushville, IN. As that was where Bill was headed I decided that God must have something in Rushville for me.

He dropped me off at a small store in Rushville and headed on home. I went into the store and, after getting something to drink, asked the cashier where I could find a church or someplace that I could sit. She directed me to a park, which was several blocks away, and said that there were some churches in the area as well. I found the park, and then walked around the area to the churches. None were open, nor had phone numbers to call, so I went back to the park trusting that God had a plan.

It was there that I ran into an older gentleman who worked

as the park patrol. Basically, he tried to keep the teens in line and help out where he could. As I didn't see any outlets in the pavilion I asked him about finding a place to plug in. He showed me where the outlets were and then told me that, if I got hungry, here was a restaurant on the corner. I was glad to find that out, as I thought I was going to have to walk back uptown to get dinner. I checked email and worked on my journal for a couple hours, then, about 6:30pm, I packed up and went into the restaurant, where I found a booth and ordered.

As I was waiting for my order, I noticed a man watching me. He looked quite a bit older than me, large, with a gray beard and ponytail. Basically, He looked like an old biker. When I looked over at him, he would look away. This happened a couple of times and,while it bothered me, I wasn't getting any sense of danger. The waitress brought me my coke and, almost immediately, the man stood up and went into the back dining room –with a Bible. Soon I noticed others come into the restaurant carrying bibles and I deducted that, maybe, there was a Bible study about to happen.

I decided that, as I was almost finished eating, I would go and ask if I could join it. Finishing my meal I went to pay, and at that moment, one of the men came out to get something to drink. I asked him if the Bible study in the back room was private and he said it was, but then asked if I wanted to join them.

I found out that the first man's name was Freddy. He was 66 and had only been saved for about three years. I also discovered that he had been watching me, waiting to see if I got something to eat. He said that, if I hadn't, he was going to come over, offer to buy me dinner and witness to me.

The group was a group of friends, from different churches and denominations, which gathered every Tuesday night to have an informal Bible study. There was an opening prayer, then one of the ladies opened her Bible and she read: *Trust in the LORD with all thy heart, and lean not upon thine own understanding. In all thy ways acknowledge Him, and He will direct thy paths.* (Pro 3:5-6). It so much described not only that day, but every day I had been on this journey. Following the lead of the Holy Spirit and finding myself in places where, while I feel I am being blessed, others are telling me what a blessing I am to them.

After a study and prayer time, Freddy announced to his friends that he was going to get me a hotel room. Everyone pitched in and then Freddie asked if I wanted a room or the money for food. As I can sleep just about anywhere, but find it hard to eat a bed, I opted to use the money for food.

Freddie's sister, Mary, said she may have a place to set my tent up and made a phone call. Then we caravanned a few blocks to where Mary lived with her daughter and son-in-law. Mary's son-in-law offered to plug in the camper, parked in the back yard, so I could sleep in it. I decided to use the tent, the ground was level and the grass thick. Just before I retired for the night Mary offered to wash any dirty clothing I had. I went to bed feeling so blessed by God, and was anxious to see what else He had in store for me.

**Wednesday-June 24, 2009**

I had already decided that, as I was ahead of schedule and behind in my journal, I would stay in Rushville for the day. So I slept in a little and then spent some time reading the Bible and praying. Soon Mary came to the back yard and asked if I wanted some scrambled eggs and toast for breakfast. I accepted and, as she made them, I let her know that I would be spending the day at the park typing. After breakfast she drove me to the park.

As we were getting into the car Freddie called her and wanted to tell me goodbye. He told me again, what a blessing and inspiration I had been to them. I don't know what all Freddy's past involves but I do know that, with Christ in his heart, he was about as gentle and caring as a person could be. It never ceases to amaze me how God works. Even though I am one person in billions of people on this planet, God has taken the time to arrange for me to meet people like the Bible study group of the Park Restaurant in Rushville, IN.

The rest of the day I sat at the park, typed for a while,

watched parents and children enjoying the day and, towards the end of it, made my way to the edge of town where I found a spot to set up my tent.

## Thursday-June 25, 2009

I made my way out of Rushville and headed towards Connersville, IN. At about 10:30 I came into a small town with only a small gas station and a bar & grill on the main road. I went into the Bar & Grill and sat down. The place was empty except for the barmaid/waitress, and I ordered a Hamburger and a glass of water. I had a chance to chat with her about God, and, when I left, I prayed that God would send someone to water the seed that I had planted.

About half way to Connersville, a vehicle going the other direction made a U-turn and pulled up beside me. The female driver asked if I wanted a ride. Her name was Phyllis. Phyllis asked where I was headed and I told her. She asked if there was a certain place to drop me off and I said any church in town. She started naming all the Baptist churches in Connersville, then she said "I'm a Baptist, can you tell" I smiled and said that I was starting to suspect she was. She dropped me off at Calvary Baptist Church, then she gave me a few dollar love gift.

I made contact inside the church with a secretary, who told me that the pastor was on vacation and the Asst. Pastor was out of the office. She called the assistant pastor –whose name was Jason –and passed along my request of staying on the church grounds. He didn't have a problem with it and said that he would be back in the afternoon.

Later, I met Jason and, after just a few minutes of talking, it felt as though we had been friends for years, but hadn't seen each other for several months; as though I was just catching him up on what I had been up to for the past year.

Jason offered to let me use a shower, washer and dryer they had at the church, then asked if he could take me to dinner that evening. We agreed to find each other at about 5:00. I found a place to read and work on my journal, then at 5:00 went to the office and found Jason, who told me that his wife and children would be joining us.

We went to an old-fashioned Drive-In called Kupkel's. It boasted that it had been in business since 1954, and it didn't seem as it had changed much (other than prices of course).

Jason introduced me to his wife, Hanna, his sons A.J. and Ethan, and their baby girl, Macy. We had a great dinner, and afterward showed them pictures of my Honduras kids on the computer and told them the kid's stories.

Later, we went back to the church, and after getting a photo, minus the baby who had fallen asleep, Hanna left to go grocery shopping. With the help of A.J. and Ethan, I got my tent set up. Ethan wanted to know if I was going to build a campfire to roast marshmallows, but I told him that it might get his dad in trouble if I did that.

Once I was set up, Jason asked if they could pray for me before they left, which of course was fine. He called the boys over and they stood, one on either side of their father, with me in front of them. Jason had Ethan pray first. This little 5 year old started praying like a prayer *warrior*. It wasn't the 'Jesus be with Dennis amen' that you would expect from a 5 year old. It was a detailed, point by point prayer. A.J. prayed for me next and then Jason. As Jason was praying, Ethan reached his hand out and took one of my fingers in his hand, and then tried to take my whole hand in his. When his father finished praying Ethan pulled me down to his level, gave me a great big hug and said "Dennis, I'll never forget you." I gave him a hug back, telling him that I would never forget him either. Jason and the boys left and I started getting ready to do the update.

I put everything up on the air conditioner that was near the tent; set up like an outdoor office desk. And of course, the air conditioner decided to come on. Everything but the computer went about 6 feet into the air and landed on the ground. The only thing I thought was "Good job Mixer, what did you expect." It had been a hot day. It was a no brainer that, at some point in time, the air conditioner would come on. I did the update, too embarrassed at the time to tell anyone what had just happened.

As I was finishing and prepared to go to sleep, I noticed the thunderheads building in the distance.

## Friday-June 26, 2009

I knew the storm was coming. I didn't look at the time, but figure it was the early morning hours when it hit. At one point the flash and boom were simultaneous. There was a downpour for a couple of hours, accompanied by high winds. Once it ended, I slept better and ended up not waking up until after 6:00. It wasn't until later that I found out how bad the storm was.

At the edge of town I found Alquina Rd, the road I needed to get me to Oxford, OH. It was as though there was a 'no hills allowed' sign at the city limits, because as soon as I was out of town the hills began. I'm not talking about little hills either. They reminded me of Honduras, except that they were paved and smooth.

Although the storm had cooled the morning air, it was fast becoming hot again. I walked for three hours before I came to anything and, when I finally came to a town, there was only a bait shop, but it wasn't open. I walked another 2 ½ hours into and through a forested area. I came to an area where the grass at the sides of the road was neatly mowed –which reminded me of a State Park.

I found the entrance, and registration station, which I went up to and asked about refilling my water bottles and about where I might get something to eat. The only place around was half a mile up the road and I headed for it. Up another hill I found Dave's Triangle, a kind of everything store. They carried fishing supplies, hunting supplies, snacks, drinks, antiques and food. After a bite to eat and some good conversation with Dave and his mother, Hazel, I headed back down the road to my next turn, about a mile ahead.

I got to the turn, and ahead of me was a steep upgrade that went as far as I could see. This made me consider stopping for the night and tackling the hill after a good night's sleep, but there was nothing around, and it was early afternoon. So, up I started. There wasn't any shoulder on the road and, at times, the side of the road only offered a foot or so before it turned into a steep embankment.

I would walk a couple hundred yards and then stop and rest, climb for a couple hundred yards, rest and so on. I finally made it to the top, thinking about the fact that, in a week or so, I would have days like this as I got to the mountain range.

NOW someone stops and offers me a ride. It was a scenario I was now familiar with; a vehicle coming from the other direction had passed by me, turned around and came back. This driver's name was Richard Hughes. He was on his way home with a cake and birthday card in the back seat. He asked me where I was headed and he drove on as we talked. We passed through another of those small towns that time seemed to have forgotten and soon we were in Oxford, where he dropped me off at a restaurant. As I was getting out, I asked him if he was coming this far. He just kind of smiled and said "Not really". I thanked him and he left, returning the direction we had just come.

I spent an hour planning the next day's travel and then looked for a church online. Finding one that was on the outskirts of town, in the direction that I would be taking, I decided to go there. When I arrived, there was no one there but, I felt comfortable setting up my tent and prepared to spend the night.

About 9:00 a man showed up, and I introduced myself to him. He verified that it was alright to stay, asking if I needed anything, then told me that there was a prayer meeting the next morning if I was interested.

I later talked to David Mock, who lived in Reading, OH. He wanted to pick me up the next day and just spend time reading the Bible and pray together.

**Sunday-June 28, 2009**

David had picked me up on Saturday and we spent the day in fellowship. This morning we went to the House of Joy, and had a wonderful time. The pastor, Bishop Todd, had me get up and tell about the ministry and my journey before he gave his message. After the service, all the ministers in the church surrounded me to pray for me and a minister from Nigeria led. This beautiful woman of God anointed my head with oil, and I don't mean a dab on the forehead, I mean my whole head. When they were done, and I was back in my seat, she and another minister came and wanted to anoint my feet and hands.

**Tuesday-June 30, 2009**

I took a couple days of days of rest. In the evening David and Julie drove me east of Cincinnati to Chillicothe, OH, where Jeremy Caverley picked me up. Jeremy and his wife, Miranda, are JMC Ministries, friends I had met online. Miranda wasn't feeling well but, when I did the nightly update, I saw her online. She told me that she had been having stomach problems so we prayed over her. Jeremy made arrangements for me to spend the night on the Salvation Army Church grounds.

We talked about the plans he had for me. Jeremy and his wife had contacts all around the Chillicothe area, and he had plans for networking for the next couple days, so I decided to see where God took us. We got to the Salvation Army about 11:30pm, and I met Nate Vanderhoof the youth director for the Salvation Army in Chillicothe.

# JULY

**Wednesday-July 1, 2009**

Today started a whirlwind of activity that kept me going from morning to night. Jeremy and Miranda took me to the Christian book store, 'Praises', where I met Chuck, the Manager, and talked to him about the journey I was on. Next, we went to their neighbors' house, Tom and Bernice Whitt, who wanted to meet me. We had a nice long visit before we started looking for a church to worship in that evening.

Jeremy began going through the phone book and the third

church he tried was the first one to answer; Church Triumphant. They were having a Wednesday service, so I made plans to attend there.

Following that, they took me to a friend's house and I met Steven. Steven was a 58 year old man with Cerebral Palsy. The thing is, he never considered it a handicap. Steven had worked for the Salvation Army for several years as a year round kettle-ringer to raise funds for the children's programs that the Salvation Army in Chillicothe offered. Steven could tell story after story of the things God had done through his ministry. He had been able to witness and collect donations in places that most men wouldn't have thought about, let alone go into.

He tells one story of a biker rally, where he had been given a booth that was getting very few donations because of it's location. Not one to just sit around waiting, Steven hooked the kettle onto his crutches and started walking around among the bikers. Because of his persistence and dedication he raised more than $1,000 over the weekend. He was a true inspiration to me; an encouragement to keep going and never give up.

The Time came to head for the church. When Jeremy had called about the service he was told that they had a special activity lined up for that night. We arrived to find this country church packed out and discovered that the 'special activity' was a visit by two members of Team Xtreme, the Christian power team. The two were Bubba and T.J. –both of whom had dynamic testimonies.

At the end of the night they gave an altar call and, after the main group went up to the altar, one of the team told everyone to ask the person next to them if they needed to be at the altar. I looked at a small group of kids in front of me, but then the Holy Spirit told me to look behind me. Directly behind me was a young man, standing there alone. I looked him in the eyes and I knew that the Spirit of God had been convicting him. I didn't ask him if he should be at the altar, I told him "You are supposed to be up there." It was as though he was just waiting to see if anyone cared about him. He just slightly nodded his head and together we slipped out of the pews and went to the front.

The church was very well organized for the altar call; they had their counselors ready to give each person a Bible and get their information. I was impressed, so often I see altar calls where, when they're done, everyone goes home and no one even knows anyone's name to follow up on the commitments made. In all there were probably 50 people that went forward that night.

I had received permission to set my tent up beside Steven's house that night, as the alley beside the Salvation Army had a lot of traffic. We stopped at the Salvation Army first, as Nate wanted to get me some items for breakfast. While we were there Jeremy pointed out two men sitting at the picnic table whom he said were homeless; they had gotten kicked out of the shelter because the one had been drinking. We went over and Jeremy started talking to them. He shared his testimony of being homeless at the age of 19 and how, even being homeless, God led him to go on a mission trip to South Africa. Despite his circumstance, he'd worked 20 hours a week and, with that and seeking donations, saved the $3,000 needed for the trip.

We prayed for the men and then we headed for Steven's house, which I discovered was built on top of the Old Erie Canal, Which explained why the street was named Canal St.; So I can now say that I slept on the Erie Canal.

**Thursday-July 2, 2009**

Another day in Chillicothe! Jeremy and Miranda showed up and said that a friend named Lacy and Miranda's grandmother, Mary Steinhauer, wanted to meet me. first drove to Waverly, OH to her grandmother's home, where I also met Miranda's uncle, Tim Steinhauer. They lived on several acres of woodland where Mary's late husband, Bill, had been born and raised. Bill Steinhauer passed away on January 10, 2009.

While we were there, we learned that a local church had a Thursday night service, which we decided to attend later in the evening. We then headed towards Lacy's house, only to discover that Lacy's grandmother had been taken to the local hospital. We headed to the Hospital and I met Lacy, her brother and grandfather. We got the opportunity to pray with them before leaving for the Gospel Lighthouse Church in Waverly.

At the church we met Pastor Joey Sandlin, who is also a DJ for the local Radio Station, WXIC Waverly AM 660. During the service he asked me to share my testimony, and afterward invited us to stop by the radio station the next day.

### Friday-July 3, 2009

At the radio station, which focused on Southern Gospel music, Joey Sandlin talked on the air about Ministry of the Sheep, and what we are doing for the Lord.

Miranda's friend, Carmen Cooper, called as we were heading back to Chillicothe and we went to her house so I could meet her, her husband Gary, and their children, Gabby Cooper and Kayla Leon. Carmen had become a Christian a few months earlier and cited Jeremy and Miranda as the reason she turned her life over to the Lord.

We later had dinner with Miranda's mom, Becky Fannin, who works in a shelter for women who were homeless due to domestic violence. After dinner we went back to Steven's and I did my live broadcast online. Then Jeremy opened up JMC Ministries' live broadcast and I was able to give my testimony and also take questions from the chat room.

### Saturday-July 4, 2009

We stayed at Steven's all day and had a cook out. That afternoon I finally met Steven's wife Leona. At 4:30pm we left to attend a Saturday night Service at Beulah Chapel with Randy Rinehart. When we arrived I met Miranda's cousins, the singing duet "The Carter Sisters"; Bev and Vel. At that moment they were preparing the music for the service; Vel on piano and Bev on guitar.

During the service Jeremy and Miranda sang and shared testimony and then I shared my story. Later, we had snacks in the Fellowship Hall and talked with Randy and his wife, Chris

Rinehart.  Others were coming up to greet me and, many donated small amounts to help me on my way.  After refreshments several from the service went to Randy's house to watch Fireworks.

## Monday-July 6, 2009

Jeremy and Miranda had driven me to Athens, Ohio Sunday night and I got set up in a field to sleep.  During the night, there was a heavy fog and the tent was saturated with water.  By the time I had carried my backpack and tent out of the field to a parking lot, my pants were soaked from the dew on the tall grass.

I was ready to once again to get on the road.  I noticed that there was a trail, which led straight to the road that I would need to exit Athens on, so I followed it –it led to an Assembly of God Church.  I discovered that there was a prayer service going on and decided to join them.  When it was over I got a bite to eat before leaving Athens.  It was after 2:00 pm by then, but I only had about 8 miles to cover to be in Shade, OH., where I had planned to be that night.

That's not what God had planned for me though.  I was only about 3 miles outside Athens when a pickup pulled beside me and I was offered a ride.  I don't remember the man's name, but God knows who he is.  He was from West Virginia.  The first thing he told me was that he normally doesn't pick people up along the road, but he saw me and felt that he was supposed to pick me up.  He asked where I was headed, and when I told him, he asked if it would matter if he got me closer towards West Virginia.

It turned out that he had delivered something to a woman in Athens a few days earlier and, when he did, he felt that he was supposed to witness to her about Jesus.  He didn't then, but, when he got back to West Virginia, he discovered that he had forgotten to have her sign the delivery paperwork completely.  He told his employer that he would do it on his own time and in his own vehicle and was on his way home when he came across me.

He dropped me off at a store called Twin Oaks, in a place

known as Five Points. I went in to get something to eat and pulled my netbook computer out to upload photos from my camera. There were a couple ladies and a man there eating and, as they finished, one of them asked how I liked my computer. She introduced herself and gave me a card. Her name was Sheila Arnold and she was a gospel singer/songwriter whom, I later found out, was the worship leader at her church.

As we talked I told her about the ministry and my journey and she said that I needed to meet her pastor. She also told me that there was a prayer meeting going on at her church that evening. I found out that the church was about 8 miles up the road in a town called Coolville.

I figured I would head out, and, If God wanted me at the prayer meeting he will provide a ride. I didn't get a ride in time for the start of prayer meeting but, I did get a ride from one of the store employees, who had gotten off work, and was headed home. I got to Faith Harvest Church at about 8:30 and went in. They were still in the meeting, but soon the pastor came out and greeted me. Pastor Beasley and I sat for over an hour chatting about the ministry and doing what God tells us to do.

**Tuesday-July 7, 2009**

It was another night of heavy dew. I got up and moved everything off of the wet grass and onto the parking lot. I also noticed a garden hose and faucet on the building, so I took the liberty of a garden hose shower.

Once I got back on the road the day was fairly uneventful. The road was flat and easy to walk and I made good time; walking into Belfry, OH at about 5:30. I continued down the street to find a church. I walked into the first one I found and was greeted by the sounds of a gospel quartet singing "God of the Mountain".

There were 3 men at the back of the church chatting so I just stood there enjoying the music. Shortly, one of them acknowledged me. He turned out to be Pastor Jack Berry. I told him who I was and what I was doing and he warmly greeted me.

After talking to the three men for another several minutes he showed me where I could set up my tent.

We continued to talk as I was setting up, and he gave me a gift to buy breakfast with. One of the other men came up and gave me what he called a "Hallelujah handshake" slipping me another love gift. The pastor also offered to let me use the shower in the morning before leaving.

**Wednesday-July 8, 2009**

Once the pastor arrived, I took a shower; then walked to the Redwood restaurant, where everyone said that I needed to try the biscuits and gravy. After breakfast, I headed towards the edge of town and to the bridge that would take me into West Virginia.

I hadn't walked for five minutes when a car pulled up beside me and a young man asked where I was heading. I told him and he offered me a ride. His name was Jeff. He said that he had been up all night, unable to sleep, and decided to drive around. Jeff said that he had been brought up in a church, but wasn't living for God; so I got a chance to encourage him to get his heart right with God, and shared the part of my testimony where I had walked away from God and lived for myself, and the consequences it brought.

Jeff dropped me off on U.S. Highway 50, on the east side of Petersburg, WV. I started walking, and soon I hit the foothills. There wasn't anything along Highway 50 for miles and miles, and I had to keep reminding myself that, what is hours of travel to me, is just a few minute's drive in a car.

I did finally find a place to stop and get something to eat; an antique shop that also served hot dogs and ice cream. After eating and resting for a while I headed back down the road and, about 4 miles later, made it to Deerwalk, WV. Here there was nothing one church and an 'everything store'. There was no one at the church, and no one knew how to get hold of the pastor.

It was recommended to me that I go to a park about a mile outside town, so I walked back to Highway 50 and headed east again. I found the 'park'; a campground called Mt. Wood Family Park, and there found some men working. I asked about a campsite, and a man named Mark informed me that the cost for primitive campsites was $20.00 a night, but said they had another one about a mile further that was $16.00 a night.

I explained to him that I was on a journey of faith and didn't have the money to spend on a campsite. Mark told another man there, who I later found out was called Scooter, to take me to the other part of the park, and tell them to set me up for the night without charge. Scooter took me there and I met John and Darlene, the caretakers of this part of the park.

John assigned me a spot and I went about getting my tent set up. By the time I got everything up, Scooter was back and gave me a few snack items and bottles of water. A short time later, John and Darlene came over with a Chicken pot pie, fruit and Grape soda for my dinner. I thanked them and they left.

While I was eating a van pulled up with a woman who introduced herself was Mark's wife. Her name was Ruth, and she told me that she and Mark had moved there from New York. She shared that she was a 'Christian Clown', and had a ministry there at the park for the children on weekends.

**Thursday-July 9, 2009**

I finally got around to leaving at about 8:00am, stopping on the way out to thank John and Darlene. Once again, there were miles and miles of nothing but forest and hills. The vastness of the forest gave me a sense of awe similar to the one I had, seeing the vastness of the farmland, in Minnesota. It just went on as far as I could see. By mid-afternoon, my feet were sore and my legs were screaming at me for making them carry me up and down the hills.

I finally got to Ellenboro, WV, where there were places to eat. It was already almost 4:00pm and I decided that I would find a Laundromat, and then spend the night there. I asked the cashier of a store about a Laundromat and she said there weren't any in Ellenboro; the closest was in Pennsboro, 4 miles away –by way of the back road which ran beside the store.

I gathered my things together and headed down the back road towards Pennsboro, going less than half the distance before hearing a voice calling from a house. A man in a patriotic shirt was commenting on my load. He asked where I was headed and I told him that I was trying to get to the Laundromat in Pennsboro before it closed. He offered to drive me there and I, of course, accepted.

The man, whose name is Sam Crites, was the pastor of Pennsboro Baptist Church and another inspiration. He explained that he had a bicycle accident a few years earlier, and suffered a head injury which left him disabled. He had been an interim pastor at Pennsboro Baptist some 20 years earlier. After his head injury, he'd received a call from the board of the church, inviting him to return as their Senior pastor. Sam told them that he couldn't and explained that, due to the head injury, his thinking process was messed up. The board responded, telling him that they didn't care. They had been in prayer and God had told them that *he* would be their pastor. Sam continued sharing his story of God's grace and provisions.

As Sam dropped me off at the Laundromat, he asked where I would be spending the night. I told him that I wasn't sure, but God would lead me to a place. He asked if I would like to sleep inside the church, citing that it would be more comfortable than being outdoors. I couldn't argue with that, and so accepted, telling him that the laundry would take about an hour and a half. He said that he would be back then. True to his word, as I was folding the last of the clothes, Pastor Crites returned.

After getting me set up in the nursery, where the floor was carpeted, he left me there –making sure that I knew to pull the door closed tight when I left. At update time I let everyone know how I had been blessed that day and then went to sleep.

## Friday-July 10, 2009

I woke a little later than I had been. I hurried to get things packed before walking to the family restaurant that Pastor Crites had told me about the night before. Heading out after breakfast, I walked about a mile to get to U.S. Highway 50, then turned east.

After about three miles, a car pulled up in front of me and a young man asked where I was headed. I told him and he said he could get me that far. I usually talk with people a little before asking about their spiritual life, but as I was getting into the car, I heard the Holy Spirit say "Hit him with it". I reached over, shaking his hand, introducing myself to him and said "So, Where are you spiritually?" He looked shocked, but then he said, 'Until a couple years ago I was an atheist; but I had an accident where the car rolled, like 8 times, and they said I should never have lived through it.' He held his elbow up and said, 'I got 5 stitches in my elbow and that was my only injury. So, I know there has to be a higher power and there has to be a plan for me, I just don't know which religion is right.' I said, "Let me tell you about my Jesus." and for the next 45 minutes he listened and asked questions. When offered a ride I normally only accept it as far as a day's travel, but, knowing that this was more important than stopping, I continued on with him.

He ended up driving me almost twice as far as planned, and, when he got to his destination, I gave him a track that I had written the ministry website on and asked him to read it and also visit the "R U Saved" page on the website. It wasn't until we had parted that it dawned on me that we had been so wrapped up in talking that I had never even asked his name.

I was now in Clarksburg, WV, about half a day ahead of schedule. There was a Church on a corner, and I went there to try and get my bearings. Figuring out where I needed to go, I started back out. After walking a few feet down the sidewalk, a man flagged me down to ask about my backpack. I had started telling him about my journey when he told me that there was a mission just down the street and recommended that I spend the night. I thought it was odd that, at noon time, he would be recommending staying for the night, but, feeling led, I headed to the mission, which was simply called the Clarksburg Mission.

I was greeted by Angel Pritt, who was in charge of the

dorms, and she introduced Lisa Hartline, who was the housing director. I was told that, if I wanted to eat, I would need to hurry before they stopped serving. I found the dining room and went inside. There were a variety of people there; a few older people, a couple of young families, and some that seemed somewhat emotionally unbalanced, who probably struggled just to get through each day.

Several of the men there were curious about my journey and wanted to know where I was headed the next day. I told them, and they brainstormed to figure exactly what I would be facing. They tried to talk me into staying on Highway 50, assuring me that it would be easier traveling, and I would get more rides. I later talked to a couple of friends on the phone that told me the same thing.

At 11:00 everything was locked down, no one in or out until morning, and the lights were turned off.

**Saturday-July 11, 2009**

I was up and ready to head out at 6:30AM. I grabbed a junk food breakfast at a gas station, and was on the road by 7:00.

Since everyone advised me to stay on Highway 50, I felt that maybe I should, and had just about decided to do that. When I came to the road I was supposed to turn on, it was marked with a sign that said 'Dead End' and I thought "That solves that dilemma." –but shortly I came to Road 76, which the other road was supposed come out onto.

Suddenly I thought of a passage in Matthew; *"Go in through the narrow gate, for wide is the gate and broad is the way that leads to destruction, and many there are who go in through it. Because narrow is the gate and constricted is the way which leads to life, and there are few who find it."* (Matthew 7:13-14 MKJV)

This journey wasn't about getting rides; it wasn't about getting anywhere faster. It was about being in God's will, whatever that was. If he wanted me to get somewhere faster or easier he would make it happen; If I got out of his will, who knew what I would miss?

I turned on Road 76, which took me to the South about one mile and then turned back to the east. It was a long road that had nothing but houses, woods and long, steep hills. The shoulder was nearly non-existent and at times the hill dropped off beside the road.

At one point a young dog started following me. At first it held back 50 yards or so and gradually moved closer until it was walking beside me. It would push its head into my hand like it thought it was my dog, or I was his human, whichever way it works.

In time I came to Bailey Memorial United Methodist Church, near Rosemont, and took a break there. Next to the church was a historical school. The sign said that it was the first school for African-Americans in West Virginia, established for the children of Black Miners.

The pastor of the church showed up and we talked for a while. Then, after filling my water bottles, I headed back down the road, still being followed by the dog.

A mile later I came to the town of Flemington, WV, where the roads changed. The roads were not marked very well and I wasn't sure if I was to go straight or turn. There was a church on the corner, with several young people there, apparently having a work day. I asked about the roads and got directions, then I asked about the dog. One of the young people recognized it as belonging to a neighbor and said they would take it home later. I thanked them and headed out walking.

I walked about 1½ miles more when a pickup, with a picnic table in the back, pulled over beside me. There were 3 people in it, a man named Dave and his two teenage kids. Dave asked where I was headed, and I told him that I was supposed to turn onto Flag Run Road, about a mile ahead. They took me to the intersection and asked if I was sure that was the right place; telling me that the road didn't go through anymore, and that it was broken up and overgrown. Then, he offered to drive me 4 miles, to U.S. Highway 119, which would put me a little north of where Flag Run would have come out, if it were open.

After dropping his kids off Dave and I traveled the 4 miles, talking about the importance of, not only raising the kids in church, but raising them to be servants of God. Soon he was dropping me off at the intersection of County Road 13 and U.S. Highway 119.

The road from that point was, to say the least, a challenge. Like the roads I had come off of, it was narrow, often times with almost no shoulder to walk on. It was also full of steep, curving hills. I walk on until about 7:00pm, before I came to the Southern Baptist Church of Philippi, about one and a half miles outside of the city of Philippi WV.

By now I was drained. I figured that I had walked 28 miles and then the few that I had been given a ride. All I had to eat was some crackers and peanut butter, so I was debating whether to stay there or just take a break and then walk the rest of the way into town to get something to eat.

The church had three buildings. One was the church, one was a modular, probably used for classrooms, and the third looked like a fellowship hall and had a sign that read "Angel food Ministries". The modular had a small deck attached to it and I sat down and ate a few crackers with peanut butter, then laid back to rest, but ended up dozing off.

I awoke to the sound of a car door closing and sat up to see an elderly man and woman carrying groceries into the fellowship hall. I checked the time and discovered that I had slept for almost an hour and it was now after 8:00pm.

I introduced myself to the man, who said his name was Bill, and, telling him of my travels, asked about setting my tent up for the night. Bill said that it was alright and told me that there may be others coming in later. Bill went on to explain that, there were about 40 people coming from Florida, to help build an addition onto the church. As soon as Bill said that I had the impression that I was supposed to stay and help in some way, but didn't mention it right then, as I wanted time to pray about it.

One concern I had if I stayed was meals. There didn't seem

to be anything around where I could get food; but I knew that if God led me to stay he would take care of that. When I did my update online I told them what I had felt and asked everyone to pray with me about it. I fell asleep praying that night, listening for an answer.

### Sunday-July 12, 2009

I awoke this morning certain that I was to stay and help at the church in some way. Right after I got my tent down and everything packed, a few people started showing up at the Fellowship Hall. I went in, introduced myself and asked if I could use the bathroom to clean up before the service. Once I got cleaned up, one of the women asked if I had eaten anything for breakfast, and, when I told her that I had not, offered me a sandwich and hash browns that she had brought with her.

When Bill arrived, he greeted me and I told him that, if it was okay with them, I would stay an extra day to help work on the church. He said that would be fine and introduced me to a couple of people. Everyone greeted me warmly and I knew that this was a church that didn't just preach the Christian life, but lived it.

The group, I learned, were mostly from the First Baptist Church in Milton, FL, though there were some there from The Carolinas and one couple from Colorado, who had brought a young man with them that had only been in God's Family for a couple of months.

Bill began the service and, after the normal openings and recognizing of the groups that had come, he introduced me. After explaining what I was doing, they took a love offering for me.

The sermon was presented by Pastor David W. Spencer, the pastor of First Baptist Church in Milton, FL, and afterward I was invited to eat with the missions group. I was accepted in as though I had been part of the church from the beginning, right down to getting one of the mission trip T-shirts. The afternoon was spent in fellowship and sharing testimonies. We had an evening service, then we finished the day with a dinner before the team headed to the hotel.

## Monday-July 13, 2009

There wasn't any sleeping in this morning. The team's bus arrived bright and early. The women started making breakfast and the rest of "us" started building. I say "us" since the group was so well organized that there really wasn't anything for me to do. So, I started taking photos of the team and the work in progress. By the time breakfast was ready, the three outer walls were up and braced. By the end of the day the team had everything done that could be, until more material arrived the next day.

After dinner Blackie, who was in charge of the group, and his wife drove me into Philippi. I figured I would make my way to the other edge of the town so as to get a good start the next morning. As I hadn't seen any churches, I started looking for a place along the road to set my tent up on, finally finding a flat area up the hillside beside the road. While it wasn't the most comfortable looking spot, I had slept on worse.

## Tuesday-July 14, 2009

I don't know how long I had been asleep, but I woke up cold. It was colder than it had been in a month. I was up before the sun, packed and ready to hit the road by first light. I walked about 6 miles before I came to Nestorville, WV. There were only two businesses that I saw, a service station and an automotive shop. Fortunately, the service station had a few convenience items and hot coffee. By now it was starting to warm up enough to take my sweatshirt off, but had it not been for the walking and the sun's rays, I would have been chilled.

I continued on State Road 38 towards Valley Furnace, which I discovered was so named for the smelting furnace that had operated there in the 1800's. A ways past it, I came to an area where a man was mowing grass. He shut the mower down and greeted me, offering a place to rest and something to drink.

His name was Perry, and he told me that he and his wife retired there a few years prior. We talked about different things. About how peaceful it was there, about the economy, his neighbors. I got the feeling that, while he was happy living where he did, he was a bit lonely for people to just sit and chat with. After a good half hour or so I told him that I should be going and he said he needed to finish the mowing, so we said goodbye and I headed back down the road.

An hour or so later, as I was thinking about taking another break, a car pulled up beside me. It was Perry, who had finished his mowing and decided to drive me closer to my destination. We went about 10 miles, to West Virginia State Road 72, which put me at about 6½ miles outside of Parsons WV.

On to Parsons-- By now the air had warmed and it was quite nice outside, but once again, the road was steep and there was little shoulder. I walked to the top of the foothill and took a break, at what looked like it had once been a western tack store. After that I walked another two hours or so before coming to Parsons.

I headed for a church I saw across the river. The river was about as picturesque as you could get. It had a rock basin and the water was crystal clear. The old town and hills made for a perfect backdrop.

I found St. Johns Methodist Church just across the river. At the parsonage, the door was answered by the pastor's wife, whose name was Donna, and she directed me to the back, where I met the pastor, whose name was John. I explained myself to Pastor John and He welcomed me and showed me where I could set my tent up in front of the church.

As I was setting up the tent John asked if I wanted something to eat. Donna provided me with a plate heaped with homemade spaghetti and garlic bread; then she let me know that there was a ladies' Bible study late, inviting me to help myself to snacks and desserts after their study was over.

After dinner John excused himself, as he was headed out to

do some fishing. I too excused myself, retrieving my camera from my tent, headed out to take some pictures of the area. After that I put on some swimming shorts, and headed for the river. It was one of the most refreshing rivers I had been in. Because it was so shallow and had a black rock basin, it was almost warm. I found a spot where the bottom lowered a little to where I could sit down and have the current pulsating against my back, almost like a hot tub. After getting relaxed and refreshed, I spent the rest of the evening writing and visiting with the ladies of the church.

## Wednesday-July 15, 2009

The morning was quite pleasant. I was awake at first light and ready to go. I had been told the night before what to expect today. It was 16 miles to Thomas, WV, which was on the top of Thomas Mountain, and the ascent would begin about 2 miles outside of Parsons. After a quick breakfast, I began my trek towards Thomas Mountain.

The first mile and a half wasn't too bad. The road was wide and level for the most part. Then I came to where U.S. Highway 219 and State Highway 72 split. Highway 72 looked level and U.S. 219 started uphill. My route took me on U.S. 219, and I walked, uphill, for a good hour.

Suddenly, there was a pickup truck beside me and an elderly man shouting, "Whatcha doin out here?" I told him that I was trying to make it to Thomas today. He responded "Shoot, that's another 12 miles, straight up." I told him that I was aware of that, and that I had been praying for a ride. He tells me "Well, put your stuff in back and let's stop wasting time then."

In the truck I was welcomed by gospel music that my parents listened to 40 years earlier, and I thought was old fashioned back then. This man, whom I learned was 80, was Don Pace. He had a "get things done, don't dilly-dally around" attitude. He said there were too many things to do for God to waste time talking about what to do. Listening to Don was like listening to me.

Too many people have been "waiting to hear from God" for

years. In the meantime, they come across, and ignore people every day that the Bible tells us to minister to. If you feel God has something special for your life, by all means, seek it out through prayer. But if you see someone in need, fill that need. Don't go around saying "Well, God hasn't told me what to do yet." He told us, in his word, what every believer is to do. Some have been given special tasks, but we are all expected to share God's love.

Don dropped me off at the top of the mountain, just on the edge of Thomas. He would be heading north on U.S. 219 and I would be going the other way, on State Road 93. Before I got out of the truck we prayed together and I thanked him. What had looked like a full day's journey turned out to be only a few hours.

I found a restaurant, sat at a table and, checking my route, I ordering a meal. I saw that, once I left Thomas, the next town was Davis, just a few miles away. After that it would be about 16 miles to the next place that showed any population. A peace came over me at the thought of a 16 mile afternoon walk –so I finished eating and headed out, going through Thomas and turning onto State Road 93 just before entering Davis.

For the next 3 hours, there was little to nothing but trees, rock and an occasional vehicle. The road was basically all downhill, but it was still slow traveling with the backpack on.

An older car passed me, stopped and then backed up. There were two young men in it and they offered me a ride for a couple of miles. They were, of course, inquisitive about me being there, walking. They didn't seem to understand why anyone would give up anything to do what God told them to. I got the feeling that they looked at God as something to believe in as a child, call on when in trouble, and look to when you're old and afraid of dying. I had a chance to tell them about the God that had a plan for each person created. I never did get their names. The ride only lasted a couple of minutes, but I did get a chance to plant a seed and gave them each a different gospel tract to read and share. They dropped me off at the entrance of the coal mine they worked in, and I continued on my descent of

Thomas Mountain.

Some four hours later I came to a power plant that seemed to rise out of the mountain forest, and, past that, the first houses in nearly 16 miles. At the very first house a man was outside loading a vehicle. When he saw me he opened a conversation concerning my burden and the distance I had just covered, then offered me something to drink, which was much appreciated. As I was enjoying the ice water, he listened about my pilgrimage.

When I finished he told me that he had been there for a funeral, and was just getting ready to head back to his home state. He said that he would be passing the church where the funeral had been held, and offered me a ride there. I readily accepted and, once everything was loaded, we headed towards Falls Assembly of God church –about 10½ miles away.

We arrived at the church about 6:30PM and there were people gathering for service already. I found the pastor, Vivan Watts, and asked about setting my tent up for the evening. He gave me permission and then asked about my journey. Later, during service, he introduced me and had me tell the members about my journey, and at the end of the service they all gathered around and prayed over me. Afterward, Pastor Watts wife suggested I stay in the Evangelist Quarters, which was basically a one bedroom apartment in the church.

### Thursday-July 16, 2009

This was a "God day" though I didn't know it at the time. I didn't wake up and think, "This is one of those days when God does great things" –though I have since realized that every day is a "God day".

I had slept later than I had planned. I had actually awaken about the time I would usually get up, but decided to lay in bed for a while; and I ended up dozing off to sleep again. I finally got up and got myself together and, after a breakfast, I went out the door that Pastor Vivan said would lock behind me.

I walked a mile or so and, as I was passing a small, homestead-looking farm, an elderly man came outside. I thought he looked familiar and, when he greeted me by name, I realized I had seen him at the church the night before. He had figured that, at some point during the day, I would be passing his house, and was waiting to offer me a ride for a short distance.

He drove me a few miles to the next intersection, Patterson Creek Road, and I headed south to Lahmansville, WV. The area looked like it hadn't changed much in a hundred years. There was a small, two room building that looked like a school and an old shack with a mailbox on one end and a portable outhouse on the other. The sign on the side announced that it was the Lahmansville post office.

After five miles or so, I turned onto a road that took me to an area that was uphill and wooded. I hadn't seen any vehicle for about an hour, but, all of a sudden, there were two vans. The first one stopped beside me and I could see that it was full. The second van stopped behind it and waited, so I assumed they were together.

The driver of the first van began talking to me and asking me what I was doing. I shared some of my journey and they seemed amazed at it. There was something very familiar with the way they presented themselves and I had a suspicion, which was confirmed a moment later when I was given a copy of "Watch Tower" the Jehovah Witness' magazine. Once I started talking about the Divinity of Jesus, the driver apologized that they were full and couldn't take me anywhere, and left.

To my surprise, the second van, which I had assumed was with the first one, pulled beside me and stopped. This one had a young man in it and, he too asked where I was headed. I told him that I was attempting to make it to Moorefield by night time. He told me that was where he was headed and offered me a ride.

His name was Lee Short. Lee lived in the area and was headed to Moorefield to shop and take care of some business. Lee and I talked about the things of God as we slowly made our way up, down and around the hills. He told me what church he attended, and it sounded like a good, Bible based church. I let him know how blessed he was to be raised in a Godly environment. I shared with him the importance of maintaining his relationship with God; adding that too many have turned from the faith they grow up in, only to make a mess of their lives – Myself included.

We made it to Moorefield and Lee dropped me off where I could get lunch and figure out where I needed to go from there. While online, in search of a route, I looked out the window, trying to get my bearings, and saw a sign for the turn I needed to make onto State Highway 55, just outside the window. It looked like the next town was about 15 miles away, and, while it didn't look like there was much between the two towns, I figured I could at least find a place to fill my water bottles.

Done eating, I headed east on Highway 55, walked about one mile, and was picked up by a young man in a pickup truck. His name was Zack and he was only going to the next exit, which was about 2 miles ahead. I didn't get much time to talk to Zack, but I did let him know of my faith in God and gave him a witnessing tract that I had picked up in the church the night before. Zack dropped me off at the top of the ramp and I continued on down the other side of the bridge.

I was barely back onto the highway when a car pulled over in front of me. As I approached on the passenger side, the driver, a middle aged man, called out and asked if I wanted a ride. I noticed that there was a cross hanging from the mirror which, with his age group at least, meant that he had some kind of Christian belief. I commented on it once I got into the car and learned that he was a pastor from Moorefield, who was headed to Winchester, VA, to visit a church member in the hospital there. He offered to take me as far as I wanted. Winchester was several miles up the road and, to get there you have to go through Stephens City, which I would be going through. I considered riding all the way with the Pastor, but didn't feel that I was supposed to, so instead I asked to be dropped off in Wardensville, WV. He let me out at a Laundromat and continued on his way.

I spent the next couple hours doing laundry, and then headed further into town. There was a man and a few teenagers sitting in front of a house on the main street. We struck up a conversation, and I was directed to a church, on the opposite end of Wardensville, which had a large area around it.

After getting a few things to eat at the local convenience store, I headed for the church. It was an Assembly of God Church, and it did indeed have a large lot. I also noticed on the sign, that it had a Thursday evening service, instead of the usual Wednesday service. It was almost 6:00pm, so I sat on the step of the church and waited for people to arrive.

The pastor and his family were the first to arrive. I let him know who I was and what I was doing, then asked about setting up for the night. After getting permission, I commented about the service and he told me that it would be an unusual service, as it was preparing for an outreach they were doing over the weekend, during a city fair. I told him that I would help in whatever way I could and, as others arrived, we gathered in the sanctuary. The 'Preparation' was a prayer service, which, in my opinion, was quite appropriate for preparing for an outreach.

At the end of the prayer meeting I was shown where I could set my tent up; a wooded area that was apparently part of the church property. While I was preparing my tent several of the men stood around talking with me and I learned that, in the early days of the Assemblies of God, Wardensville was a revival hotspot. Where the woods are now, had once been an open field with a large barn in it. People would come from miles around for the revival meetings, which started in early spring and went late into the fall. They would bring what they had to offer –be it dried beans, fresh vegetables or meat. Everyone would work together to make meals and, no matter what you brought, be it nothing or the finest meats, everyone was equal. It seems to me that that was how the early church might have been. It made me want to be able to visit the past to see what that was truly like.

## Friday-July 17, 2009

I was up and on the road early today. The weather was cool and cloudy. As the morning went on the clouds became thicker and it began sprinkling. Soon it was pouring down rain. I was too far away from Wardensville to go back and miles from any other town; so I just wrapped up in my poncho and kept going until I came to the Virginia State-line.

There I found a spring. that I had been told of in church the night before. The water was gushing out of a piece of PVC pipe that someone had wedged into the rock. so the water came out away from the side of the hill instead of down the rock. I filled my water bottles and drank my fill of the cold, fresh water. The only way it could have been better would have been if it was hot that day instead of rainy.

While I was there, an old pickup truck from the 50's pulled in and a man got out. He looked like he could have been in his mid-nineties, though I never did find out. He pulled out several water jugs and began filling them. We started talking about the area, and he said the water there was the only water he had ever drunk. Once his bottles were filled, he said that he needed to get home to milk the cows.

I continued along U.S. Highway 48 and in mid-afternoon, a car pulled to the side of the road. It was one of the ladies from the church in Wardensville, who was headed to Stevens City, VA. She dropped me off at a fast food restaurant and I spent the rest of the afternoon writing and then looking for a church.

What happened next was the first instance where I was rejected by a church. I am not here to lift one denomination up, nor put one down, so I will refrain from naming the church. There were people there when I arrived and I quickly located the pastor. Introducing myself and giving him one of my cards, I explained that I just needed a place to set my tent up for the night. He took me to the back of the church which had a nice, big yard surrounded by a wooded area. I thought the pastor had brought me back there to show me where to set up my tent. I was surprised when he started out by saying, 'Now see, the kids like to come back here and party on the weekends.' I told him "that isn't a problem; I'll invite them over for a Bible Study".

Then, pointing to a housing area, he said 'Well, see that

house over there? The lady that lives there will call the police on the kids and they'll come.' I responded, "I was an officer for 20 years, I know how to 'cop talk'." He quickly added, 'Besides, the men have a function early in the morning and when they find you here they will wake me up to find out who you are.' I asked "Oh, are they having a Bible Study?" As he answers, he kind of rolls his eyes and says 'No, a men's breakfast..., but they'll call and wake me up, and besides, the deer graze back here and one might step on you in your tent.' At this point I'm thinking of all of the churches where they would have said 'Of course, you can set up back here, and by the way, the men are having a breakfast in the morning. Why don't you join us as my guest and have some fellowship?'

But this man, claiming not only to be a man of God, but to be the shepherd of a flock, tells me that there is a campground a couple blocks away, where I might be able to set up my tent. When I re-explained that I was living on faith, and wondered if they might donate a spot, I was told that if they didn't, to return and then he would see what he could do for me.

This was my first, fully negative experience with a church and I was greatly disheartened. As I prepared to leave I told the pastor, "The ministry is named after Matthew 25:31-46. Going by that scripture, you just told Jesus to go into the world and, if the world rejected him, then you might help him out." Then I turned, kicked the dust off my feet symbolically and walked away.

The campground was a quarter mile away and, as there was no one there to give permission to set up a tent, I ended up sleeping in a clump of trees, about half a mile from there. I prayed for that pastor that night. Perhaps because of our encounter, his eyes would be opened.

### Saturday-July 18, 2009

It rained again during the night, but, by the time I got up, the sky was clear. I ate a few crackers and peanut butter for breakfast and headed East on State road 277.

No Mere Coincidences, a journey of faith

The day turned into one of the nicest days I had seen. It was cool and there was a nice breeze, not too windy, just right. As I walked through the countryside I came to a man who was working a few yards off the roadway on his property. He called out and told me that there was a water spigot, with ice cold spring water, at the side of the road if I was thirsty. Seeing the faucet, I thanked him and started filling my bottles. He came over after a few minutes and introduced himself as Dennis and I introduced myself as having the same name, giving him a card.

We talked about mission work and Dennis told me that he had been to Africa on safaris and told me about the school there that his wife had adopted. Every year she would send enough pens and paper to supply each of the students for the year. Before I left Dennis gave me a love gift which would provide a day of meals for me.

As I continued my journey I couldn't help but notice the countryside was becoming more and more 'Colonial' looking. Stone fences, some stretching for miles, had been built there hundreds of years earlier, erected by the people who had cleared the land. Men would dig the rocks up and the women and children would load them onto wagons, and then move them to the edge of the property, where others would build the walls. These fences had no mortar to hold them together, just the skill of the men putting them in place, and had stood through storms and battles. I wondered what it must have been like then. I know that most of the work was done by slaves and that, in itself, showed the integrity of these men. To be forced into labor and yet, do their jobs with such pride, that the walls were there hundreds of years later.

I came to the intersection of U.S. Highway 50, where there were a few businesses, and stopped to get something to eat. About 5:00 I was picked up by a man named Christian. He was another one who passed by me then turned around. Christian drove me about 7 miles to Middleburg, VA and dropped me off in the center of town.

Middleburg was a small, rustic town, kept in the Colonial-

Era style –full of small shops and restaurants. I found Middleburg Baptist Church on the edge of town. It was a beautiful, old, historical church, surrounded by graveyards with headstones dating back to the 1800's. As there was no one around, I set my tent up behind the church and then, grabbing my camera, started walking around the old cemetery that made a horseshoe around the church. After getting several pictures, I walked up the street and found a small pizza shop, going inside.

My camera was still around my neck and the man inside asked if I was the photographer for the Bluegrass event. I told him that I wasn't and started telling him about the journey I was on. He said that he didn't believe the Bible because it was just a book written by man. I explained that it had been inspired by God Himself. He said that it may have been, but man had written it down and then changed things in it. I let him know that I disagreed, explaining how the Dead Sea scrolls had been found more than 300 years after King James had the scriptures translated into English and, when the Dead Sea scrolls were translated, there was very little difference. He seemed to have a "my mind's made up, don't confuse me with facts" attitude, but there were a couple others in the restaurant that seemed to be listening intently.

I bought a slice of pizza, thanked the man and left, soon coming upon a street music festival. I listened to the Bluegrass music for a few minutes before walking around the rest of the little town, then returned to the church.

**Sunday-July 19, 2009**

I walked to a small gas station for coffee and a sweet roll. Then, returning to the church, I washed up at a faucet before people to started arriving.

The congregation was warm and friendly. I met the pastor, Dr. Bill Thipen, and he invited me to join his Sunday school class. It was an in-depth study, designed for maturing Christians, giving the meat of the Word. The service was about going where God calls you, whether it's across the world, across the country or across the street, often referring to me as an example. I've wondered if it's God's planning or if pastors change the sermon topic because I'm there. It seems that many of the sermons I've attended have been on service to God or on having faith.

It was almost 1:00pm when I finally got back on the road. The rest of the day was basically uneventful. Travel was easier now that I was out of the mountains, though there were still some hills. I walked until about 7:30 before coming to Stone Ridge, VA; where I found a place to eat, but, unable to locate any churches, ended up in a field off of the road. I was still 5 miles from my goal of Chantilly, VA so I decided to get an early start the next morning.

**Monday-July 20, 2009**

I hadn't walked much more than a mile this morning when I began wondering if I had awakened in Mexico. There, at the side of the road, was a gas station with a large banner that read 'Pupusaria Hernandez'. There were several Latinos standing around the store. I went inside and they did, indeed, have *Pupusas*, so I enjoyed a couple for breakfast before continuing.

It was a very humid day and by the time the sun got very high, it was quite warm. It wasn't long before I was totally soaked in sweat, from head to toe, to the point that my feet squished when I walked. I finally made it to Fairfax, VA, where I took a break at a shopping mall.

As I started back towards the road, a lady in an SUV pulled beside me and handed me an ice cold bottle of water. I thanked her as I accepted it and thought, "This is what being Christian is about… seeing a need or a way to help others, and doing it without hesitation."

Not much further along, a man in an old pickup, sitting at a traffic light, indicated for me to climb in if I wanted. He drove me a couple miles to the Fairfax Circle and, as he dropped me off in the parking lot, he pointed out a mission where I could get lunch if I wanted. I thanked him, and continued on my way, reaching Arlington about 5:30. I made my way to Rosslyn, VA, where I got a sandwich at to eat before crossing the Potomac River into Washington DC.

That night I did the update online from the steps of the Lincoln Memorial. There were several people with bags marked with the Christians United for Israel logo on them. They were with World Vision from New York. Most of them were young people, but I found one of the adults and interviewed her.

After the update, I made my way past the Washington Memorial and stopped to watch the end of Close Encounters, which was being played on a Jumbo-Tron in the park. As the people started clearing I wondered where I would sleep that night. There were no churches nearby that would have lawns and I didn't think I would be able to set my tent in the middle of the park. I finally laid on the steps of the Smithsonian Museum of Natural History, and shortly I was asleep.

**Tuesday-July 21, 2009**

I awoke at 5:00. Surprisingly, I slept undisturbed all night, though not soundly. It amazed me that I could sleep there and not be noticed. I walked up 9th street towards the Convention Center. finding a McDonald's, I went inside and got breakfast, buying an extra sandwich and a few pies to eat later.

Soon I made my way to the convention center and found a few people going in. I was hoping to get a picture inside but, as I didn't have a pass, wasn't allowed in. So I sat outside for a while and watched as people filed into the convention center, walking past people sleeping on the lawn of the building across the street. These people were obviously homeless, and were probably wondering what they would eat for breakfast. I engaged in conversation with one of the men on the lawn across the street and ended up sharing my sandwich with him.

I left there and began making my way towards the Capital. I was sitting on the steps of a fountain when a jogger stopped and said that he had seen me walking in Fairfax the previous day. We talked for a while and, as he parted, he said that he would keep me in his prayers and would also tell his church about me and

Ministry of the Sheep.

From there I headed towards the Holocaust Museum on 14<sup>th</sup> Street. I had been to most of the museums while stationed in the area in the early 80's, but the Holocaust Museum hadn't been built yet; when I was there in 1997, for Stand in the Gap, I didn't have time to visit it.

There was a long line when I arrived at 10:00. So I waited, managing to get a ticket for entrance at 11:30. I decided to go to the snack shop –which was in an adjacent building –to get a drink while I waited. I knew things had changed since September 11, 2001, but I was surprised when I had to pass through Security to get into the snack shop. I carry a clip on knife in my front pocket and had another knife in my backpack. I was told that if I turned them over to Security, I wouldn't get them back. I ended up going across the street, where there was a clump of bushes and pine trees, and burying them in the pine needles.

At 11:30 I entered the museum. On the first floor I was given identification papers, like they had to carry at the time, with the history of one of Hitler's victims. Then you enter elevators, the entrance of which is made to look like the entrance of the gas chambers, and they take you to the top floor of the museum.

From the first exhibit I was choking back tears. How one group of people could hate others for any reason, let alone race or religion, is nothing short of demonic. I had read of the propaganda claiming that the Jewish people were cheating and trying to take control. What I hadn't realized was that there was only a 1% Jewish population in Germany. The country was hardly on the verge of a hostile takeover. I would encourage anyone that gets to the Washington, DC area to visit this museum. I have read books and seen documentaries on the Holocaust, but it became so much more real when I stood beside a bed, brought from Auschwitz death camp, knowing that the people that had laid on that bed had been murdered en mass.

I left Washington, DC, passing Arlington Cemetery, and headed south on U.S. Highway 1, walking until just before

9:00pm. I stopped just past the Pentagon and Crystal City to get something to eat and do the nightly update. After the broadcast I went another mile or so, where I found a thick grove of pine trees at the side of the road. I crawled under it and, lying on top of my sleeping bag, fell into a deep slumber.

**Wednesday-July 22, 2009**

Another humid day! Even though there was a slight chill in the air when I woke up, I was already sweating. Then, it got hot.

As I walked, I came to an area that had been fenced off and had several signs along the fence. One sign announced that a Freeman's Cemetery Park would soon be there. I stopped to read more and learned that the area had been used as a cemetery for black slaves that had made their way to the area to escape slavery.

The cemetery had been used for just three years, but in that time over 1,500 former slaves had been buried there. Over half of them had been children under the age of 10. With nothing but wooden markers, the rest had soon been forgotten. Roads had been built over it and, in the 1950's, a gas station had been erected on it.

I continued on my way, passing Fort Belvoir. I had been stationed there in 1984 and, being on light duty because of a motorcycle accident, placed in charge of vehicle registration.

It was a 9-5, Mon-Fri office job. I am not a 'sit in the office' type person. Everyone working for me thought it was great, having evenings and weekends off. I hated it. My roommate and other friends were Road M.P.'s and worked rotating shifts, so most often I was alone in the barracks or had to be quiet so they could sleep.

I made it to Woodbridge, VA about 4:00pm, tired, hot and still 5 miles short of my destination of Dumfries, VA. I came to a small mall which had a Laundromat in it. I thought that I would do my laundry, find a church and call it a day.

Again, God had other plans. I walked into the Laundromat and it was crowded. There were two women inside shouting and cussing at each other and an attendant that was just ignoring them. In one aspect, I knew that this was a place that needed to see God's love and, may have been a place that Jesus would have gone into. On the other hand, I didn't feel that it was where I was supposed to be. I left and headed back to the road, following the sidewalk of the L shaped mall.

As I approached the doors of the last store, a young man walked out, and seeing me, jerked back, as though I had caught him by surprise. Then it was my turn to be startled. Without so much as blinking, and as quickly as he had jerked back, he asked "Can I take you somewhere?" It was so abrupt that I think *I* jerked back. I told him where I was headed and he said "It doesn't matter where; I'm just supposed to take you somewhere." Without any further conversation he led me to a pickup truck and helped me put my backpack in the back of it.

As we got into the truck we made our introductions and I learned his name was Daniel. It turned out that Daniel was a Marine stationed at Quantico –but, before he entered the militaty, he had been the assistant youth pastor at his church in Texas.

Reaching Dumfries, he deposited me at a gas station, where I inquired about a Laundromat. Leaving without the information I sought, I saw a young police officer and asked him. He said that he wasn't sure, but he thought there was a Laundromat in the mall at the other end of town, about 1 mile away. I found it, started my laundry, then sat down at a table near the window.

What I saw amazed me. There, across the parking lot from the Laundromat, was... The Dumfries police station. My only thought was, "I hope that officer never gets an emergency call here. It would be embarrassing to have to ask its location."

I talked to the attendant, a young man named Jonathan, who was in college. As we talked, I told him about Ministry of the Sheep, and Jonathan said that he had been feeling led to be a missionary. We talked about this for a while and I encouraged him to earnestly seek God's will for his life and that God would reveal it.

**Thursday-July 23, 2009**

It was another hot, humid day and my stomach was upset, so I found myself stopping often to rest. By 6:30pm I hadn't even made it to Fredericksburg, VA. I found a church, named Covenant Family Church. When I found no one there, I tried to call the phone number on the church sign, getting voice mail. I left a message in hopes that someone would check it. Then I put my backpack behind the church and walked to the corner where there was a convenience store.

I got a dinner from the deli, and returned to the church with my meal. Taking out my netbook, I looked up the church's website online and liked what I saw in the Mission Statement. Soon, a Lexus pulled up with a young couple in it. I introduced myself, telling them that I had been trying to get ahold of the pastor for permission to set up for the night. The response I got from the man was "You can't just walk up and ask something like that. You need to submit a request and wait for a response." That left me disheartened. From what I had seen on the website, I was led to believe that this was a Bible based, Bible practicing church. When Jesus told Zaccheus to come out of the tree, he didn't say "I'd like to come to your house for dinner next week." When people came to him for healing, he didn't say "Let me consider it and I'll get back to you later."

The man left and I repacked my computer and was about to leave when I felt that this one man doesn't represent the church. So I sat back down on the steps and within minutes another vehicle arrived.

I asked the driver if he knew how to get ahold of the pastor. He told me that he did not, but, that another man would be arriving soon that could help me; describing what kind of vehicle it would be and where he would park.

A few more people arrived, including the first man I had talked to. I could tell by the way he looked at me that he was upset that I hadn't left yet. But, as I looked at him, I had compassion on him. God allowed me to see that *he* was why I was there. He was a man who longed to be like Christ, but he was caught up in Pomp-and-Circumstance, appointments and schedules. I was there so his eyes could be opened to the ways of Jesus.

A short time later the vehicle I had been waiting for pulled in and parked right where I was told it would. I introduced myself and explained my situation to the man. His name was Darvon and, I later discovered, that he was the pastor's son. He told me that it shouldn't be a problem, but that he would check with the pastor to make sure. When he returned a few minutes later he let me know that it was fine. Behind him was the first man that I had been in contact with. He extended his hand and apologized to me. I took his hand and let him know that I understood.

I got my tent set up and was doing the video update online. I was concluding my recap of the day's activities, and had just told everyone online that I was low on funds; having only enough for one more meal –but letting them know that God is faithful and I knew he would provide. Just at that time, the activity at the church came to an end and the people were leaving. The man from the Lexus walked up, apologized once more and, as he shook my hand, slipped me a $20.00 bill. It was as if God had planned that out so the people in the Chat-room could see God's faithfulness.

**Friday-July 24, 2009**

I was awakened at about 4:30am by a trash truck emptying the dumpster, and felt like I should get up and get an early start. This was one of the times I didn't listen to God, thinking it was my own thoughts, and instead, decided I would get up about 5:30am and get on the road.

I should have gotten up. At 5:00am the sprinkler system kicked in. There was nothing I could do but lay in the tent while it got soaked with water. When the sprinklers shut off I moved my backpack into the parking lot, shook the water off the tent, and moved it into the parking lot as well.

Once packed, I headed into Fredericksburg, VA and, once again, thought I was lost. At the very south end of town was a

Pollo Campero; a fried chicken restaurant that I had seen only in Honduras. I had just eaten not half an hour earlier, but I went inside to see if they had Flan, and indulged in a serving of the caramel topped custard.

I continued south and before long a Utility truck, with a bucket on top, pulled to the side of the road a hundred yards ahead of me. The driver got out and started arranging things in the back end. As I approached, he said "if you don't mind riding in the back, I can take you to Richmond." Once again God had provided. I had stayed in Washington, DC an extra day to see the Holocaust Museum and now, I would have a ride that was over a day's journey.

I don't remember the man's name, but as he was driving a company truck, he probably prefers to remain nameless anyway. He drove me to Richmond, VA dropping me off near several fast food restaurants, where I was able to get online and plot my way through the city.

It wasn't even 4:00pm. It was too early to stop for the day and it was only eight miles through the city, so I headed on my way, and just before 8:00pm, I got through the city, found a church, setting up my tent in the back part of the property.

**Saturday-July 25, 2009**

Another morning waiting as the tent dried in the parking lot. As I was sitting there, writing in my journal, a Latino man walked by. I greeted him in Spanish and he returned the greeting, commenting that I spoke Spanish. I let him know that I spoke very little Spanish, but with the little I knew and the little English he knew, we had a good conversation, and I ended up showing him pictures of the kids in Honduras.

As we were standing there talking, a man arrived at the church. He walked over and asked who the tent belonged to. I told him that it was mine and I introduced myself to him and, as I was explaining my journey, he cut me off and asked if I would be leaving soon. At that point I was ready to leave. I don't know if this man was the pastor as he hadn't bothered to introduce himself

96

to me, but it was clear that he wasn't welcoming me as a brother in Christ.

I started walking south and walked about six miles, until I came to Bermuda Baptist Church, which had a couple vehicles in front of it. I decided to stop and see if I could rest for a while. I was warmly greeted and given a glass of ice water by a woman, which I later learned was the pastor's wife. It turned out that they were having a church cleanup and also had a small building project going on.

I had been sitting there for a while, resting and working on my journal, when the ladies started setting up tables and chairs. I figured they were setting up for a function later and, as I started putting my things away, told them that I would get out of their way. I was told that I wasn't in their way and that, in fact, they were setting up for lunch, and they asked that I join them.

Men started filing in from the outside projects they had been working on, and I discovered that three of them were from the Southside Baptist church in Suffolk, VA. Their names were Jeremy, Jeff and Greg. During lunch, they began asking about the R.V. Park next to the church and were told that it had started out being an overnight stop but, had become a low income housing area. Jeremy, Jeff and Greg decided that, after lunch, they would visit the park to talk to the residents and invite them to the church. I decided to tag along.

The church had some witnessing new testaments, and we took several of them. Jeremy and I went one way and Jeff and Greg the other and we started knocking on doors.

We came to one man sitting in a lawn chair outside his trailer and introduced ourselves to him, inviting him to the church the following morning. He told us that He knew God better than any preacher did. It was soon apparent that this man was deceived by his own (lack of) understanding. He was the type that had heard it all and gave well-rehearsed answers.

I commented that he seemed to know God pretty well, but then I asked if God knew him. This threw him a little bit. He had never been asked if God knew him, and wasn't sure how to answer. He asked what I meant and I explained about the sheep and the goats in Matthew 25:31-46. How both groups were calling him Lord, yet, in the end, only the sheep were allowed to pass into eternal Life, the rest were cast into eternal punishment. I also drew his attention to Matthew 7:21, where the people emphatically called 'LORD, LORD' and yet God said he never knew them. When we left, we made sure that he knew there was an open invitation to the church, and started walking the dirt road again.

Soon we ran into a lady carrying bags in her hands and stopped to talk to her. Her name was Linda and she invited us into her trailer for ice tea. In the trailer, it became apparent that Linda was fighting her own demons, demons that we call schizophrenia. The walls of the trailer were covered with writing, some of it was scriptures of comfort and some it was random thoughts. Some were neatly painted and others scribbled with crayons and pen.

Linda told us of a son that tried to get her to check herself into a hospital and had 'disowned' her. Talking to her more about it, I understood that it wasn't that he had disowned her; he wouldn't allow his children around her because of her personality changes –not multiple personalities; she would just become mean or paranoid at times. Before we left Jeremy and I prayed for Linda and encouraged her to seek help.

We ended our door to door knocking, met up with Jeff and Greg, then headed back to the church. After discussing who we had visited with the members of the church so they could do follow-up on them.

I packed and headed back down the road. A minute later Jeremy, Greg and Jeff left, honking as they passed. Five minutes later they were back, offering me a ride south. They said that they could give me a ride to Emporia, VA, if I was willing to ride in the back of the pickup truck. I gladly accepted and we headed on down the road.

I don't know why, but I haven't had so much fun riding in the back of a truck since I was a kid. It may have been me, feeling blessed and having fun, or maybe it was the Holy Spirit. As we drove down I-95, it was suddenly like I was in a parade. I don't even know if I started it or someone else, but as we passed vehicles and vehicles passed us, everyone was waving at me and me at them. Kids would crowd the passenger side of cars and vans to make sure I saw them waving. I waved at a grumpy looking old man and he got a great big smile on his face and waved back. One man woke his wife up, saying something as he pointed at me and they both smiled and waved. It was like God had put a sign on me that said 'New creation in God's grace' or something.

I could have ridden a hundred miles like that, but sadly, we had to exit the interstate and stop. Before I could get my pack out of the truck, all three men had come to the back, wanting to pray with me before we parted. So there, at the back of the truck, on a busy road, Jeremy, Jeff and Greg laid hands on me and prayed, each in turn. As they left, I felt a little lonely. I guess having the fellowship for the afternoon was kind of like going to the amusement park as a child. You know it's only for the day, but you hate to leave it.

I walked into Emporia and found Calvary Baptist Church. Going to the door of an attached building I found people inside, getting ready for a Kid Crusade. One of the men was the church custodian, and he contacted the pastor for permission for me to set up my tent there.

**Sunday-July 26, 2009**

I didn't sleep well during the night. The back of the church faced the police station and the ambulance department was next door to the church. To top it off, the fire department used a siren to alert the firemen, which went off twice during the night.

I got up at 5:30am, as the custodian said he would be there about 6:00 to open the church and I would be able to wash up. By 6:00 I had my tent down and packed up. I found a gas station and got a cup of coffee, then returned to the church.

The custodian didn't arrive until 7:30. I got my things and

went into the small men's room and proceeded to clean up. I cleaned my partials (upper front teeth) and was letting them dry so the denture cream would stick better. I had washed up and was standing there in my swimming shorts, no shirt, getting ready to shave, which I hadn't done for 3 days.

In walks Dr. Walter Lester, the pastor. He introduced himself and welcomed me. All I could do was wonder what he must be thinking; me standing there, unshaven, half naked with no front teeth. But he was very dignified and, if my appearance shocked him, he didn't let on. I told him how much I appreciated being allowed to camp out on the church lawn, and that I was looking forward to his sermon.

A few minutes later I was standing outside the restroom, talking to the custodian, when Pastor Lester walked up. The custodian started to introduce me, to which Pastor Lester responded that he had met me in the restroom. I commented on how I must have looked and we all got a good laugh.

The Sunday school class was a joy. It was the men's class and I was the youngest there. Everyone else was in their 60's. Before class these men had stood around talking bass fishing, hunting and cars. They poked and prodded each other in friendly jesting and it was fun being included. Often (even at my age) we think of older people as being stuffy and no fun to be around.

The pastor's wife played the organ for the service, but during the offering she played an awesome piece on the Piano. I have heard many people playing the piano, and Ellen Lester could easily have made a living as a concert pianist.

Not surprisingly, Dr. Lester's sermon was about faith, and not giving up when things look dim. The illustration used was George Müller, the Englishman that looked out at the street orphans and, though he had no money himself, ended up caring for 10,000 orphans over the next 60 years. At times he would have the children sitting at the table with nothing to eat. They would pray and wait in faith for food... and it would arrive. Müller kept a prayer journal and recorded over 30,000 prayers that had been answered in those 60 years.

# No Mere Coincidences, a journey of faith

After the service I headed out, thinking that I would be able to walk about 10 miles that afternoon. I'd only gone about half a mile when I saw a C-Store and decided to grab something there for lunch as there didn't seem to be anything else around.

I had noticed a small church beside the store, but didn't think too much about it. Then I walked past the side of the building and could hear music coming out a window. I could feel the Spirit of God flowing with the music and, as I got closer, realized that the singing was in Spanish. Finding a door on the other side I went in. I figured that the service must be over, but just wanted to bask in the presence of God for a few minutes.

I later learned that the church was Iglesia Cristiana Pan de Vida (Bread of Life Christian Church), and they shared the building with another congregation. As it turned out, the Latino service wasn't ending, it had just started. I was greeted by an usher and sat in the back of the church.

A couple minutes later a lady in the front of the church went up to a younger lady, whom I later learned was the pastor's daughter, and said something. The young lady looked back at me then picked up a microphone and started translating the service. This service was about going the distance, completing what God set before you to do, finishing the race.

After the service I met Celso and Olga Mendoza, the co-pastors, and was invited to stay for a lunch, which consisted of sandwiches and soup. The soup brought back memories of Honduras. The soup was almost identical to the soup that was made at the orphanage.

As we ate, I shared with the congregation about the journey I was on and the orphanage I worked at in Honduras. I ended up pulling my computer out, showing pictures of the kids in Honduras, sharing the histories about them. As things wrapped up, I went into the restroom before leaving and, when I came out, was told that they wanted to pray for me before I left.

Everyone gathered around me and prayed, then I got a surprise blessing. While I was in the restroom they had taken up a love offering for me, and Pastor Celso presented it to me.

It doesn't matter how many times this happens, I start crying. It so touches me that people, that I have known such a short time, will reach into their pockets to help me out.

As I walked out of the church, I heard my name being called from behind. One of the young men was headed south and wanted to give me a ride. I thought he said Roanoke Rapids, which is in North Carolina,

While we traveled, he told me his testimony, though it was difficult understanding because of his accent. We drove passed Roanoke Rapids, but I felt that this was a part of his testimony that he had been longing to share, but had been afraid of being judged for. I let him know that we had all have things in our pasts that we wish weren't there and, that God had set us free of them when we turned out lives over to him. Those things are cast into the deepest parts of the sea, never to be remembered against us again.

He ended up stopping in Hickory, NC, about 16 miles north of Rocky Mount, which is probably what he had said when he offered me the ride. We pulled into a truck stop there and, after I prayed for him, he headed on his way.

The truck stop had a restaurant in it and I spent the next couple hours catching up on my journal, which I had come to realize was almost a full time job. I never thought it would take so long just to write down the things that happened and my thoughts for a day.

I found a small church about a half mile from the truck stop, pitched my tent behind it and, after doing my broadcast, fell into a deep sleep.

**Monday-July 27, 2009**

I hadn't plotted my route the night before, so I went back to the truck stop. Sitting down, I got some breakfast, plotted the route and worked on my journal some more before starting to walk for the day.

The morning was mostly uneventful. The weather was warm, but not overly hot; the road was wide with good shoulders and lightly traveled so the walk was easy. A few miles outside of Rocky Mount, a pickup truck pulled over. The passenger got out, offering me a ride. I was dropped off at a shopping center and, as I was getting my backpack out of the truck, the driver came out. I thanked him for the ride and he asked if there was anything else he could do for me. I told him I only accepted what God led people to do. He was somewhat shocked and at a loss for words. It seemed like a catch 22, he had left it open for me to ask for anything I might need, but all I could ask for was water and a place to set my tent. He had the passenger get a couple bottles of cold water out of the truck and, after I thanked them, they left.

**Tuesday-July 28, 2009**

After getting a breakfast sandwich, I began to plot out the day's travel. I decided that it would be a good day's travel if I made it to Kenly, NC –which was due south on US 301. There isn't much to say about the morning other than it was yet another hot humid day. I did get a ride from an elderly man for a few miles to Wilson, NC and walked into Kenly about 5:30 PM.

I saw a steeple about a block away and headed for that church. It was an Original Free Will Baptist, and there were two men inside. After I introduced myself, I asked about setting up my tent, and got permission to set it up in a field across the street, which the church owned. I set up the tent under a couple of trees and was laying in it, as the insects were already out and biting.

About 25 minutes later two police officers came up –first time I had been checked by the police in about 1,500 miles. They were Lt. Hendren and Sgt. Parrish, and they asked what I was doing there. I told them that the church had given me permission to set up there and told them a little about my journey.

They verified that I didn't have any warrants and then told me that I wasn't in the best place to spend the night. Apparently, the drug addicts and gang bangers used the field to cut through. I told them that I wasn't worried about them, that God takes care of me; but they said that they would feel safer if I wasn't there.

Lt. Hendren asked if I had to sleep in a tent and I told him that I didn't, but all I asked for was the basic need of a place to set the tent up and the rest was up to the church to follow however God led.  He then asked if it would be alright to put me up in a hotel room.  I was like, "you mean I would have to sleep in a *bed*?  I guess I could suffer through that for one night."

Sgt. Parrish Waited while I broke camp, then he took me to the police station to fill out paperwork for Ministerial aide, then took me to a small hotel.  It wasn't anything special, but it was better than what I lived in Honduras, and, it had running hot water, so I was happy.

### Wednesday-July 29, 2009

I didn't hurry getting around this morning.  I lay in bed until almost 6:30am.  When I did get up, I turned the computer on and, as soon as the internet booted up, Bobby from India was calling, so I spent some time chatting with him.  After getting packed, I got some breakfast, then headed South on U.S. 301.

I had only walked for about an hour when a man in a pickup turned around and offered me a ride.  His name was Jimmy and he gave me a ride into Smithfield.  I learned that he belonged to an interdenominational church, and we had a good talk about spiritual matters as we traveled.  He dropped me off at a Salvation Army thrift store, then gave me some money to get something to eat.

I continued south, without any real destination in mind other than sticking to the route, that would eventually take me into South Carolina.  By about 3:30 I found a church.  There was a vehicle in the parking lot, but I wasn't able to find anyone.  I figured that I would rest for a few minutes, and if no one showed up, head along the road a little further.

As I was resting, a large, fluffy cloud settled behind the steeple of the church.  I got my camera out and took several beautiful photos before the cloud passed.  As I was putting the camera away, a car pulled up.

Greeting the male driver, I told him who I was and what I was doing, then asked about setting up my tent for the night.  The man, whose name was Linwood, told me that, normally, it wouldn't be a problem; but they were having Vacation Bible School activities, and would be using the grounds that night. He told me of another church nearby, and was sure they would let me set up there. I thanked him and started down the road.

This road didn't have any shoulder to speak of. The pavement ended about 4 inches past the white line, and the grass was over a foot tall beside the road. There was a lot of traffic, but it didn't seem there would be a problem unless two semi-trucks were meeting. I'd walked about half a mile, staying close to the road, as the grass was a little shorter there, when all of a sudden I felt something hit my arm, right above the elbow. Reflexes threw my hand up –into the mirror of a pickup. I looked at my hand and saw that it had basically torn off a strip of skin about a quarter inch wide and 4 or 5 inches long. I've had worse, but the mirror on the truck had shattered, and the driver kept on going for a good quarter mile. He finally turned around and came back, and as he did, I saw that the truck also had front end damage. I figured that I wasn't the first thing he had hit and felt thankful that it was his mirror and not his bumper.

As he pulled over beside me, I said, "I think you'll need a new mirror." He asked what happened and I said "You clipped me with your mirror, that's what happened." It dawned on me that he had never even seen me and probably thought he had hit a rabbit or something until he tried looking in his mirror, and didn't have one anymore.

He asked me if I was OK and, holding my bleeding hand up, told him it was just a flesh wound. He just said "OK" and left. Normally, when you are in an accident, you go into shock. It wasn't the accident that shocked me; it was that this man could injure someone and then just drive away.

About a mile from there was a country store. I cleaned my hand, then asked about the church I was looking for; Stone Creek Advent Christian Church –which I found out it was still another 2 miles ahead. A man, who had been in the parking lot chatting, offered to drive me there.

After being dropped off I went to what I thought was the parsonage. I didn't get an answer, but I found a water faucet on the outside of the church and washed my hand up again as it hadn't totally stopped bleeding. Shortly, a man pulled up in a white pickup and asked if he could help me. I assumed he had something to do with the church, although he didn't offer any information. I shared about my journey with him, and then asked about setting up my tent for the night. After he gave me permission, I verified that they had a Bible study that evening. I set my tent up behind the church and then went back to the faucet to use it to clean up a little bit before the service. By then people had started to arrive.

We had a great study. The pastor, Doug Abel, had apparently been briefed about me; he mentioned me and my journey, and asked me tell a little more about it. After the Bible study Doug asked me if it would be too much trouble taking my tent down and, if not, I was welcome to spend the night at his house. He had a meeting so, while he was in it, I packed up and carried my things to the front of the church.

There was an elderly couple there and they struck up a conversation with me; asking several questions about the journey. Soon the man reached out his hand with a love gift for me.

Once Pastor Abel was ready to leave we went to his home and I was shown a bedroom. His wife had made sweet & sour chicken, and I was offered a large plate of it. After I had eaten, Pastor Abel and I sat up until almost 11:30, just talking about spiritual matters. It was a one on one fellowship that I rarely get and, it was both relaxing and refreshing. When we were done talking, I took a shower and went to bed feeling fulfilled.

### Thursday-July 30, 2009

The smell of coffee brewing woke me at about 5:30, but I couldn't bring myself to get out of bed. I just lay there for a good half hour praying and talking to God.

When I finally got up I found Pastor Abel and his wife in the kitchen. He said that he wanted to take me to breakfast, and then get me closer to my destination, so after getting packed, we went into Four Oaks, NC for breakfast.

After that, we headed to Dunn, NC where we prayed together before parting ways. I headed out, continuing south on U.S. Highway 301. I was a couple of miles outside of Dunn when I saw an old pickup, truck headed the opposite direction. It was an early 70's two tone brown with a spare tire strapped to the top of the cab. As it passed, I thought, "There's your ride Dennis." And then I thought "Oh sure, it's just headed in the wrong direction."

A short distance later, as I walked past a house, I heard someone calling to me. I turned and saw a man in his early thirties on the porch. He asked if I was OK and if I needed anything. I told him that I was good, but he wanted to know if I was hungry or needed a shower. I let him know that I had showered the night before and had just eaten a good breakfast, so he asked if I would like some ice water.

Ice Water is always good, so I accepted. He invited me into his home where I met his father, girlfriend and their little boy of about 3 or 4. After offering me a seat he then got a glass and a jug of water from the refrigerator.

As I drank the water we talked about the Bible. He had a lot of knowledge of the Bible, but lacked understanding. I explained that much of the writings were in parables and allegory. He hadn't thought of that, and I suggested that he pray for understanding before reading the Bible and search for a church that *taught* the Bible, not just preached. We sat there talking for a good 45 minutes before I left.

Leaving there, I started back down U.S. 301 and, had walked about a quarter mile, when what should pass me? The same two tone truck that I had seen earlier. It pulled into the next intersection and stopped. As I got near it, the driver got out and asked me where I was headed. I told him Fayetteville and he offered me a ride, which I gladly accepted.

His name was Jimmy, and he told me that he had been headed into Dunn, to sell some scrap metal, when he had passed me earlier. He said that, when he saw me, he felt that he should give me a ride so he decided then that he would pick me up on his way back if I was still on the road.

After he dropped me off in Fayetteville, I checked my route then headed down the road. About 4:00 I decided to rest for the afternoon and started looking for a church. I came to a little convenience store and, while drinking the cold water I'd gotten, I noticed a church just down the road from the intersection.

When I arrived, there was a pickup truck in the parking lot at the back of the building. As I approached it, a man came around the corner. I asked if he was the pastor and he said that he was, so I introduced myself. Giving him a ministry card, I made a request to set my tent up for the night.

This man just chuckled and said "But I don't even know you." Then he started making other excuses. They had just been there two years and didn't want something to happen, etc. etc. Then he said, "I know what we're supposed to do…and maybe, once I've had time to check out your website,..." All I could do was think, "How sad it is that this pastor could say what he just said." In Matthew 7:21 the people are claiming to be believers and believing they were doing God's will. Here is a man, claiming to be a shepherd of a flock, who is saying "I know what I'm supposed to do BUT..." I was wondering how much harder it would be on him, than those that thought they were doing His will.

Then I thought, "Have I been any different?" I may not have verbalized it to people's face, but how many times had I passed someone, broken down or walking, and not stopped because I didn't know them or I was in a hurry? How could I take the splinter out of my brother's eye until I removed the log from my own? More and more I was realizing that this wasn't just a journey of faith, but also a time of refinement and polishing for me. As I headed back down the road I asked God to forgive me for every time I had the chance to help someone but didn't.

I went on for a couple of miles before coming to State Highway 71, then turned and walked a couple more. The clouds were getting thicker and I could hear thunder rumbling in the distance. I knew that I would have to find a place to set my tent up soon, or I would be caught in the storm. I kept praying that God would hold the rain off until I got to the next town, a few miles ahead.

As I approached an intersection, a pickup truck pulled up to it, started to go, but then waited. When I reached it, the driver asked how far I was going. I told him that I didn't know the name of the town ahead, but that I was headed towards Florida. He told me that he could get me south, so I got my backpack in the truck and off we went. We hadn't traveled a mile when the clouds burst open and it was pouring down rain.

The driver told me his name, but added that no one knew him by it. Everyone called him 'Jaybird'. He owned his own business and had been headed into Fayetteville, to make a delivery, when he had first seen me, and decided to pick me up on his way back if I was still on the road. This was the second time in one day this had happened.

Jaybird drove me 40 miles to Laurinburg, NC and took me to a convenience store where I could get some food from the deli. When I went to pay for it, the clerk told me that Jaybird had already told her that he was paying for whatever I got. I thanked him and, as we headed back outside, Jaybird pointed to a church and said that it was the one he attended; but then asked if I wanted to spend the night there or if I would like to go a couple more miles further south. I told him a couple miles further would be great and we got back into the truck.

He took a couple back roads, and soon came to a highway and pulled into a hotel parking lot. I asked/stated –with some surprise –"You're getting me a hotel room?" Jaybird just said, "Well, it's supposed to storm more tonight and I'll sleep better knowing you weren't in a tent." He got me a room, helped me get my backpack out of the truck, and then, as we said goodbye, gave me money for food the next day.

I wasn't going to waste this blessing. I found the laundry room, started my clothes washing and then slipped into the hotel pool to cool off.  Once my clothes were done, I showered and then worked on my journal until it was time to do the update.

**Friday-July 31, 2009**

I stayed at the motel until almost checkout time, trying to catch up on my journal.  It has become more and more difficult to do as I continue my journey.  God was doing so much that it was hard to write down *all* the events of a day.

As I headed out, as I do every morning, I asked God to lead, guide and protect me.  This morning I added "... and Lord, I could use a couple days to catch up on my journal."  I headed down U.S. Highway 15 and, hadn't walked 100 yards when my sleeping bag, which I had strapped onto my backpack everyday for the last 60 days, fell off.  I picked it up and walked another hundred yards to a convenience store.

I got the sleeping bag strapped back on, set the pack against the wall and went inside the store to get something to drink.  While I was paying, the customer that had been in front of me walked outside and then came back and asked if that was my "stuff" outside.  I told him that it was, and he said that he was headed to Society Hill and wondered if I would like a ride.  I asked if that was south and he said that it was, so I accepted the offer and we got into his car.  I introduced myself and he told me his name was Chris.

Chris said that he was headed to work, although he usually worked the late shift; but, because his company was doing inventory, all employees had to be there in the afternoon instead.

Then he started talking about a problem he had that I see more and more now days; he and his wife, having raised their own kids, were now trying to raise a grandchild; a 14 year old boy that had been raised with no responsibilities, and no respect for others.  We talked for the next twenty-five minutes or so about it.  As Chris dropped me off at a gas station, I prayed that God would grant him the wisdom and patience in dealing with his grandson.

At the gas station I checked my location and found that I

was on a straight shot to Florence, SC on U.S. 52 so, I headed out –not even getting a half mile when a car pulled over in front of me. This driver's name was Josh, and he was headed to Florence.

As it turned out, Josh owned a heating and cooling business and, one of his customers was a church, whose air conditioner had gone out, and he needed a part to fix it. If he ordered the part it would be Monday before he got it so, in order to have it fixed for Sunday, he had to drive to Florence for the part himself.

Josh dropped me off at a group of restaurants and hotels near I-95, where I found a restaurant, ate and worked on my journal. It started raining, and soon the sky opened up and it poured down the rain, with the wind whipping it around in sheets. It was almost five hours before the clouds thinned enough that I felt safe in leaving.

I had walked for over an hour without finding a church and it was now dark. I came to a road that was marked "No outlet". There was a bank on one side and a house on the other, but I could see nothing past them. I headed into the dead end, and found that it was a cul-de-sac, that had not been built up yet. An area of about 30 feet had been mowed and past that it was wooded. I found a level area, and set up my tent up in the dark. The spot was secluded and I slept, uninterrupted.

# AUGUST

### Saturday-August 1, 2009

I woke up this morning feeling refreshed. The storms had passed and the air was cool for a change. As I praised God for the day, I had a peace fall upon me, like the Father was saying Good Morning son, welcome to the new day.

I was on the edge of Florence and had passed all the restaurants and convenience stores, so headed south on 52 Highway. A couple miles later I saw a gas station, on the opposite side of the highway, and headed towards it.

# No Mere Coincidences, a journey of faith

I had just crossed over the highway and was walking in the parking lot when a pickup truck, that I had just seen leave the store, pulled in again. The passenger, whose name was Tina, asked where I was headed to and I told her Manning. The driver, Glenn, said that they were headed to Kingstree, which would get me south 40 miles and then I would just have to go west to Manning, about 20 miles.

They had the back seat of the truck full, so I climbed into the bed and we started to Kingstree. When we got into town, Glenn turned west and took me a couple miles to a road called Manning Rd, and we pulled over. As the couple were getting out of their truck, I got a gospel tract, with my website on it, to give them. Glenn told me that Manning Road was a straight shot into Manning. Tina handed me a bag that had some mini donuts and a drink in it, then she handed me some money, telling me that it was for something to eat once I got to Manning.

I gave Tina the tract and told them that I was on a 4,000 mile journey of faith. Glenn looked at me, said "get back in the truck; we'll take you to Manning. He added that he needed to get some gas so, we went back into Kingstree and, while getting gas, Glenn was asking me about my journey. He also rearranged the back seat so I could sit inside the truck the rest of the way.

We had almost made it to Manning, when Glenn received a phone call, telling him that his horses were out, and next to the road. He apologized and pulled into a country store a couple miles outside of town. As they dropped me off I told them how much of a blessing they had been and let them know that I would keep them in my prayers.

Walking the rest of the way into Manning, I found a place to eat lunch and figured out the next step of the journey, which was Summerton, SC. I walked into Summerton about 6:30pm, and I soon found the Summerton Baptist Church.

The only person around was a lady and her kids, who were cleaning the church. She was unable to contact anyone, but didn't think it would be a problem if I set up my tent for the night.

## Sunday-August 2, 2009

The Summerton Baptist Church had three morning services; the first one starting at 8:30, so I made sure I was up and packed by 8:00am. The church had a special speaker that day. Reverend Roger Orman was a 60 year old man that had more energy than most 30 year olds. He had been a youth pastor for 20 some years and there wasn't a dull moment in his sermon.

Afterward, I joined a Sunday School class that made me feel right at home. One lady was talking about "Bald Peanuts". I said that I had just learned about Boiled peanuts a few days earlier, and wondered what Bald Peanuts were. Her husband, who was a Military Chaplin, calmly said, "They're the same thing, just think of a peanut with no hair and that's how they pronounce it here."

Sunday School was over at about 11:00 and I was scheduled to do a broadcast to Waverly Methodist Church, in Waverly, GA at 11:15. I got my netbook out of my backpack and started setting it up. As I was setting it up, one of the deacons came up to me and said that he knew I had expenses and explained that, because of a situation at the church, it wasn't a good time to take up a love offering for me. He gave me a love gift, though I don't know if it was out of his pocket or if the deacons had decided to give it to me out of the church funds. God knows and will award accordingly.

A few minutes later Preston, one of the men from the Sunday School class, came up and invited me to dinner with his family. I did the broadcast right on time, then went to dinner with Preston, his wife Rosie and their two daughters.

After a delicious dinner, Preston and Rosie endured me showing them pictures, and telling the stories of the kids in Honduras. They had plans for later that afternoon, so after I thanked Rosie and said goodbye; Preston drove me to Santee, SC and prayed for me –also giving me a love gift to help me on my way. He kept saying that he felt guilty just dropping me off, but I assured him that he and Rosie had been a true blessing to me and that I would be fine.

# No Mere Coincidences, a journey of faith

I went online to find a church that might have an evening service. As I was planning to spend the next day catching up on my journal, I tried to find a church close by. Finding none, I decided to just start walking down the route I would take, at least until I found a place to set up my tent for the night. After walking a good mile, I came to an old motel that had been converted into a church/deliverance center. There was one car parked outside and I went over to what appeared to be a chapel area, only to find that it was locked.

I started knocking on doors and was rewarded when a man, whom, at the very least, had been kicked back, relaxing, if not sleeping answered the door. I told him who I was and asked about setting my tent up there. He pointed down the road and asked if I saw the revival tent, about 200 yards away, and said I could probably set up there as it wasn't being used. I thanked him, assuming that he had something to do with the tent and walked to it.

As I was taking my backpack off, I heard gospel music in the distance and, looking around, saw the tops of cars, above a cinder block wall, a few buildings away and figured that had to be where the music was coming from. It was a few minutes after 7:00, so, figuring that a service must have just started, I put my pack back on and walked towards the music. I found Healing Temple Ministries at the end of a small mini-mall.

Going inside I immediately felt out of place. It wasn't that I was the only white person there, but that everyone was dressed up. I'm talking vested suits and double breasted suits, Women in fine dresses and hats. Even the children were in suits and dresses and, the place was packed. Before I had a chance to turn around a lady motioned to a place where I could set my backpack and then a man moved a chair where I could sit down. I joined in the worship and fully enjoyed the sermon.

I later discovered that they were celebrating the pastor's sixteenth anniversary with the church. Her name was Lillie Gadson and, from what I could gather, she had touched the lives of people from New Jersey to Florida, and it seemed there were people from every place in between represented there.

The sermon, not surprisingly, was about faith and finishing what God has set before you. It was dynamically delivered by Pastor Johnell Cancer of Rehoboth Ministries International, out of Charleston, SC. This was my first experience in an African-American church, other than what I had seen on TV, like T.D. Jakes and Tony Evens.

Pastor Cancer was just as I would have expected. He delivered the message with so much passion and energy that, when he completed one thought, I was afraid he would pass out before he caught a breath of air for the next one. Towards the end of the sermon he went into a melodic monolog, that would sound funny coming from anyone other than an African-American pastor.

During the sermon, Pastor Cancer would have us go to different people and tell them things like "You have to keep the faith to stay in His grace", God doesn't lie, it's just not His timing yet". When we did this, little kids would come over to me and give me hugs. One little boy, of about 4, kept running over to me, give me a hug, run back to his mom giggling and then a minute later be back for another hug.

When Pastor Cancer was finished, Pastor Gadson delivered her own message. By the time service was over it was almost 9:30pm, and, I was about to put my backpack on, when an elderly lady said, "We're having a dinner, aren't you going to stay?"

After a mouthwatering, home cooked, southern style dinner, I went back to the revival tent where, to my surprise, there was a meeting going on.

I slipped into the back of the tent and sat down, as inconspicuously as possible, being the only white person in another African-American congregation.

As the pastor preached, he made his way to the back of the tent and was soon standing next to me. He reached up, removed his lapel microphone and, bending over to where only I could hear, said words that I will never forget.

"Man of God, I've just had a vision,

and it's a vision of a ministry whose
seeds have already been sown.
Those seeds will take root and it will grow
and blossom and you will influence thousands
of young people to serve God unselfishly."
Then he clipped his microphone back on and continued to preach.

I later found out that the pastor was Apostle Ingram and that the church, Outreach to the Unreached Ministries, had just finished a 14 day revival meeting.

The service went until almost midnight. I asked Apostle Ingram about setting up my tent for the night; he recommended that I set it up inside the revival tent, as it was supposed to rain that night. I helped carry the chairs and audio equipment into the church, then set up my tent getting to sleep at about 1:30am.

### Monday-August 3, 2009

Being up late didn't help. By the time I woke up and got ready to go, it was already 9:00. It hadn't rained during the night, but it was hot and humid.

I headed South on U.S. Highway 15. Soon after starting, I passed a house where four men were sitting at a picnic table. One of them called out, and, as I walked closer, he offered me some cold water, which I accepted. I sat there for a while, talking about God, my journey and the ministry, and then headed back on my way.

It wasn't long before I needed another break. The problem was, there wasn't any place to take one. There was nearly nothing after Santee but a few scattered houses. My breaks consisted of finding some shade and bending over to take the weight off my shoulders. This went on for the next ten miles. A couple times I did take my pack off, removed my shirt and wrung the sweat out of it.

I had finished all my water and had been looking for someplace to refill the bottles for about an hour. When I saw a home near the road with a garden hose, I headed for it. The front door was open so I went up and called out.

No Mere Coincidences, a journey of faith

A lady in her early thirties came to the door and I introduced myself, learning that her name was Vivian. When I asked about filling my bottles at her water hose, she said yes, but asked if I would like some cold water. I told her that cold water sounded wonderful and she disappeared back into the house.

I proceeded to fill my bottles and soon Vivian was back with a gallon of cold water, some snack cakes and some fish. She said that there was nothing ahead on the road for several miles and wondered if I would like a snack. As I drank the better part of the gallon of water and ate, Vivian and I talked. When I had finished, I thanked Vivian and told her what a blessing she was.

I headed on back down the road and hadn't even gotten out of sight of Vivian's house when a van pulled up behind me and tooted its horn. The driver, a young man, asked where I was headed, to which I answered that my destination was St George, SC. He looked somewhat concerned, as though it was further than he had planned to go. I quickly let him know that any distance would be a blessing and every mile saved me half an hour of walking. He said he would take me to St. George and I put my backpack in the back of the van. As I got into the front seat he moved a Bible from the seat to make room for me.

I introduced myself to him and he said his name was Quinton, and asked if I had family in St. George. I told him that it was just a point along the way, going into the story of my journey, and the ministry, and about how it was based on Matthew 25:31-46.

As I talked I could tell by the expression on his face that he was shocked. I asked him if he was alright and he responded by saying "This might surprise you, and you might think I'm crazy." I said, "Oh, please, try to surprise me."

Quinton proceeded to tell me about a dream he had, about two months earlier. He said that he didn't understand the dream until just then, but had shared it with his pastor. In his dream he was driving the van, talking to a white guy, "Like you" he added. They were talking about God's will and the kingdom of heaven when all of a sudden the man pointed and said "There it is, the Kingdom of Heaven."

Quinton said that he understood now. In the example Jesus gave to pray he said "...Thy kingdom come, Thy will be done, on earth as it is in heaven..." What is God's will? We are told both in Isaiah 58 and in Matthew 25. It's caring for others. Not socialism, where the government takes everything and makes everyone equal, but where people freely sacrifice to help others, out of love for God and their fellow man. Without even thinking of what I was saying, I said "And there it is, The Kingdom of Heaven."

Quinton dropped me off in St. George, NC at a little, walk-up food place with a few picnic tables. We prayed, then Quinton turned around and headed back the way we had come. It was still early afternoon, but too hot to walk much. I sat at one of the picnic tables and worked on my journal in the shade.

After a couple hours, I went up to the window to get something to eat. I saw that this little place had combo specials, so I ordered a Bacon Cheeseburger combo. The elderly African-American lady working there just said, "OK, but we out of bacon, so you just get the cheese burger." I almost laughed. It was like being at an aunt's house. "You can have what you want, but this is what we've got, so be happy with it!" As I waited for the burger, I noticed that they had handmade, old fashion, milk shakes and decided that, after I ate, I would get one.

I finished my burger, went back to the window and, looking at the flavors offered, asked for a strawberry shake. The lady looked at me and said "Ain't got no strawberries, you want vanilla or butter pecan?" I couldn't help myself, and let out with a laugh. She asked me "What's so funny?" I told her she just made me feel like family, at which time she pointed her spoon to a sign and said "That's why the sign say 'Home Cooking'."

After downing a butter-pecan shake I thanked the lady and headed to a street that had a church sign pointed down it. Finding the church a few blocks away, I knocked on the parsonage door and, getting no answer, I wrote a note to the pastor, introducing myself, then set up my tent behind the church.

## Tuesday-August 4, 2009

I woke up and was on the road by 6:30am. I wanted to make sure I got a few miles before it got unbearably hot. It didn't work. By 8:00 the sun was full force and the humidity was worse than it had been on Monday. The only good thing was that the road wasn't as barren as it had been the day before.

I walked about 6 miles and came to a little town called Grover, which had a little store that reminded me of a Pulparia in Honduras. It had water, pop, chips and a few other items, but that was about it.

I got a cold bottle of water and a snack cake, then talked to the owner for a few minutes while I ate and drank. I told her about the ministry and the journey I was on, then we talked about the heat. She told me that there was a river about three miles further on the road, with public access, that would be a good place to cool off.

Sure enough, about an hour and a half later, I came to a bridge crossing a river, and there was a boat ramp, with a dock there. The way the bridge was made provided an excellent area for changing and soon I was in shorts and in the water. The river was clear and indeed refreshing. I sat in the water for a good half hour, just enjoying being cool.

I had been walking again, for about an hour, when a car went past me that looked wet and then another one; then a tractor-trailer went past, with a spray of water coming off of it. I turned around and saw a wall of rain headed towards me. Ahead of me was a pillar at the entrance of a driveway and I quickly made for it. I got there in time to pull out my poncho and cover the backpack up before the rain hit. The pillar, while it didn't keep me totally dry, did block some of the rain, that was pushed by the sudden wind that came with it.

Fortunately, the rain was short lived, and within minutes I was back on the road. I walked another ten miles or so and, was about three miles outside of Walterboro, SC. A pickup truck pulled over ahead of me, waiting for me to get closer. As I approached, a man got out of the truck and asked if they could give me a lift. I was more than ready to accept a ride and quickly got my backpack into the bed of the truck.

The man introduced himself as Tom, then his wife Becky, son, Brad and their baby, Destiny. As we went down the road, talking, Destiny, whose baby seat was in the center of the back seat, would look at me and start giggling. She did this several times, apparently finding me extremely amusing.

It turned out that Becky had just picked Tom up from work. Tom's company had just been shut down by OSHA and he didn't know when he would be able to return to work again. Even with the uncertainty of his employment, they saw someone in need and, acted to care for that need. We didn't have time to talk about God much but, with their understanding & compassion, and their calmness in their situation, I suspected that they not only knew about God, they Knew God. As they dropped me off in Walterboro I asked if I could pray for them and asked God to bless them and provide in their time of need.

Passing a parking lot, I saw a young man pulling wheelies on his bicycle, and commented that if I were to try that I would fall on my butt. We started talking and he immediately said that he liked my cross, then, as an afterthought, commented about it being inside a Star of David. It was unusual, as most people comment on the star before they notice the cross.

The young man's name was Louis and he said that he had given his life to Christ, but was still learning. I let him know that learning and growing in Christ was a lifelong venture. The important thing was to never take your eyes off of Jesus, and strive to live the way He taught us to live; loving God first, and others as ourselves. Louis told me where I could find a church and I set off to locate it, but as it was time for my nightly update, I sat at one of two tables outside an Ice Cream shop and set up my computer.

There were a few new people at the update and I recapped the last couple of months for them, letying them know how God had been providing for me. Shortly after I started the broadcast, a couple of teenagers sat down at the other table and stayed there during the rest of the broadcast. While I was packing up my computer one of them began asking me what I did. I shared the ministry and my journey with them. Giving each of them a gospel tract, I headed out to find the church.

Finding the church and a spot in back of the church parking lot, I set up my tent and was soon fast asleep.

**Wednesday-August 5, 2009**

I had already decided to take the day off, do laundry and catch up on my journal. After packing everything I walked to a gas station, got a cup of coffee and asked about a Laundromat in the area. I was told that there was one a few blocks away. I headed there and cleaned up a little while my laundry was going. I found a place to sit and spent the majority of the day writing.

Later that evening, I found a Wednesday service at Faith Baptist Church, near the intersection I would need to turn on the next morning. People started showing up and I talked to one of the men, who said that the pastor would arrive soon.

The pastor arrived. His name was Tony Jones, and, after introducing myself, received permission the tent up after the service.

The service started and the pastor sang –southern gospel – along with the choir, which was comprised of the youth from the church. Then the pastor and his wife did a duet

Next, the pastor's visiting father delivered the sermon. His name was Johnny Jones and he was a *lively* speaker. He was in the pulpit, out of the pulpit, in the pews and between the pews. He wanted everyone to know that the message was for them.

The service ended right at 9:00pm and I went outside and started booting my computer for the update. I was a few minutes late and there were several people there. Pastor Jones came out to show me where I could set my tent up and I was able to introduce him to the viewers.

After the update I set up my tent next to a palm bush and

went to sleep.

## Thursday-August 6, 2009

It was an absolutely beautiful morning. The sun was shining and the air was cooler than I remembered it being for a good month. I started out the day by taking a couple pictures of my "campsite" before starting the day's journey.

I started southbound on U.S. Highway 17. I had walked for an hour or so when I came to a church which was named Great Swamp Baptist Church. It was built in the classic early 20th century style and, had probably been built then.

With the sun getting higher it had started to warm-up quite a bit; and I was about ready for a break so I took my pack off, got my camera out and snapped a few pictures. As I putting the camera away, an older gentleman walked over from an old house across the street.

He introduced himself as John Cravans and asked about my destination, and where my journey had started. We started talking about the economy and end-times, and had probably been talking for a good half hour when I mentioned that I should be getting down the road, before it got much hotter.

John asked if I needed any water and insisted on filling the one bottle that I had emptied. When he came back, he asked if I would like a breakfast of eggs and grits. Accepting the offer and we walked across the street to his home, where his wife, Jan, had fixed the meal.

As I mentioned before, it was an old house and the couple lived a humble life. There were no big TV's or stereos, just a cassette player in the kitchen with a few tapes stacked beside it. The furniture and decor looked like they were from the 60's or 70's. It was plain, but homey.

We shared a wonderful home cooked breakfast and John gave me a couple of Slim Fasts for the road. I prayed for them before I left and then headed back down the road.

I was grateful for the Slim Fast; it was well after noon before I came to a place to get anything else. It was a little store that, once again, reminded me of a pulparia in Honduras. I got a bottle of water and a sweet roll and the owner invited me to spend some time at the "tables" in the shade. The tables were old cable spools, that had been set on end, and it was evident that they were probably surrounded by people, standing there with their cold drinks in the evenings.

There were three men there at the moment, two of which had heavy accents, as though they, or maybe their parents, had emigrated here from Africa. The third man came over and started talking to me, asking where I was headed and why I was walking.

Once again, I was asked about being a veteran and I had to ask how he knew I had been in the military. He commented on the discipline to, day after day, put on a heavy pack like I did. We didn't have time to talk much more. His ride arrived and he left so, with my "military discipline" I hoisted up my backpack and headed out.

About an hour later a car went past me, did a U-turn and came back. The driver asked where I was headed and I told him Point South. He said that they could get me to Yemassee so I climbed into the back seat.

He introduced himself as Maurice, and the passenger said his name was "Darl". I asked him to repeat it and again he said "Darl". I asked how it was spelled and he said, "D a r r e l l". I said "Oh, Darrell" and he said "Ya, Darl". I asked him to excuse me, explaining that I was a northerner, and had just learned what "Bald Peanuts" a few days earlier. We all had a good laugh and were soon in Yemassee.

I thanked them, started walking again and, had walked about four more miles, when a pickup with three men in it pulled over and offered me a ride into Point South, dropping me off at a fast food restaurant. Their names were Darrell (pronounced Darrell), James and Dennis.

I got some dinner, then located a church named Family Worship Center. Finding it, I got permission from Elder Barnett to set up for the night.

## Friday-August 7, 2009

I stopped and ate before leaving the area, then began walking down the outer road of I-95. The road was straight, long and nearly deserted. As it paralleled the interstate, the only traffic was from the few locals that lived on the road, logging trucks and an occasional utility truck.

The temperature rose quickly and it wasn't long before I was saturated with sweat. The trees on both sides of the road had been cut back 25-30 feet and there just was not any shade. To make matters worse, there was no shoulder and the grass along the road was a good foot and a half tall. With the road next to the interstate, I couldn't walk the road and then move off when I heard a vehicle coming because, all I could hear were the cars on I-95. To top that off, the grass was seeding so every quarter mile or so I would have to take my shoes off and shake the seeds out of them.

I finally came to an area where there was an exit from I-95 which had a couple of gas stations. Going into the first one I refilled my water bottles and got lunch. I noticed that the water had a sulfur taste to it, but it was cold, and that's what mattered.

Refreshed from the few minutes of rest, I went on. As I walked the water got warm and soon it tasted like swamp water and, before long, was cloudy. I wondered if it was safe to drink – in Honduras the water didn't smell that bad and we didn't drink it because of parasites –but I didn't have much choice; it was so hot out and the water was finished before I got to Ridgeland, SC., three hours later

I found a place to get something to eat and filled my bottles with filtered water. With fresh water I headed back towards U.S. Highway 17, my intent being to find a church for the night. I walked on, for two or three hours, down a heavily wooded area. I saw a clearing in the woods, about 30 yards off the roadway, where I could set up my tent. The area was obviously a bog, but it had been a dry year. I cleared as many of the branches and stick from the area as I could and set up my tent.

By this time it was dark and I was exhausted. I fell asleep

instantly, and slept soundly for about two hours. What awakened me was the fact that the ground had settled; I was laying in a foot deep indentation, with sticks, and who knows what else, poking me. Then there was the traffic. I was in between the interstate and the highway and the traffic was non-stop. I lay there the rest of the night, never getting into a deep sleep.

### Saturday-August 8, 2009

As soon as there was enough light to see by, I got up, packed and was headed down the road. An hour and a half later, I came to an intersection that went towards the interstate. There were several hotels and restaurants here and I walked to a fast food restaurant and order breakfast.

Later, as I passed through the city of Hardeeville, I found a Mexican market and went inside for a break. I spent my last dollar on a Coke that was made in Mexico; which meant still made with sugar instead of corn syrup. Chatting with the owners for a while felt like I was back in Honduras.

They had two young boys, about 6 and 8 years old, who were staring at me like they had never seen a white person before. Their dad told them to leave me alone; but I assured him that they were OK and shared my Honduras experience with them. I gave them my website, telling them where they could show the boys photos of the kids I worked with in Honduras.

Heading out, I figured that my dinner would be crackers and peanut butter no matter where I stopped for the night; so it didn't matter if I was in a town or at the side of the road again. But, I had walked for less than an hour when an SUV pulled to the side of the road in front of me. When I got beside it, a young woman asked if I'd like a ride and added that she was headed to Garden City, GA. That was on my route so I accepted the ride, introducing myself. She said her name was Shana.

It still amazes me how often God gives me *something* to connect to people with. Shana had just picked up a Plecostomus for her aquarium. I'd maintained a 75 gallon aquarium for years and one of the fish had been a foot long Plecostomus, which I had gotten when it was about 2 inches long. Shana also worked with Emergency Medical Services, as I had for years. I was able to have conversations with her, leading up to talking about God.

Shana dropped me off at the intersection where I was supposed to turn in Garden City. My destination for the day had been Silk Hope, GA, but, as she didn't know where that was, she couldn't tell me how far I was from it. As it seemed to be no more than a spot on the map, I wasn't sure if it was ahead of me, or if I had already passed it.

I decided to just keep walking the route that I had written down and see where I ended up for the night. Once again, I hadn't walked long when a car pulled over in front of me and the driver, who said his name was Mark, asked where I was headed. As I wasn't sure I just told him south. I explained that I had gotten a ride to Garden City and hadn't had time to check my exact location, adding that, at that point of the evening, I was just trying to locate a church to set up at for the night.

Mark asked about my journey and about how I got involved in ministry. When I told him that I had spent most of my life in law enforcement he chuckled, adding that he had been involved with the law most of his life too —on the other side of it.

He went on the share his testimony with me. Mark said that he had spent 8 years in prison, and how he had come to know God through a prison ministry, adding that, while many of the inmates went to chapel just looking for an early parole, he had wanted God to be made real in him. Since getting out of prison, he had gotten married, had kids and, he and his family were living for God.

He asked if I had eaten and I let him know that I had basically just had breakfast. He pulled a few dollars out of his pocket and handed them to me, telling me to put them into my pocket, then pulled into a McDonald's asking me what I wanted.

Once we had the meal he asked what church I wanted to go to. I told him that it didn't matter, and he took me to a large church —Savannah Christian Center —where there was obviously some activity going on; the parking lot was full, with people directing parking. Mark pulled up at the front door and prayed for me before I got out of the car.

There were three men standing outside of church, and I asked what type of function was going on and was told that it was a service; learning further that there were two Saturday evening services and two Sunday morning services.

I explained to them who I was, and asked who to talk to about setting my tent up on the property. One of the men took me inside and showed me to the information desk. There, I again explained my journey and asked about setting my tent up. I was told that they would find out once the second service was over. I was asked if I would like a shower, which I did, and a security guard, named Noel, showed me to a restroom that had a shower in it.

Shaved and showered, I entered the second service, which had just started. The worship music was wonderful and the pastor spoke on passionate prayer. Afterward, I was introduced to one of the Board Members.

After hearing about my journey and my request, he told me that they wanted to help me out, but, because of liability, couldn't let me set my tent up on the property, and asked if a hotel room would be okay. Then he invited me to join the small group which was meeting at a home for a meal.

I accepted the invitation and, besides getting a good meal, spent a couple hours in good Christian fellowship. I did my broadcast from there and, once the group broke up, I was taken to a hotel that was on U.S. Highway 17, on the south edge of Savannah. I was also given a love gift that would allow me to eat for a couple of days.

Even though I was exhausted by now, I went online to see exactly where I was. It turned out that I was about 14 miles from Midway, GA, which was my goal for the next night. I also looked on the map to find churches along the route, and saw that there were three about a mile and a half away.

**Sunday-August 9, 2009**

I got up and headed towards the churches I had seen online. Before long was offered a ride by a young man, whose name was Marcus. I told him that I was just heading up the road to a church and he said he was headed for a church himself, bringing me to ask which church he attended. He told me that it was one in Savannah, which was the other direction. I asked what church he was headed to now, and was caught off guard by the answer. It turns out that he fixed pianos and organs as a side job. He had repaired an organ for a church –and hadn't gotten paid. Marcus was going there to pull the repairs he had done.

I figured that talking to Marcus was more important than attending one of the churches I had seen online, so I asked him if he was a Christian. When he said that he was, I asked if disabling the organ was something he thought Jesus would want him to do.

We talked about it while Marcus drove a few miles and then he abruptly pulled over at an intersection. He told me that this was where he needed to turn, adding that, he would think about what I had said. I encouraged him to, at least, talk to the pastor to find out why he hadn't been paid before taking any action to disable the organ.

By now it was about 10:15am, and I was well past the churches I had seen online. But, I had seen a sign-about a mile back- for a church. I decided to walk back to it. I walked the mile, only to discover that the sign said that the church was *two* miles ahead.

I debated whether to walk back north another mile, where I had seen a church or, continue towards Midway. I felt led to continue on and soon was walking past the intersection I had been dropped off at some 40 minutes earlier.

Continuing on, I soon saw a church that had people going into it and, as I got closer, saw that it was Beach Hill Missionary Baptist Church. I also noticed that the service started at 11:30. A glance at my watch showed that it was 11:20 –I figured that this must be where God wanted me this morning.

I soon discovered that it was an African-American

congregation, and the church's 130th anniversary; having been established 14 years after the end of slavery. I also learned that the congregation from Peaceful Zion Baptist Church was there to help them celebrate and the church was packed.

The message was delivered by Rev. Robert Thorpe, the pastor of the visiting church. Afterward the service I was invited to stay for a meal, during which I spoke to several of the congregation, telling them of the ministry and my journey.

I was told that they were having another service at 3:30pm was invited to stay. I went back into the sanctuary and spent some time in prayer. An elderly man came over and greeted me. His name was Freddy Baker and I learned that he was 85 years old.

Freddy sat down and we started talking about the changes over the years. He remembered when the church had a full choir, the pews were full and they had an active youth program. He said that now, people don't attend church; they don't even send their kids. Then they sit around wondering why our country has fallen so much and why there was so much violence. As he talked, it was almost like he was speaking the heart of Jesus. He was so saddened by the lack of believers that he started crying.

The second service was organized by the First African Baptist Church from Riceboro, GA. Their choir sang and the Rev. Neil Dawson delivered a powerful message. After the service I was greeted by more people, including the pastors.

As I was putting my backpack on, one of the ladies came up to me with a takeout container "in case I got hungry later." I thanked her, put it inside my backpack lid, and headed down the road. As I was about to walk out the door a man came up and slipped me a love gift, telling me to have breakfast on him in the morning.

I had considered spending the night there, but the church didn't have much space around it. I headed out, in hopes of finding another church, and hadn't walked far when I found Fleming Baptist Church. An evening service had started about 15 minutes earlier, so I slipped into the back pew.

It turned out to be just a short Bible study that was over by 7:00pm. When it was done, I introduced myself to the pastor and asked about setting up my tent for the night. I got his permission and then spent some time talking to a few people that were interested in my journey.

**Monday-August 10, 2009**

My intent for the day was to get into Midway, find a Laundromat, and then find someplace to work on my journal. I found a Laundromat to do my laundry but, as there were no tables to sit at, I didn't get to work on my journal there. When my clothes were done, I asked about a fast food restaurant and was told that the nearest was by the interstate, three and a half miles off my route, or Riceboro, GA, five miles ahead, on my route. I decided to stick to my route, and, about three hours later, finally came to Riceboro.

There was a small church on the edge of Riceboro that had a bench in front of it, so I took a break there before continuing into town. Passing through Riceboro, all I saw was one small convenience store and a lot of places that had been shops or restaurants at one time but, had long since been closed down. I decided that, if there was a McDonald's there, it was obviously in a different part of town or possibly, like so many other areas I had seen, miles outside of town at an exit for the interstate. I walked on – into a long, straight stretch of road.

I can't say the road was deserted as there was some traffic, but most of the vehicles were coming towards me. Some time later I could see what appeared to be a bridge across the road with heavy traffic on it, but it was another mile before I was able to tell that it was definitely the interstate. It was still another hour to get to it; and I had finished all my water, which made it seem that much further.

I eventually came to a work crew, spraying the weeds along the road. They allowed me to fill my bottles and I thanking them. I continued towards the bridge, and when I finally arrived, was very happy to see an interchange –with gas stations and a restaurant.

I got a meal and then went to find a place with an electrical outlet. I found one outside of the Convenience store, near a picnic table, just in time to do my update. When Gary Neese, from agapejesus, found out where I was, he told me to try and get to Brunswick, GA by noon the next day. He and his wife would be there for lunch and would be able to pick me up there.

I cut the broadcast short as I was getting bitten, by what I thought were mosquitoes, and set out to find a place for my tent. Even laying inside the tent, I was still getting bitten, which I didn't understand. While I was doing the broadcast I was next to the interstate, keeping me from hearing mosquitoes, but now, there wasn't the constant noise and I still couldn't hear any. I later found out that they were sand gnats; worse than mosquitoes, as you could feel them bite, and the skin was irritated for days, like from chigger-bites.

## Tuesday-August 11, 2009

I was awake when the sun started coming up. After taking down the tent and packing, I got a couple of breakfast sandwiches and filled my water bottles with the filtered water.

Once again, the road was long and straight with not much on it. Here and there was a home or an old building, that had once been a business when Highway 17 was the main road. I did come to Memory Park Christ's Chapel, which is listed as the smallest church in America. I took a break there for a few minutes.

I had walked for a couple more hours when a car turned onto a crossroad, a good hundred yards ahead of me, and just sat there. I didn't know if they had pulled up there to use their cell phone or what, but as I was about to walk past, it backed out, onto the shoulder of 17 Highway.

The elderly, woman driver rolled her window about half way down and asked where I was going. I told her I was trying to get to Brunswick and she asked "You're not a serial killer, are you?" I assured her that I was not, and that I was actually a minister. Her response was "Okay, I don't know why I'm doing this, but I'll give you a ride to Darian. Go ahead and put your things in the back seat."

I opened the back door and, as I was putting my backpack in the car, heard the last words of a broadcast. It was only three words, but the voice was unmistakable and, as I got into the front seat, I asked, "Was that J. Vernon McGee I just heard?" She said "Why yes, it was." This put her at ease. I'm sure there are few, if any, serial killers that would have recognized his voice. J. Vernon McGee was known as "The Bible teachers Bible teacher" and had a radio program called "Through the Bible". Even though he had passed away in 1988 his programs are still aired today.

This lady's name was Fran and she gave me information on the radio station, which also broadcast online. I shared my story with her and, as we got into Darian, she said "This is Darian, but I'm taking you on to Brunswick." I thanked here and told her what a blessing she was and we continued talking. She commented on how many churches just seem to be in the business of entertainment now days. Ones that feel that all there is to serving God is to sing a few contemporary songs and give an uplifting sermon. Very few that really got into the Meat of the word.

When we got into Brunswick, she asked where I needed to be dropped off. I told her any place would be good and she took me to a Burger King, and then pulled into the drive-thru, telling me that she was buying me lunch. After getting the meal I thanked her and went inside to eat. It was well after noon and I figured that Gary had already left Brunswick, so I decided to work on my journal for a while then find a church where I could set-up for the night.

I found a church online and was packing my computer up when the phone rang. It was Gary, who was wondering if I had made it yet. I told him where I was, and he said that he was just a few miles away.

After knowing each other online for months, I finally got to meet Gary, Peggy and their niece, Rebecca, who was living with them. They took me to their home in Kingsland, beginning a week and a half of Georgian Hospitality.

## Wednesday-August 12 – Saturday-August 22

I was awake before anyone else, so I made a pot of coffee and started working on my journal.

When Gary got up, we went to the Living Waters Christian Bookstore. Here I met Mark. Mark had been a faith missionary. He had felt led to go to Africa. He bought a plane ticket, went there, and then lived on faith; ministering to the local people.

After talking to Mark we talked to the owner of the bookstore who, after hearing about my journey, asked if I would still be in the area following Saturday. He said that, if I was, he would like me to speak at the bookstore's Grand Opening. After spending a few minutes in prayer, I asked Gary and Peggy if they would put me up for an extra week. They said that they would and I let the owner know that I would stick around for a week.

Gary and Peggy were remodeling a house which belonged to Miss Lauren, who attended Waverly Methodist Church, and I went with them on Friday. The home sits on the inland waterway –so I did a little fishing.

On Sunday I spoke at the Waverly Methodist Church. They took a love offering for me and Miss Lauren, learning that I was staying for the week, invited me to spend it in her guest room. The plan was for me to use the peace and quiet to catch up on my journal, but, I found it hard to write with a fishing pole in my hand. I did get some much needed rest and particularly enjoyed sitting on the dock, praying and watching the spectacular sunrises.

On Friday evening I returned to Gary and Peggy's home with them for my last night in Georgia.

## Saturday-August 22, 2009

We arrived at the bookstore just before noon, and I was

first on the agenda to speak. A short time later, my cousin Jeanette and her husband Milton showed up. Jeanette and Milton are the parents of Dawn, whom I had met in Lebanon, IN. They live in Fernandina Beach, FL and had offered to host me for a couple days. After saying goodbyes to Gary, Peggy, and everyone else there, I headed to Florida with my cousins.

Once at their home Milt cooked steaks on the grill while Jeanette set out salads and side dishes and we had dinner, after which they offered me the "25 cent" tour of the town; beginning with the Historic waterfront and then to the beach. Once we got back to the house we sat up and Milt told stories about my mom when she was a child.

**Sunday-August 23, 2009**

Today we went to First Baptist Church of Fernandina Beach. The pastor gave an awesome sermon on family, directed mainly to the men, emphasizing how you can be a good witness at work, but people will always look at the family to see how you really live your life.

Later, during the evening service, the member of the church who gave the closing prayer mentioned that I was there and encouraged people to greet me. Several members did, asking more about the journey, giving me their best wishes, and one lady that came up gave me a small love gift.

**Monday-August 24, 2009**

After a big breakfast of biscuits and gravy, Jeanette and I said our goodbyes. At that time Milt and Jeanette gave me a gift card to help me on my way.

Milt was heading to Jacksonville, FL and offered me a ride. So we headed south on State Route A1A, taking a ferry across the water, to get to Jacksonville Beach, FL. We pulled into a parking lot, and after praying together, Milt left, and, once again, I was on my own.

Milton and Jeanette had recommended that, if I wanted a more relaxed and scenic route, that I stay on Florida A1A, which paralleled the ocean. I set out walking and soon was out of the business area and into an area with large, ocean front homes. This went on for a couple of hours, and I figured that I should be coming upon some type of convenience store or something soon.

No such luck! The houses ended and there was a sign prohibiting parking along the road for the next four and a half miles. I had walked into a nature preserve, and I wasn't about to walk back. I asked God to provide a place for me to rest, and walked on for about a quarter mile. Here I saw a sign for a parking lot for a beach.

The parking lot was on the right side of the road and on the left side were wooden stairs that went over a hill. There was no shade around the parking lot, so I climbed the stairs. When I reached the peak, I was greeted by a *breathtaking* view of the Atlantic Ocean.

I quickly descended the stairs, lowered my backpack, took off my shoes and socks and walked out into the cool salt water. It had been a week and a half since I had been walking, and my feet were tired and sore. When the cool water hit them, it was like a fire being put out. I could almost hear them sizzle and see steam coming from them.

There were a few people on the beach; some were lying on the sand, and there was an elderly couple who were surf fishing. Another couple saw me and came up to talk. They had seen me on their way to the beach, and had thought about offering me a ride, but as I wasn't hitchhiking, had continued on.

I told them about my journey and told them that I do accept rides when God leads people to stop and offer them, then shared my vision with them for a while. I finally began preparing to continue down the road. I really hadn't rested much, but I did feel refreshed.

After climbing the stairs over the dunes and back to the highway, I continued my journey south, and had walked half a mile, when an old pickup passed me. I felt that the Holy Spirit was telling me that it was my ride, and so wasn't at all surprised when, a few minutes later, the truck was coming back towards me. It went by and I made eye contact with the driver, and knew that they had indeed returned for me. It went on up the road, and a moment later was back again. The female passenger asked where I was headed and I told her that, at this point, I would be glad to get out of the nature preserve and someplace where I could get something to eat.

They had me climb into the bed of the truck and we headed on, towards St. Augustine, FL. As we traveled I became more and more grateful for the ride. We got out of the nature preserve soon enough, but there was still several *more* miles of nothing but houses along the road.

Finally getting into an area where there were businesses, the truck pulled into a parking lot and I got a chance to introduce myself. I learned that their names were John and Tammy, and I told them of my journey and added that God had shown me that they were going to pick me up. John looked dumbfounded and I don't think he knew what to think about this.

I asked which way to get something to eat and they directed me a couple blocks south. I thanked them and walking the two blocks, finding a place to eat, then later, a church to spent the night.

### Tuesday-August 25, 2009

I don't know what time it was, but I was totally shocked when, here, in a city, a rooster started crowing.
People have this perfect picture of a rooster, sitting on a fence post, announcing the rising of the sun. Wrong! They start crowing in the middle of the night, *hours* before sunrise, and this one was no exception.

I finally gave up trying to get back to sleep, and instead got up, rolled up my sleeping bag, dismantled my tent and walked to a McDonald's –grateful that it opened at 5:00am, as I had seen some that didn't open until later.

I got a couple sandwiches and was answering emails when a man walked up, asking about my computer. We started talking and he told me that he attended the local Assembly of God

Church. We talked for quite a while, and before we parted, he asked to pray for me and then gave me a love gift to buy my lunch that day.

I finally got headed down the road and knew right away that, with the temperature already in the 90's, I wouldn't make it far on my own. I would later be ashamed for thinking this –as I have learned that, when I'm in God's will, I'm never on my own.

I went on through St. Augustine, stopping at Costillo De San Marcos National Monument for a break before heading out of town, still following the coastal roads. I was barely outside of the city when an SUV pulled up beside me. It was a young couple who wanted to know where I was headed. I told them that I was going south, towards Daytona Beach, and they helped me get my backpack into the SUV.

Their names were John and Ilene. I was sharing my journey and the ministry with them and, before I knew it, we were in Daytona Beach and I was being dropped off. I asked if they lived here and Ilene said that they lived in St. Augustine. It was then that I learned that they had actually been headed into St. Augustine after visiting the beach and, when they saw me, they felt that they should help me. John, Ilene and I joined hands and prayed, then John gave me enough money to buy a meal before they left.

I know that I shouldn't be so amazed, because God is good, but I can't help being awestruck at the number of people God has put in my path to help me on my journey.

They had dropped me off at a convenience store and, as I looked around, I found that it was directly across from a ramp leading to the beach. It had been hot the last couple of days and I hadn't had a chance to bathe so, I went to the beach;.getting into the water. I just kind of laid there for a while, cooling off, relaxing, and letting the waves massage my back.

After a while I gathered my things together, then headed back into the asphalt jungle. I came to a man sitting on a bench, who, judging by his appearance, was homeless. I asked him about a fast food restaurant and he told me that there was one a couple blocks south. As I talked to him I noticed his hat on the bench next to him, with a note in it asking for change. I dropped a dollar bill into the hat, explaining that I was living on faith or I would give more.

As I headed for the restaurant, I began to feel guilty. Twice that very day I had been given enough money to buy a meal; yet *I* would only give a dollar and an excuse. I thought about what Jesus had said to his disciples, "Freely you receive, freely give. When I got to the restaurant, I bought a meal and returned to the man on the bench, letting him know that God had been taking good care of me, and apologized for having been so selfish. He thanked me and I returned to get a meal myself and plan the next day of the journey.

About 7:00pm I looked for a church, finding one, but there was no one there; but, a lady next door, told me that there was a Salvation Army, just up the road, that would offer me shelter. It turned out to be about a mile away, and I arrived about 8:15pm, only to find that it was full. So off I went again, following a main road, and soon found Central Baptist Church.

Going around the back of the church, I turned around and caught a glimpse of a man disappearing around the corner of the building. I returned to the side of the building and saw the man standing at a pickup truck that hadn't been there a moment before. I introduced myself and, learning that his name was Steven, asked if he was associated with the church.

He said that he worked there and I asked about setting my tent up for the night. Steven immediately said yes, and showed me where I could pitch my tent. I had just gotten set up when he returned, letting me know that he had contacted the pastor to let him know I was there; the pastor recommended he ask me if I needed a shower or food.

I replied that I had already eaten, but did need a shower. It had been hot and humid and, other than the ocean water, I hadn't had any place to bathe since Monday morning. Checking the time and finding out it was 8:50, I let him know that I had to do the update at 9:00. He said he would show me where the shower was, leave it unlocked and then return later to lock it back up.

I did the broadcast and then shaved and enjoyed a nice long, hot shower before going to bed.

### Wednesday-August 26, 2009

It was supposed to rain, and rain it did. Not the wind-blown rain that I had expected, but a heavy downpour that lasted most of the night; often accompanied by heavy lightning and thunder. The good thing was that the ground here was sand, so it soaked in instead of pooling.

The rain ended somewhere around 6:30am and I got up, packed. Once that was done, I had to decide which way to go. I had traveled west the night before, looking for a place to sleep, and figured that I was probably closer to U.S. Highway 1 than I was to Florida Highway A1A. I saw a busy intersection about 3 blocks west and headed for it. Sure enough, when I reached it, it was U.S.1 so, I turned southbound.

The rain the night before had not only failed to cool things down, but *added* to the humidity, and, by the time I found a place to eat breakfast, I was hot and drenched in my own sweat. While I was sitting in a restaurant a man came up and began asking me about my backpack. I told him about my journey of faith and he had a lot of questions. When we were about done talking, he told me that the city bus went right past the restaurant and said that it would take me several miles south. I told him that I couldn't take the bus and he said, "You take rides when offered, right?" I confirmed that I did and he said, "So, if I give you $1.25 specifically for a bus, it's like offering you a ride, right?" I couldn't argue with that, and he added that there might be someone on the bus for me to minister to as well, which I couldn't argue with either.

When the bus arrived, I climbed onto it, asking the driving it to let me know when it got to its southern most point. I sat in the front seat after putting the backpack down, and the driver started asking me about it; I was able to share my journey with her, as well as several other passengers, who were listening in.

Several of them wished me luck or said God Bless You as they disembarked the bus. Eventually, the driver turned onto a side road and announce that this was as far south as she went. I thanked her and, as I got off the bus, she told me that she would keep me in her prayers.

I continued walking south on U.S. 1 Highway, but only for about ten minutes. A car pulled to the side of the road, and an elderly lady got out, waiting until I was almost there. As I approached, she asked if she could give me a ride, and I let her know that it would be a great blessing. I put my backpack in her car and then introduced myself to her. She said her name was Maurice.

She told me that she was a Caregiver, adding that one of the people she cared for had passed away, leaving her with only 10 hours of work a week. Her son had talked her into going to a food pantry for groceries and it was from there that she had come.

As she talked, she turned off of U.S. 1 and continued talking, pointing out Trinity Lutheran Church as the church she attended as we passed it. Then she said that she was taking me to her home, where I could shower and wash my clothes if I needed to, and then she would take me on down the road further.

This was a pleasant surprise. I didn't have a lot of dirty clothes –but I did have several pairs of damp socks.

It had only been about 14 hours since I had last showered but, with all the sweating I had done, it felt more like it had been days. When I was done showering, there was a large bowl minestrone soup waiting for me. Maurice had me say the blessing and we shared a meal. The experience reminded me of the widow; having just enough oil and flour for her and her son, she fed Elijah anyway. I prayed that this Godly woman's supplies not run out until her famine was over.

Once my clothes were dry and the backpack loaded, Maurice drove me several miles south, dropping me off about half way between Scottsmoor, where she lived, and Mims, FL. I was extremely grateful for the distance she had taken me, as there seemed to be nothing between the two towns.

I walked the rest of the distance to Mims and came to a convenience store, where I got some cold water, and asked how far it was to anything. I was told that the next convenience store was about 3 miles south and I headed that direction.

About an hour and a half later I came to an intersection that hosted a couple convenience stores and entered one that had a fast food franchise, getting a sandwich for dinner. As it was now about 6:00pm, I also asked about churches in the area, and was told that there was one right on the highway a short distance up.

The church was Mims House of Prayer, and according to the sign, it had a Wednesday night service that would be starting shortly. Within minutes people started arriving. Everyone greeted me warmly and soon the pastor came in. During our introduction I learned his name was Pastor Tiller, and I asked about setting up my tent for the night. We had a great Bible study on being a servant of Christ. Pastor Tiller used one of his own as an illustration. I don't remember the man's name, but will never forget the story.

One of the church members had been active in a prison ministry. His end was near as he lay in his hospital bed. On a Sunday morning, in the final moments of his life, a man entered the church meeting; saying that the man had told him to go to the church when he got out of prison. The man listened to the sermon and, being shown God's plan for salvation, the former prisoner accepted Jesus and was reborn into the family of God – about the same time the other breathed his last breath on this earth.

At the man's funeral, prison guards and former inmates stood, side by side, as brothers in Christ. One of the prison guards spoke at the funeral and said that their friend had entered the prison to minister to the prisoners, but never forgot that the guards needed Jesus too. --Oh, to leave a legacy like that.

After the service, those who hadn't met me came up to greet me and I was asked to stay for fellowship. It was almost 9:00 by now so, I grabbed my computer, planning on doing my update from the Fellowship Hall. As I was booting my netbook , a couple people, that had been watching me, commented on my "Honduras kids'" picture (I use it as my wallpaper), so I opened my pictures and started showing the photos of my Honduras kids, telling their stories. All of the sudden I realized that I'd had an A.D.O attack (attention deficit... Oh, look at that funny rabbit). I quickly logged into the chatroom and found several people there chatting, wondering where I was. I apologized and did a quick update, letting them know where I was and some of the events of the day before signing off.

As people started to leave Pastor Tiller came up and gave me a love gift, then took me to the food pantry, where he gave me some crackers and peanut butter. I thanked him, then went outside. While I got my sleeping and tent off of my backpack, several of the men gathered around, and were talking to me. One of them, whom I had met at the church, was Billy. He came over and told me that I was welcome to stay at his house. That sounded a lot better than sleeping in the hot, humid air, so I accepted.

Once at his house he offered to change the sheets on the bed so I could sleep in it while he slept on the sofa. I assured him that I was used to sleeping on the ground and that the sofa would be like a king's bed to me. We talked for a while and then retired for the night.

**Thursday-August 27, 2009**

I slept later than usual this morning. I thought I'd heard rain during the night and, sure enough, it had rained. After a breakfast of coffee and cereal, Billy took me back to the church. I sensed that there was something on his mind that he wanted to talk about, but I felt that it would be in his timing when, and to whom he talked to. Still, I made sure he had my email address and phone number and let him know that he could contact me at any time, after which he left me at the church.

I had checked the map and was looking at a good five hour trek before I got to anything so, as soon as Billy was gone, I started walking. Soon a vehicle pulled up beside me. It was Billy again. He had decided to drive me up the road a ways.

As we drove he opened up, and began telling me the problems that he was going through. We talked, and soon he was pointing across the water, telling me that was Kennedy Space Center.

All week Gary and my cousin, Jeanette, had been keeping me updated on the space shuttle launch. When it was, when it had been scrubbed and when the new launch time was. Here I was, in Titusville, FL, about 14 hours from the next scheduled launch, looking at the launch site. I decided to stay there the rest of the day, and Billy and I got to spend the next several hours in fellowship, talking and ministering to each other.

We were sitting in a park and I was sewing on my backpack, while we talked. A man came up and said that he had gotten some cans of soup from a food pantry, and wanted to know if we would like some. Talking to this man I learned that he was homeless and went around to different places to find food. When he had more than he needed for the day he would share it with others in need.

At 9:00pm I did my update from Billy's vehicle with an excellent view of the space center. The night was clear and, though it had been windy in the afternoon, the wind had died down. I was looking forward to seeing the launch. We were talking about it online, and someone said that they thought the launch was canceled. Jeremy went to the NASA website and, sure enough, it had been. So, when the broadcast ended Billy took me to a local church that seemed suitable for me to set up at. After Billy and I prayed together, we parted ways.

### Friday-August 28, 2009

When I awoke this morning, I considered staying in Titusville to work on my journal and then watch the shuttle launch, which had been rescheduled for that night. After praying about it I knew that it was time to leave; so, I packed up and headed out, returning to U.S. Highway 1.

I soon came to the edge of town and, suddenly, a green pickup truck pulled up beside me. It was an older, small size pickup, like a Ford Ranger or Chevy S10. As it stopped, I saw the driver's arm stretching across the passenger, who was leaning back, looking like he didn't know what was going on. From the look on the passenger's face, you would have thought the driver had a gun in his hand. It wasn't a gun, but a $20.00 bill, sticking out the passenger window.

I took it and said "Thank You" and in unison the driver and I said "God Bless You", and they were gone. There was no chance to get his name or find out why he felt compelled to give me the money, but I was definitely feeling blessed, and continued on my way, thanking God for his grace and goodness to me.

About an hour and a half later I was more than ready for a break. I was soaked from sweating and I wanted to at least find a place to wring the sweat out of my T-shirt. There wasn't much around where I could sit down, but I did find a church, which was in a building with several businesses. It was called Sovereign Grace Church and it was on the north end of the building. The front doors were locked, but there were large air conditioning units, where I was able to park my backpack.

I drank a bottle of warm water, then walked around the back of the building to see if, by chance, someone was parked there, using a back door. There were no cars there either, but I did find a garden hose and, taking my shirt off, rinsed the sweat out of it. As I was doing this I saw someone walk around the corner of the building, then, turn around, going back the other way. Quickly wringing the water out of my shirt I returned to my backpack. There was a car in front of the church now and I went up to the doors.

Just as I was reaching for the door handle, the door opened, and there was a young man standing there, with an ice cold can of Sprite in his hand, which he handed to me –apologizing that he couldn't find any cold water for me. I thanked him and he invited me inside, out of the heat. He introduced himself as Chris and then introduced another young man as Josh.

No Mere Coincidences, a journey of faith

I don't know why but, when Chris said Josh, it just came out of my mouth; "Josh, Joshua, Yashua, that's quite a name to live up to." Josh said that he knew, and I introduced myself to them. Chris, whom I believe was the youth pastor, asked several questions about the journey I was on. I spent about half an hour there, resting and talking to them and, after filling my water bottles at a drinking fountain, I prepared to leave.

Chris asked if they could pray for me before I left so, the three of us stood there in prayer for a minute. I started walking again and, hadn't gone far, when a vehicle pull alongside of me, the driver asking where I was headed and then offering me a ride.

His name was Mike and he was a fellow believer. I asked where he lived and he told me the name of a town, which I had passed a couple days earlier. I asked him where he was headed and he told me, "where ever God leads me."

I learned that Mike, when he wasn't working, drove around, looking for people to help. He told me that I was the first one that he had picked up who was just walking. Usually he finds motorist that had run out of gas or broke down, gives them a ride and takes advantage of the situation to witness to them.

Mike drove me to Roseland, FL, which was a good 45 miles from where he had picked me up, and, after we prayed together, he dropped me off at a convenience store. As it was still early I continued walking and had gone a couple of miles when a Black 4door pickup pulled over beside me.

The driver was a young Latino man and, though he spoke very broken English, conveyed to me that he was going to Vero Beach and was offering me a ride. I walked to the back of the truck to load my backpack into it and noticed a bumper stick that said "Honduras" on it. As I got into the truck I asked him if he was from Honduras and told him that I had spent 6 months in Comayagua, working at an orphanage there.

His name was José, and he was from just outside of Tegucigalpa, Honduras. He spoke very little English, but with what English he spoke and the little Spanish I spoke, we managed to have a good conversation.

José, like so many others, had passed by me and felt that they should give me a ride. But then, Satan started throwing reasons why *not* to help me at him. He said that first, he thought, "Maybe he has drugs in his bag and if he gets arrested I might be deported." Then he thought, "No, I'm supposed to help him!", and he started to turn around. But then he thought, "What if he has a gun and robs me and steals my truck?" But, once again, he decided that he was supposed to help me and returned to offer me a ride.

I told José more about my journey, and as we talked, he pulled a bill out of his wallet and handed it to me. I thanked him, knowing that, most likely, as with many, he probably supported family back in Honduras –what he gave me would be equivalent to a week's pay there.

By now we were well into Vero Beach and José dropped me off at a convenience store. As we parted, José gave me another $5.00 to buy dinner with. I could feel a tear swelling up in my eyes and said "Gracias y bendición de Dios" (thank you and God bless you).

After supper I headed out in search of a church, and within a few blocks saw a sign that said "Resource Jesus". There were a few people standing outside of it, so I went up, asked if it was a church and was told that it wasn't, it was an outreach ministry. They were about to show a movie and I was invited to stay.

It was a nice evening, relaxing in the air conditioning. Later I learned that the ministry served breakfast and also had a shower I would be able to use in the morning. While talking to some of the men there, I was directed to a place that I would be able to set my tent up for the night, and after the movie I found the area, set up and fell fast asleep.

## Saturday-August 29, 2009

I got up about 5:30am, packed and returned to Resource Jesus. When I arrived there, there were three men waiting outside. After greeting them, I sat on a bench, pulling out my notebook. One of them asked where I had come from and I shared my journey with them. Two of them left, but the third one, whose name was Eddie, stayed and continued talking to me.

I started asking more about him and learned that he had crossed the country on his bicycle, stopping here and there when he found some temporary work. He didn't consider himself homeless; he was just a free spirit that didn't like to be stationary.

I did find out that he was in need of some socks. I had bought several pair before I left on the journey, so I gave him a package of new socks as well as a couple cans of soup that I had acquired a few days earlier.

Soon we were allowed into the building. after a quick breakfast, I took a shower and was back on my way again; traveling a couple of hours before coming to a convenience store.

While I was taking a break, it started to sprinkle and thunder. It was more of an electrical storm than anything, and soon I was on my way again. I hadn't made it far when I could see more rain headed for me – obviously *not* just a rain shower. I hurried along a short distance to a small motel that had a carport, where I took cover. I made it just before it started pouring down rain. It was an hour and a half before the sky lighten up and the rain stopped. Unfortunately, while the rain had cooled it off, the Sun quickly evaporated the water, making it twice as humid.

I had been walking for another hour or so when a pickup, coming from the other direction, made a U-turn and pulled up beside me. This truck had a young Latino couple with a child and baby. The driver, whose name was Jesús, offered me a ride, so I climbed into the back of the truck and was taken about five miles, being dropped off in a shopping center parking lot. After thanking Jesús and wishing God's blessing on him and his family, I went in search of food.

When I headed back out, I was planning on stopping at the first church I found. I had just started walking when a van pulled to the side of the road, and the female driver offered me a ride. Her name was Dawn and she started asking me where I was from and where I was headed. Then she asked me where I sleep at night, and I told her that I usually found a church to set my tent up. I let her know that, when possible, I would obtain permission, but if no one was around, and the church claimed to be of God, I would assume that it was OK.

Dawn suggested that she take me to her church and I agreed to go, so we headed to Port St. Lucia, FL. The church was having an activity that night so there were people there. Dawn told someone of my situation and they went to find someone else that could help me. While waiting I looked around and saw several banners and fliers advertising that the church was starting a series on discipleship the following Sunday.

I was introduced to a man who was in charge that night and made my request. He said that he would contact the pastor and get back with me after the activity was over.

The activity was a variety show fundraiser for a mission trip to Africa. Afterward, I went and found the man again, only to hear that he had talked to the pastor –who had said no; The reason being that they had been having break-ins lately, so the police were watching the property and would arrest me if they found me there. This made no sense to me, but, this man was just the messenger and I wasn't going to debate it with him. I left, sad because I had found yet another church, that apparently didn't understand God's ways.

Walking back towards the highway, I found Walton Road Baptist Church. It had a large field in back of it. by now, it was late –so I set my tent up and went to sleep.

**Sunday, August 30, 2009**

I didn't sleep well during the night. I kept thinking about the banners, advertising the discipleship series, the church was planning on starting the following week. I had prayed throughout the night, and knew that I needed to go back to the church to speak with the pastor, so I rose early and packed. Finding a gas station, I went into the bathroom, shaved, washed and put on clean clothes.

Somehow, I knew that there would be people at the church early –though I don't recall seeing anything with a schedule of the services. When I arrived, I asked the greeter if I could see the pastor. We went looking for him and found him at the Sound-booth in the sanctuary.

When he was free he shook my hand and I handed him a ministry card, and told him that I had been the one looking for a place to set my tent up the night before. Then I told him that God wanted me to let him know that, according to Matthew 25, Jesus had been looking for a place to rest and had been turned away.

The pastor asked "God told you to come back here?" I told him yes and he said "That's debatable! So, God told you to come back here and chew me out?" I said "No, not to chew you out, to let you know that you're not practicing what you are supposed to be teaching." Then the pastor said "I want to tell you something-- and God told me to tell you, though you probably won't believe that." I responded by saying, "If it's in keeping with God's word I would take it to heart." He continued by saying, "We've had a lot of break-ins, and we couldn't very well call the police and tell them that you were spending the night here." I asked why not and he said "What are they supposed to do; Track down every patrol car to let them know it's Okay for you to be here?" I told him that, I had been in law enforcement for 20 years and they usually used the radio for that. At this point he got flustered, thrust the ministry card back at me and walked off.

I had done what I felt God had told me to do and I left, saddened and fearing for this man's soul. Unless this pastor had a change of heart, he would be standing before the throne one day hearing "Depart from me, I never knew you." And if he taught what he lived, he will have several of his congregation standing in line behind him. Not only was he not living the way that Jesus taught, but had mocked the message I had given him; disbelieving that it could be from God. Then took it a step further, claiming that God was telling him to tell *me* something, which had no biblical basis.

I'm very careful about saying that something was from God, and have no problem saying "I feel that..." Letting them know that, it may not be straight from God, but from my understanding of the scriptures, and I try to back up everything with scriptures. To say something that contradicts scripture, claiming it's from God, is playing with eternal fire.

In any event, I returned to Walton Road Baptist Church, where there was now a car outside. The door was unlocked, and I entered, calling out "hello" so as not to startle anyone. A man came out of an office area, and greeted me.

He was the pastor, who introduced himself as Steven Moore. I introduced myself to him and told him that I had spent the night camped out behind the church. He assured me that it was fine and asked where I was headed. I started telling him about my journey and he offered me a cup of coffee and invited me to sit down. As I drank the coffee, he listened to my story of how I came to be on a 4,000 mile journey, and when I finished, commented on how inspiring it was. Eventually he told me to help myself to more coffee and excused himself to finish preparing for the service.

I poured another cup of coffee and then pulled out my journal and began writing. It seemed God had been doing so much lately that, by the time I got one day written down, two days had passed.

People started to arrive for Sunday school and most of them came up to greet me. The teacher was wearing scrubs and I assumed he worked in the medical field and had either just gotten off work or had to be there immediately after the service. Judging by the questions people were asking him about his wife, it became evident that there had been a miracle in their life during the last week.

Between Sunday school and the service more people came up to welcome me. Pastor Steve delivered a wonderful message, then called on the man who had taught the Sunday school and his wife to give their testimony.

It turned out that he worked at a cardiac clinic. His wife had to have a procedure done that would send a Laparoscope through her femoral artery, into the heart, to check on it. They had scheduled the procedure so that she would be ready to leave about the time he got off work.

As he was preparing to leave, it came to his attention that one of his co-workers needed a break, and he volunteered to stay. As he was going about, filling in for his co-worker, a nurse ran into the room he was in and told him that his wife had coded. Her heart had gone into fibrillation, but they had used the defibrillator in time, and she had lived.

Had they left when he had gotten off work, they would have been miles from the nearest help and she would most likely have died. But, because this man had thought of another person's needs, his wife was where she could get the medical attention needed to revive her.

After their testimony, Pastor Steve wanted to recognize me and asked if I would share a little about my journey. When the service was over, many of the people came up to me and asked questions about the ministry and my journey. Then the pastor's wife, Beth, wanted to know if I would join them for dinner. A home cooked meal sounded good to me, so I accepted and Pastor Steve said that I could either take my backpack with me or leave it at the church. Thinking that there was an evening service I asked if it was OK to camp out behind the church another night and, with that being approved, I left my backpack at the church.

In the car I met the pastor's son, Nathan, and his "unofficial son", Evan, who spends Sundays with them. At the house I met the rest of the family; Katy, Emily and Claire, who all made me feel more like a visiting uncle than a stranger that had walked into their church just a few hours earlier.

Pastor Steve and Beth's family were tight-knit. Everyone worked together to get things done, and when dinner was over, everyone pitched in to clean up. After that the kids wanted me to play a card game with them, and we ended the afternoon by watching a movie. Everything reminded me of times past, when families were families and not a group of strangers living together.

After a fully enjoyable afternoon, I learned that there was no evening service, as most of the congregation had migrated north for the summer. We had supper and then Pastor Steve said that he would take me back to the church, but recommended that I sleep inside the church, instead of in my tent. He also said that he would pick me up in the morning for breakfast with the family before I headed on down the road.

I asked if it would be OK for me to wash up in the restroom of the church, and he suggested that I just take a shower at the house before I left the next day. Beth started apologizing that she hadn't thought about me needing a shower or needing my clothes washed. This wonderful woman of God, having hosted me all day, was now concerned that she hadn't done enough. She sent a plastic bag with me and insisted that I send my dirty clothes home with Steve.

We got to the church, gathered my laundry and, once Pastor Steve left, I did my update and went to sleep.

## Monday-August 31, 2009

I made sure I was up and ready to go when Pastor Steve arrived at the church. We went back to the house and, while breakfast was being prepared I shaved, showered and packed my clean clothes away.

After breakfast, Pastor Steve had everyone join hands and, starting with the one on my right, each family member prayed for me, then I for them. After saying goodbyes, Pastor Steve took me a couple miles south on U.S. Highway 1 and I was on my way.

It wasn't long before a car pulled to the side of the road and the passenger, a young woman, asked where I was headed to. I told her and she turned and talked to the driver, then offered me a ride into Hobe Sound. I accepted the offer, the trunk popped open and I loaded my backpack into it, then climbed into the back seat. To my surprise the driver was also a young woman. Both of them appeared to be in their late teens and, judging by the books in the back seat, college students.

I introduced myself and learned that the driver was Natalie and the passenger Annie. They started asking me why I was walking and I told them about the ministry and my journey. Natalie said that she wanted to work with kids in Uganda someday and, I told them about the Angels of East Africa, who went out into the jungles to rescue some of the kids that had escaped capture or escaped from the Lord's Resistance Army.

Soon I was being dropped off at the south end of Hobe Sound and began walking again. I hadn't even broke out in a sweat, when a vehicle pulled into a drive about 50 yards ahead and the driver got out, moving things from the front seat into the back. As I neared him, he asked where I was headed. Normally, I had one day travel in mind and used that as my destination. Today, however, I had looked to see where I was *supposed* to be to be back on schedule, and Hollywood, FL. Just slipped out of my mouth.

I was totally shocked when the man said, "Well, if that's where you need to go, then that's where I'll take you." At the time I didn't know how far it was to Hollywood, but I knew that I was still about 4 days behind after spending the extra time in Georgia. We got onto I-95 and passed a sign that announced that Hollywood was *89 miles.*

This man's name was Art and, as I had already suspected, God had spoken to him and told him to take me where I wanted to go. Art was a devout Catholic and he, like me, had been shown that, one thing we would have to answer for at judgment would be not caring for others, loving them as ourselves.

Art dropped me off in Hollywood, FL, a couple blocks from U.S. Highway 1 and, before he left, he gave me a love gift. We prayed together and then, he turned around and headed back the way he had come.

At about 6:00pm I found a place to eat dinner and, after eating, set out to find a place to set up my tent for the night. It wasn't easy, as everything in the area was some type of business, but I finally found a church with a large lawn and some bushes that would afford me some privacy.

# SEPTEMBER

*"God does not need us. Whether we serve & worship him or not, He is still God. We need to serve & worship Him so our lives will be fulfilled, full of peace, happiness and blessings."*
~Brother Sean Rogers~

### Tuesday-September 1

It was a fairly pleasant morning; cooler than it had been, and the humidity was low. I packed up and headed out, stopping for a light breakfast along the way.

When I came to the Miami-Dade county line, things changed so drastically, it was like going from water to land. Where there had been businesses and hotels, there were large homes with gates and manicured lawns. The sidewalk stopped and there was no shoulder on the road for about two miles, but at last I got into the businesses again and went on to Pace Park. Here, there were access points to the beach, and, by now I had been walking for a couple of hours, and was ready for another break. I got some good photos, then went in the water to cool off and relax.

I could see thunderheads moving towards land, so I headed out. Walking a few blocks to my furthest point south, I turned and headed west. It wasn't long before it started to rain and I was forced to take shelter, which happened to be a restaurant, so I ate, and wrote, while I waited out the rain.

When the storms passed, I headed on west, now in search of a church along the route. There were very few churches along the way. The ones I did find were older, with tall cast iron fences and re-enforced gates.

I also soon realized that I was in a rougher part of town. Just about the time this struck me, a patrol car pulled up to me and an officer asked my name. I told him, expecting him to ask for identification. He didn't, he just advised me to keep walking a couple miles before stopping for the night, which I assured him that I would do. It was about time for my nightly update, but, pulling my computer out there would be like an invitation to rob me, so I just kept walking.

I still didn't know where I was going to spend the night, so I continued on west, and eventually walked into Little Havana. I found an area that looked like it had been a mobile home park at one time. It was now empty and overgrown with brush, but I walked to the back of it and set my tent up for the night.

## Wednesday-September 2, 2009

It hadn't rained during the night, but the dew was so heavy that it might as well have. The tent was completely soaked and, by the time my tent was packed and ready, my shoes and socks were saturated too. I walked half a block and got some breakfast, then changed my shoes and socks before heading west on 8th street.

Finally getting to the edge of the city, I came to the intersection of U.S. 41 and Krome Ave, where there was a truck stop on one corner and a casino on the opposite corner. Beyond that was the Everglades and the Miccosukee Indian reservation. I took a break there; made sure my water bottles were full and bought some granola bars and peanut butter. I planned for the worst– 4 or 5 days walking through the Everglades.

It was only 2:00pm and too early to stop for the day. I headed out towards the Miccosukee village, figuring I would reach it by noon the next day. I walked about eight miles before stopping to rest at a roadside Restaurant/Air-boat Tour business.

I finally came to Frog Town, where I had planned to spend the night, only to discover that Frog Town wasn't a town. There was nothing there but a locked gate with a sign on the inside of it that said Frog Town. I kept walking until I came to a spot where there was an area that gave access to a utility road. There wasn't a lot of room, but it was enough to set up my tent, just as the last glow from the sun faded.

As I lay in my sleeping bag, I kept hearing what I thought were some type of frogs, and figured that was why they called the area Frog Town. A few days later, I learned that they were not frogs, but alligators.

When I learned this, I decided they were probably having a conversation something like this: "Hey, did you see that guy setting his tent up? I bet he'd be good for dinner." Then another one would say, "Na, I saw him come in. He was old, fat and carrying a big backpack. He'd be tough, stringy and greasy." Then the first one said, "Bummer. Well, let's go see if we can find a young deer or something, we'll eat him as a last resort."

**Thursday-September 3, 2009**

I awoke before first light and was packed and ready to go by the time the sun was up. I ate a couple granola bars with some peanut butter for breakfast, then headed out.

As I always do in the morning, I prayed for God's guidance and protection, but this morning I prayed for some help. I was looking at another three days of walking through the Everglades, and I knew that the road would be long and straight, which makes it seem even longer. When you see something and walk for hours before coming to it or, look behind you and see things you passed hours ago, it seems that you haven't gotten very far.

I entered the Miccosukee Indian reservation, and about four hours later that I came upon a crew working on the road –hoping they had a water cooler, and would allow me to get some. I had only finished about half my water, but it was hot out, I was hot and my water was hot. I was looking forward to getting something cold to help me cool off.

They didn't have a cooler, but one of the men gave me a bottle of cool water, which was better than my hot water. He commented that he had seen me the night before, on his way home from work, and asked about my destination, so I talked to him for a few minutes before he had to get back to work. As I thanked him, he pointed to a sign about one and a half miles away, and told me that it was a gas station/restaurant at the edge of the Indian Village, so I figured I would get a meal and fill my bottles there.

I hadn't gone far when a pickup truck pulled beside me. It was one of the men from the roadwork site; whom I had presumed then was a supervisor. He was headed to check on another crew and offered me a ride to the Indian village.

His name was Elvis and he was listening to Dr. Tony Evens on the radio. We talked for a few minutes about how few people want to listen to Bible teachings now days and, how many Christian stations don't even air them anymore, because people – even Christians –just want music to entertain them or give them an emotional experience.

As we talked, we passed the gas station/restaurant and Elvis offered to turn around and take me back, but we were in front of the Indian village gift shop and I told him that I would check it out and then walk back if I needed to.

I went inside and got a bottle of ice cold water, drinking it as I walked around the shop. They didn't have anything to eat but candy, so I asked if there was someplace to get food, and was directed to a little shack, a short distance away. I found the shack and they had a small menu, so I ordered a sandwich, ate and was back on my way within a few minutes.

As I walked through the town, I saw my first alligator in the wild. It was in a waterway between the road and the back of houses. The alligator was about ten feet long and was swimming towards me, but not like it was trying to be stealthy and sneak up on me. I figured that it was probably one that the local Native Americans fed and thought I might have a snack for it.

Continuing on out of the town, I'd made it a good mile before I realized that I hadn't filled my water bottles. I debated going back, but felt that I should press on; like the Holy Spirit was saying "Always forward, never retreat" so I just asked God to provide. I got my answer an hour later, which I believe had been in God's plan the entire time.

As I was walking, I noticed a small shack at the side of the road ahead. A minute later a car pulled in front of it, a man went inside and returned a minute later with a bag in his hands. There were no signs indicating that it was a store or anything, but I went ahead and walked to it. On the door was a piece of paper that showed the hours of operation, but nothing else. Taking my backpack off, I went inside what was, indeed, a small store. There were two men inside talking to a woman, who appeared to work there and, as I entered, she got excited and exclaimed, "We saw you yesterday, we saw you walking yesterday, but you had a backpack on!"

I told her that I had left the backpack outside. She told me that she and a friend had been headed for Miami for supplies when they had come across me. She said that her friend had called me a homeless person, but that she'd told her friend that I wasn't homeless; I was walking with a purpose in life.

I verified that I did have a purpose, and gave her one of my cards. When she looked at it, she said "I knew you were a brother, I told my friend that I could sense the Spirit of God in you." She said that they were going to pick me up on their way back, but couldn't find me.

She told me to bring my backpack inside, saying, "You're not going anywhere for a while." I retrieved my backpack, and got a bottle of water while she took care of the other customers.

Susan, as I learned her name was, wouldn't let me pay for the water and she had me sit down, asking if I was hungry. She began fixing me a meal, and as we talked, she shared that her husband had passed away the year before. She, not being Native American, was tolerated on the reservation only because of her 16 year old son. She didn't drive, and was dependent on her friends to drive her to town and church.

I learned that the only church on the reservation had been closed for some time for the lack of a pastor. She talked about the difficulty in spreading God's word to the Native Americans; they believed everything had a spirit and wouldn't embrace the idea of worshiping One God. She explained it in this way: If you were to build a house and give the keys to someone, they would go up, embrace the house, thanking it for giving them shelter, instead of thanking the one who built it –in other words, worshiping the creation instead of the creator.

A short time later another woman came in, who Susan introduced as Virginia. Susan told Virginia about my journey and about me having worked with the kids in Honduras. Virginia said that she had wanted to do work like that, but God had led her to teach at the school on the reservation. I told her that, from what Susan had been telling me, she was needed there to introduce the children to God.

Before Virginia left, she and Susan prayed for me and she gave me a love gift. A short time later I felt that it was time for me to leave and mentioned it to Susan. She said that she felt it was time for me to leave too. She said that God had something planned for me soon. Susan then placed a generous love gift in my hand and told me to use it wisely. I assured her that I would and, giving her a hug, retrieved my backpack and headed out.

By now it was 5:00pm, but the sun wasn't setting until almost 9:00. Being well rested and fed, I figured I would be able to get another six or seven miles in. I had just barely gotten out of sight of Susan's little store, when a Miccosukee patrol car pulled in behind me. A young officer asked for my identification. Amazingly, this was only the second time I had been identified in almost 2,400 miles and the first time that I was stopped at the side of the road and checked.

The officer went back to his patrol car and, after being satisfied that I wasn't a wanted person, came back and let me know that, in less than an hour, I would be trespassing. It was then that I found out that, at 6:00pm, anyone not Native American, or passing through in a vehicle, was trespassing. Although I am one eighth Ojibway Indian, my family was never registered and I, unlike my siblings, look nothing like a Native American.

I asked the officer about getting a ride off the reservation, as there was no way I could walk off it in an hour. He checked with his supervisor and was told that it was against policy for them to give me a ride, but as long as I was on the roadway and not on someone's property, they wouldn't bother me. I thanked the officer and continued on my way, praying that God would provide. Less than half an hour later, He did.

As I was walking, a van went past me, then stopped,

waiting until I was there. When I got close the driver got out, and asked if I would like a ride, which, of course, I did.

His name was Daryl and he lived in Naples, but worked in Miami. He said that he had seen me walking as he was headed home the night before, then again, headed to work that morning and decided that, if he saw me on his way home again, he would offer me a ride.

Daryl had been raised in a church, but had wandered away, recently returning to God in the wake of a crisis. I talked about the importance of a relationship with God, not just using faith as a fix, when things were going bad. Christianity is supposed to be a way of life, not a crutch to lean on in time of trouble. The time passed quickly and soon we were in Naples, FL.

I had made arrangements to stay with a family in Naples, but, I hadn't looked to see exactly where they lived. I had Daryl drop me off at the intersection of U.S. Highway 41 and Collier Boulevard, before he turned north on Collier.

I found a restaurant and checked the address, only to discover that I needed to go north on Collier Boulevard, almost 15 miles. At first, I was somewhat upset at myself for not knowing this sooner, but realized that there may be a purpose in it. I found a spot to set my tent up about a block away.

### Friday-September 4, 2009

I woke-up shortly after falling asleep, to discover that, while I was secluded from view, I was not secluded from the sand gnats, that had apparently infested my gear. I wiped insect repellent on myself, which helped and let me get back to sleep – only to be awakened again to the sounds of rain and water dripping on me. It was apparent that the waterproofing spray had worn off. I did my best to get back to sleep, but finally got up as soon as the rain stopped. By the time I got packed, a nearby restaurant was open, so I went there and order breakfast.

The family I was going to spend the weekend with was the Walter Reyes family. I had spent 2½ months with Walter (Wally) in Honduras, working at the orphanage and sharing a room, and had come to think of him like a son by the time he left. His parents, Walter and Lillian, had come to visit him in Honduras and, though we hadn't spent much time together, I felt a kinship with them as well.

As soon as it was light enough to walk the road, I headed out, north on Collier Boulevard. I hadn't walked more than a mile when a city bus pulled up beside me and the doors opened. The driver asked me where I was going and I told him "About 14 miles up this road." He thought for a minute and then told me to get in, that he would take me as far as the hospital. I had no idea where the hospital was, but figured it must be North. I also felt that I was supposed to be on this bus.

Once inside, I asked how much the fare was and the driver told me not to worry about it. Then he asked what I was doing, walking down the road and I told him that I was on a 4,000 mile journey of faith. He looked at me and said, "OK... Why?" I told him, "Because God told me to." and he replied, "You talk to God... and He talks back?" I said, "All the time." Then he asked, "Are you sure it's not just voices in your head?" I told him that, I was being led into some interesting situations if it was just voices in my head. Then he said, "I've been in church all my life and I've never heard of God talking to anyone."

I suddenly had a picture from "Green eggs and Ham" and the words "Sam I Am" flash through my head and I looked at him and said, "He wants to talk to you too Sam." He just looked at me, startled, and asked, "Wha... what do you mean?" I asked/stated, "You're a Christian, aren't you Sam?" He confessed that he was, and I continued, "And you pray every day, don't you." Again, he confirmed this. I told him that prayer is not meant to be a monolog, it is a dialog, a conversation, between us and God.

I continued, explaining that, when Adam was in the Garden, God would come down to walk & talk with him, in the cool of the evening. Jesus came to restore what had been lost, to reunite us with the Father. It's just that, most people get up in the morning, thank God for the day, ask for his favor and blessing;

161

then they run off and get caught up in the world that we call our daily lives; leaving no time to be in communion with God and to listen for His voice.

Then I said, "Besides, God has been speaking to you, you just don't recognize it." Again Sam asked me what I meant, and I asked him, "Why did you pick me up this morning Sam?" He said, "Well–, it's dangerous walking on the side of the road." "So, every time you see someone walking at the side of the road, you stop your city bus and give them a ride?" Sam said "Noooo." and again I asked, "So, why did you pick me up this morning?" His reluctant response was, "I... just felt that I was supposed to help you out." I asked, "Do you think, maybe, that it was God telling you to help me out?" He didn't have an answer, but I could tell that he was in deep thought about it.

About that time we pulled into the hospital, and Sam opened the door. I disembarked and turned to thank him, but he said, "Wait a minute, get back on, I'll help you get to where you're going." I thanked him and he asked more information on my destination, so I dug out the address and gave it to him.

Soon, we were at a transfer station and Sam told me what bus I wanted, and said to tell the driver where I wanted to go and he would drop me off a few blocks from the house. I asked how much the fare would be for the other bus and Sam said not to worry about It, and handed me a transfer ticket. I thanked him once again and got on the other bus. Shortly, I was being let out at the entrance of the subdivision that the Reyes family lived in, and walked the few blocks to the house.

Though I knew Walter Jr in Honduras as Walter, his family calls him Wally and so, to save confusion, for this book, I too will call him Wally and his father Walter.

When I knocked on the door Wally answered. I hadn't seen him in over a year and, though we had talked on occasion, I missed him like any of my other "kids" from Honduras. He asked me how I had gotten there so quickly and I told him of my bus ride. He couldn't believe it; I told him that was how my entire summer had been. Then we just sat and talked for a couple of hours. It was just as it had been in Honduras. Well, except that there was air conditioning, a television, no kids running around – jumping on us, no geckos on the walls, no smells from the market...

All too soon it was time for Wally to go to work. Before leaving, he showed me where I would be sleeping and where the washer, dryer and shower were. By the time his parents got home I had showered and my clothes were in the dryer. We spent a couple hours talking, then I was told that Walter was going to take me to Naples Pier, to see the sunset, as Lillian had a "Girls night" planned at the house.

We left and soon I was watching my first west coast sunset. It was truly breathtaking; there was a line of clouds that enhanced the colors of the sun and, even though there were people all around, it was as though God had created the scene just for me. As it turned out, that was the only sunset I would see from the ocean. Every other time I was on the ocean after that, it was at least cloudy if not storming.

When we returned to the house, the ladies were still in fellowship. Lillian suggested that I share about my journey with her friends, which I gladly did.

### Saturday-September 5, 2009

I awoke early and, as I was the only awake, began working on my journal at the kitchen table. Soon Walter was awake. He had told me the previous night that he was going to make me a Honduran breakfast, and so we had beans, scrambled eggs, fried bananas and tortillas.

During breakfast, Walter told me that he was going to their pastor's house to do some repairs, and asked if I wanted to accompany him; suggesting that I take my computer to show the pastor some pictures.

I had met the pastor's wife, Emily, the night before, and now met Pastor Jr. Walter told Pastor Jr. that I had some photos he should see and I sat in the living room showing him pictures of the kids in Honduras, telling their stories, and then told him of my journey of faith. Pastor Jr. asked me if I would share about my journey at church the following day and I told him that it would be my pleasure.

Soon lunch was being served. During lunch I found myself enjoying what I had found somewhat annoying in Honduras; I have found, when around Bilingual people, they often start speaking in English and, suddenly, switch languages, often in mid-sentence. Even though I don't speak much Spanish, it gave me a feeling of being accepted, like being a part of their family. Once they catch themselves, they apologize and we have a good laugh, especially the times I hadn't even noticed it.

After lunch, Walter and I went back to work on the windows, and were almost finished, when Lillian called; her mother was in the hospital and the outlook was bleak.
We quickly finished the windows and headed back to the house.

Walter made sure I knew that there were plenty of leftovers in the refrigerator, then he and Lillian left for Ft. Lauderdale, FL. After putting a prayer request around the world with friends online, I spent a quite evening writing and emailing.

Wally came home from work, packed, and let me know that someone from the church would be picking me up in the morning then, he too, headed for Ft. Lauderdale.

## Sunday-September 6, 2009

My ride arrived and I was delivered to La Iglesia Centro Internacional de Alabanza. Many of the people came up and greeted me, and, some of the ladies I had met at Lillian's dinner, introduced me to others.

Once the announcements were done and singing worship over, Sister Emily introduced me and Pastor Jr. translated for me. I started by telling of a missionary I had met, who had been invited to speak at a church, whose language he didn't know. He decided that he wanted to impress the congregation; so, he looked up, and studied a blessing in that language, which went "May the blessings of Heaven rain down upon you." Once in the pulpit, recited the phrase. At first there was silence, then, everyone

164

started laughing. The visiting speaker turned to the translator and asked what was so funny. The translator told him that he had mispronounced the word for blessings and had actually said, "May the vomit of heaven rain down upon you". Then I said, "With that in mind, my opening statement to try and impress you is, ''Buenos Tardes, mi nombre es Denis!" (Good afternoon, my name is Dennis)

I went on to tell them about my calling and the burden I had for people; then told them of the journey I was on. When I finished, Pastor Jr expounded on my journey, telling them that there had been churches that had turned me away; and questioned where the love of Jesus was in those pastors.

After the service I was returned to the house, where everyone was home and napping. Lillian's mother had pulled through and was doing better. Walter got up shortly after I got there and fixed us something to eat, then took me sightseeing around the area, including a nature preserve to look for alligators. This is where I found out that, what I had thought were frogs a few nights earlier, were actually alligators.

By the time we got back to the house Lillian, who works nights, was headed to work, and Wally had fixed fajitas for our dinner. For the rest of the evening we just sat around in fellowship.

**Tuesday-September 8, 2009**
Originally, I had intended to head out on Monday, but Walter suggested that I put my departure, as it was Labor Day. Walter wanted to get me back to U.S. Highway 41, and a few miles south before having to be at work. I was driven to Ft. Myers, FL, which had me back on schedule. Walter gave me a love gift, and then we prayed together before he left.

Once again, I felt alone, but knew that God was with me. I headed northbound and had a somewhat uneventful day. In the late afternoon I was offered a ride by two men in a pickup, pulling a small boat. Their names were Tom and Gil and they drove me to Punta Gorda, FL.

I found one restaurant, which was the only place to eat in the area. Like so many areas close to an interstate, most places were near the interchanges. My online search for a nearby church came up empty. I walked on, going along U.S. Highway 41, until I came to an area with some bushes that gave me a little privacy and set up for the night.

## Wednesday-September 9, 2009

I was awakened early to the sounds of large mowing equipment. The lawn service apparently started work at 5:00am, so I quickly packed, got out of their way and started walking. The day was hot and humid, which left me stopping for a break every chance I got. One of these stops was at Gospel Gifts, a Christian bookstore in Port Charlotte, FL. I was able to pick up some gospel tracts there as I had given out my last one.

I talked to the cashier for a while and asked if any of the churches there had Wednesday night Bible studies. She told me that there were none in town, adding that, Wednesday night services were kind of 'Old School'. The way she said this let me know that she didn't agree with it, but was describing the general attitude of the area. I thought how sad it was that taking time to learn about and worship God could be considered in such a way.

Back on the road, I hadn't walked far out of Port Charlotte when a pickup truck pulled over in front of me and a young woman was offering me a ride. Her name was Becky and she was headed to South Venice. Asking where I wanted to be let out; I told her that any church in South Venice would be fine.

Soon we were talking about spiritual matters and she told me that she was not a Christian. She had nothing against Christians, but didn't see where they were any different than she was. She helped people whenever she could, tried to get along with everyone and not hurt anyone.

This was a tough one. It's easy when someone is heavily involved in the world to show them where what they are doing is ungodly. When you find someone who acts more like a Christian than many proclaiming Christ do, you have to convince them that they need a dedication to Jesus for eternal life.

I told her that, even though she was a good person, because of Adam's fall, we are all separated from God and that it was only through Jesus, dying for our sins, that we could have a relationship with God.  Jesus, himself, said in John 14:6 that no one could get to the Father except through him.

We arrived in Venice all too soon and I was being dropped off at a church, but before she left I gave her one of the tracts I had just purchased, and also gave her one of my cards, asking her to read the R U Saved page on my website.

The church Becky had dropped me off at didn't have an evening service but, there were three more churches on the same block that did.  I walked past all three, but felt led to the first one, which was the South Venice Christian Church.

Inside I found the pastor, Earl Knopf, in his office. Introducing myself, I made my request of setting up my tent on the property after the Bible study.  When the study started, Pastor Knopf introduced me to the small group; then started asking about my beliefs.

This was a first.  I gave a brief summary of my beliefs and when I was finished, Pastor Knopf let me know that the only thing we disagreed on was the speaking in tongues; adding that was hardly grounds to break fellowship.

We then had a good, well prepared study on confessing our belief in God, Jesus and the Holy Spirit, and the importance of not only letting people know what you believe, but living a life that showed what you believe.  After the study I talked to several of the group and then Pastor Knopf and I discussed what being a Christian means and how to live life like Jesus taught us to.  It was obvious that the Holy Spirit had led me to this church.

Later, I was shown where I could set up my tent for the night; but, as the pastor was doing this however, there was lightning in the distance and then thunder.  This changed his mind.  He suggested that I sleep inside the building instead, in case it rained.

**Thursday-September 10, 2009**

I headed out about 6:00 and had walked about five miles when I noticed a sign for Venice Beach. I decided to walk the half mile or so off route, and was soon in the water.

After relaxing for an hour or so and getting some photos, I began talking to a lifeguard, telling her about my journey, and how I had come to love stopping at beaches along the way. She told me that I need to stop at Siesta Key Beach, in Sarasota; telling me that it was one of the most beautiful beaches in the country. I thanked her and headed out.

It took me until well into the afternoon to get to Sarasota and, once there, I found that the beach was a couple miles from the highway. I was told that a bus went to the beach, and being tired, and wanting to be on the beach by sunset, I decided to take the bus; getting there about an hour before the sun started going down. The beach truly was beautiful. The sand was pure white and the water crystal clear.

The last bus had come and gone before sunset, and I was in an area with nothing but hotels, motels and large homes, so I decided to stay at the beach for the night. Sitting at a concession stand, I worked online until about 10:00pm, and then went onto the beach, to one of the lifeguard towers. There was a narrow walkway around the sides of the towers and I laid my sleeping bag down, covering up with a light blanket. There was lightning out at sea, but the sky above was crystal clear, bright with stars. The waves on the beach were making a very soothing sound, and I was quickly in a relaxed sleep.

**Friday-September 11, 2009**

At some point during the night, I was awakened by a couple of people walking the shoreline; and again, when a young man, looking for a place to sit and think, decided that "My" life guard stand would work. Though he was reluctant to tell me his name, we did talk about his problems for about half an hour before he said he was feeling better and thanked me before leaving. Other than that, it was a very peaceful night.

About 5:30am I got up, rolled my sleeping bag, and was sitting at the bus stop when it came around. I got into a conversation with the driver, whose name was Fabian. Before long I was back on route. As I was about to disembark, Fabian told me that if I got onto another bus, it would take me to Palmetto, FL.

I don't normally ride the bus; the only exceptions I had made was when I was given fare specifically for a bus, when Sam had picked me up a week earlier and, of course, the bus to the beach the night before and again to get back on route. Now, I felt that there was a purpose for being told about the bus going to Palmetto, so I went ahead and boarded the next bus.

Once in Palmetto I found a place to eat. During lunch, It started raining, so, when I was done, I went to a park across the street that had a pavilion. As I sat there, writing in my journal, an elderly African-American man came up, and started talking to me –at first just small talk. I shared about my journey, and soon it was apparent why I was to be in Palmetto when I was –to meet C.W. Scott or "Pops" as he said everyone calls him.

Pops started telling me his testimony. Being 74 years old, he had seen a lot of changes over the years; and he, himself had changed. He told me about the difficulty of getting a good job as a young Black man, and how he had become one of the first African-American bus drivers. He said that, on his very first day of driving, he had been taken off the bus in handcuffs, because the police had assumed that he had stolen the uniform and the bus.

After being verbally abused and belittled, he was released, but this sparked bitterness towards 'Whites' in him. At one point he was hired to do odd jobs for another White man, which included, on occasion, welding lids onto 55 gallon barrels. He later found out that the man was a hitman for the Gotti family – and he had been helping to dispose of bodies. C.W. said that, when he found out, he felt as he had sold his soul to the devil himself. His association with the man almost landed him in prison, and it also deepened his resentment towards White people.

He had taken another risk when a friend told him about a job, tearing out an old deck and rebuilding a new one. This job too, was working for a white man. This man was an older, disabled man who had diabetes. He recommended that C.W. live at his house while he did the work and the two soon became friends.

One day, when C.W. Had been out, he returned to find his friend/employer crying and holding a gun, prepared to kill himself. The reason given to C.W. was that he had just soiled himself, because he couldn't get up. He said that he couldn't live like that. C.W. told me that he suddenly had a compassion for this man. A compassion he had never felt for anyone, let alone a white man. He said that he had managed to get the gun away from his friend, afterward taking him and cleaning him up. He told me that, if anyone had told him that, one day, he would be wiping a white man's butt, he would have told them they were crazy. But, for the next seven years, until his friend's death, he'd worked a part time job and cared for his white friend.

C.W. gives the glory to God for delivering him from his bitterness. He said that he would have held onto it until he died if God hadn't softened his heart. We spent the rest of the afternoon talking about the things of God, involving some teenagers that had come to the pavilion after school to hang out.

Come suppertime C.W. announced that he needed to go home, but before he left, we prayed together and gave each other a hug, acknowledging that, if we didn't see each other again here, we would in heaven; where color never has and never will be a barrier between anyone.

I got dinner and found a church a couple blocks away, getting my tent set up just as it started to rain again.

**Saturday-September 12, 2009**

It poured down rain all night, and I hadn't gotten spray for my tent, so it leaked again. My backpack was covered with my poncho, but my blanket and sleeping bag were soaked.

The rain finally stopped about 4:00am and I got out to wring the water out of my sleeping items. As I did this, I noticed a 24 hour Laundromat, directly across the street from the church. Saying a silent prayer of thanks, I shook the water off my tent the best I could, rolled it up and then made my way to the Laundromat.

Once everything was dry, I packed and headed out, Northbound on U.S.41. I hadn't walked far, when it started raining again; but I was ready for it. I had left my poncho out, tucking it between me and the backpack, to put it on quickly.

It didn't just rain, it became a downpour. There were times when it was hard to see the edge of the road because the water was ankle deep. Whenever possible, I would stop and take a break from the rain. One small convenience store had water in the parking lot that was halfway to my knees.

In mid-afternoon I was offered a ride by a young Latino man named Louis. He didn't speak enough English, nor I enough Spanish, to get beyond our names and that I would like to go to a McDonald's, but I could sense the Spirit of God in him; we were able to communicate in a manner that this world can't understand. Louis, not even being able to speak to me, had enough of God's love in him that he didn't want to see another person suffer even so much as to be left to walk in the rain.

We arrived at a McDonald's, and I discovered that we could communicate one thing in each others language. After getting my backpack out of the truck I said, "Gracias, y las bendiciones de Dios mi amigo" and Louis responded in very broken English, "God bless you also my friend."

I went inside and got something to eat. My plan, once the rain stopped, was to walk back a couple blocks to where I had seen a church. The rain finally stopped and I headed out at about 10:00pm, planning on turning south. When I got to the road, I suddenly felt led to turn North instead of South, so I walked about a mile, and found myself standing in front of Calvary Evangelical Lutheran Church.

I walked around the church and found a good place to set up the tent. Once again the ground was so sandy that, even with all the rain, there were no puddles.

## Sunday-September 13, 2009

My alarm went off at 6:30am and I stepped outside, only to find that there were already lights on inside the church; I quickly took down my tent and went to the front of the church. The doors were still locked, but I could see someone in an office, sitting at a desk. A vehicle pulled in and drove around to the back of the church. A few minutes later, the man that I had seen at the desk, was unlocking the front door; holding it wide open for me. Once inside, I introduced myself to him.

He said that his name was Jason, and that, though not the pastor, he was doing the services that morning. I let him know about my journey and that I had slept behind the church the night before, which was fine with him. I asked if there was someplace I could wash before service, and he showed me the restroom, where I washed and changed clothes.

That done, I went to talk to Jason some more and let him know that this would be my first time at a Lutheran church for services. I had spent the night at a few during my journey, but had never been in one on a Sunday. Jason told me I was in for a treat; They had three services, a blended, a contemporary and a traditional. He encouraged me to stay for all three, which I agreed to do.

The blended service had both traditional and contemporary songs, using drums, guitars and keyboard. Jason let everyone know about my journey and encouraged people to visit with me after the service, during a time of fellowship. The sermon was an analogy of Jesus being a superhero. It was very good, though a little different, I thought –but it made sense to me shortly.

As I entered the fellowship hall after the service, I discovered that the children were starting their Sunday school season and, the theme was, "Super Heroes of the Bible". I got a cup of coffee and people started coming up to greet me and ask about my journey; several giving me love gifts.

The second service began, and this time the music was completely contemporary. The kids made their entrance, in capes and painted on masks. They presented Jason with a cape to wear for the service and, once again, Jason did an excellent job at delivering the sermon. Again, he introduced me and encouraged people to visit with me after the service, which they did.

One man said that, when Jason mentioned a man doing a 4,000 mile journey, he expected to see someone in their twenties and was surprised when I stood up. Then a lady, named Trudy, asked if I had plans for dinner and invited me to dine with her. I finally made it to the fellowship hall, where others came up to talk to me and, once again, several handed me love gifts.

Returning to the sanctuary a few minutes after the third service started, I heard Jason say as I walked in, "There he is" as he had been telling the congregation about me. The third service was traditional and very reverent.

Once again, following the service, people came up to greet me, a few of them slipping me love gifts. I don't normally talk much about the love gifts but, this time I think it's relevant.

I had been sending money to India to help care for kids, who had been taken in by Pastor Job and, were now being cared for by Bobby since his father's passing. A few days earlier Bobby had posted some photos, and one of them was of the kids, playing in the cooking room, which had an open, wood fire burning. I commented about it not being healthy to have the fire inside and asked about a gas stove. Bobby checked on the cost of a stove and propane tank, and I told him that I would pray that God would provide the funds needed.

When I counted what I had been given in love gifts that morning, it was enough for the amount I normally send, the amount for the stove and propane tank, plus enough to eat on for two or three days, which is what I would normally have.

Everyone had finished greeting me, and, as if on cue, Trudy, the lady that had invited me to dinner, returned to the church. I said my final goodbyes and we headed out for a restaurant. Trudy wanted to hear the entire story of how I came to do a 4,000 mile journey of faith. After dinner Trudy and I prayed, then she took me back to U.S. Highway 41, where she gave me a love gift before I left.

I walked north a few miles until I came to Gibsonton, FL, where I found the First Baptist Church of Gibsonton. It was only about 5:00, but there were cars in the parking lot, so I went in and found the choir practicing. As it turned out, the choir director was also the pastor. When the practice was over, I introduced myself to him, learning that his name was Pastor Clements. I asked about setting my tent up after the service. Pastor Clements said that I was more than welcome to set up for the night.

The service was beautiful, the choir sang and the sermon was about living the Christian life and how lax people had become; putting God on the back burner. If nothing else is going on, they figure they might as well go to church. He talked of the days when the churches were full, both morning and evening, because Sundays were dedicated to worshiping God.

I remembered how, in Honduras, one church had a week long revival meeting, which translated, was called "Meet me on the Mountain". People walked miles, up a mountain pass; many were older people and young mothers, carrying their children. They would spend the nights there, praying and fasting before walking back down. They did this because they expected the presence of God to be there and, they weren't disappointed. I was there one night; the Spirit of God was moving among them and there were several miracles.

Many people I talk to wonder why God doesn't work like that here; it's because American Christians have become complacent, worldly and lazy —wanting God to bless them without worshiping him in Spirit and truth. My friend, Sean Rogers, says it best. "God does not need us. Whether we serve & worship him or not, He is still God. *We* need to serve & worship Him so our lives will be fulfilled, full of peace, happiness and blessings."

After the service I talked to some of the congregation and

It was just after 7:00pm when everyone was gone.  As I was setting up to do my nightly broadcast a man walked up with a bag, saying that his wife had met me at the church earlier and wanted him to bring me some meals.  Inside the bag were three "A packs", ready to eat meals like the military uses.  I thanked him and asked that he pass my thanks onto his wife; then packed them away to be used when I was not around any place to eat.

**Monday-September 14, 2009**

Being on the outskirts of Tampa, FL; I wanted to get an early start so I could get through the city.  I don't really like big cities –they are just too busy for me.  I think that's one reason I enjoyed Honduras so much, life was just slower-paced.

After zigzagging through the city for several hours, having to stop at just about every intersection.  I finally made it out of Tampa, and just south of Lutz, FL.  It was now after 9:00pm and, even though I had only traveled about twenty miles, I was exhausted and sore.

I got some food from a grocery store deli for dinner, then I found a place to get some sleep.

**Tuesday-September 15, 2009**

I was up at first light.  After walking about a mile I came to a restaurant, got some breakfast, then headed down the road.  Within just a couple of hours I was wondering if I had eaten.  My stomach was growling as though it hadn't been fed and I was feeling weak.

I made it to Land-O-Lakes, FL and came to a building that said 'Larry's Deli'.  As I walked through the parking lot, a van pulled in.  As the driver got out, he asked if I would like something to eat.  It hadn't been more than three hours since I had eaten, but, I was already feeling hungry, so I accepted the offer and he bought me a Cuban sandwich.

His name was George, and, as I told him about my journey, he started telling me about being raised in a church, and of falling away from God.  George was another one who, like me, had been raised to serve God, had chosen not to and then, when God started calling him back, bringing him down hard to get his attention. In George's case, he had been out of work for a year and, out of desperation, began seeking God again.

I thought of how many churches performed a child Dedication; not for the salvation of the child, but to dedicate the child to God and, to charge the family and congregation with the Godly upbringing of the child. I've found that many people – including myself –have been raised in a church and Godly homes, but often slip away from God; then something happens in their life, leaving them seeking the God of their youth.

The sandwiches that George had ordered were ready and he paid for them, giving me the change. Since he was headed southbound we prayed together, then parted ways. After eating half the sandwich, I put the other half away for later. I headed northbound, coming to a convenience store a mile or so later and went in to use the restroom and get some water.

As I was standing outside, drinking the water, a young man came up and asked where I was headed; to which I answered that I was trying to get to Spring Hill, FL. He replied that he and his boss were headed for Brooksville and might be able to get me in the right direction. He went into the store and, a moment later, came out with another man. This man looked at me with scrutiny, before saying that they could get me to a road parallel to Spring Hill. He added that I would have to walk about 5 miles to get back on route. This sounded fine to me, as it would save me about 15 miles of walking.

During the ride, I found out that the younger man was Matt, and his boss was Warren. Matt told me that he had been raised in The Grapevine Church in Tampa, FL, but that was about all we had a chance to talk about as Warren received a business call that lasted the rest of the trip. They dropped me off at the intersection of U.S. Highway 41 and Spring Hill Drive and I headed west, towards Spring Hill and U.S. Highway 19.

It had turned into another hot, humid day and there was no shade along the roadway. About the time I needed a break, I saw

Spring Hill Bible Church. The only shade was a covered front entrance, and headed for it. I was eating the remainder of my sandwich, peering in the front door, when, much to my surprise, the office door opened. The man inside saw me, and, appearing as surprised as I was, he quickly regained his composure and came to unlock the door. I apologized, and told him that I had just stopped to eat my sandwich in the shade. He let me know that it was Okay, and invited me into the cool air.

There were chairs in the foyer, and, despite me being sweat-soaked, he encouraged me to sit down in one of them. I took him up on his offer, and then introduced myself and asked about the church. As I had already concluded, this man was the pastor, and he introduced himself as Roy Herbster.

Letting me know that I could rest as long as I like, he told me where there was a drinking fountain and a restroom I could use; then he excused himself and returned to the office. I finished my sandwich, used the restroom and then checked out some of the literature in a tract rack on the wall.

I headed out and had walked about and hour when a storm quickly approached . I heard thunder in the distance, and then a strong wind came up, and, by the time I got my poncho out of my backpack, it started –the sky opened up, the wind whipped the rain in circles and there was lightning all around me. There was no place to get out of the rain, so I just held my poncho down and kept pressing on.

Before long I was walking in ankle deep water and, at one intersection, it was up to my knees; but it finally stopped –and then the sun came out making it hot and humid again.

Pressing on I continued walking, knowing that I couldn't be far from U.S. Highway 19, and came across a crew, that had been doing some work at the side of the road. They had apparently taken refuge from the storm in their vehicles and had just finished picking up equipment to leave.

One of the men asked where I was headed and I told him that I was turning northbound, when I got to Highway 19. I didn't get his name, but he offered me a ride if I didn't mind riding in the back of the truck. I climbed in, and soon we were in an area with business' and I figured I would be dropped off there. But, when we came to Highway 19, the truck turned north and we started up the highway, towards Crystal River, FL. I was taken to Homosassa Springs, FL, which was half way to my next day's destination.

### Wednesday-September 16, 2009

The area I had set-up my tent was on the north outskirts of Homosassa. The only place to eat was a convenience store. So, after a junk food breakfast, I continued on U.S. Highway 19.

As I was already half way to Crystal River, FL, it was only about 2:00 when I arrived at my destination. I found a restaurant, spent the rest of the afternoon working on my journal and, towards evening, started looking for a church that would have a Wednesday evening service. I found a Baptist church nearby and headed there, only to discover that they were having a business meeting that night.

I asked about being allowed to wash up and was shown to a restroom where I would have some privacy. By the time I had washed and changed clothes, the meeting was over and I was introduced to Pastor Tim Lantzy, who had no problem with me setting up for the night. Some of the church members came over to talk to me as I set up my tent, and one young man, named Matt, brought some bottles of water, chips and crackers for me. Another asked if I was going to be headed out early the next morning, and I said that I would take time to find a Laundromat. They suggested that I use the washer and dryer that the church.

The church used part of a school across the street from it and Matt had told me that there was an outlet, under an overhang that I could use. I had just set up to do my nightly update, when it started to pour. It rained for a good hour and then, it was another half hour before the water in the street had receded enough to cross the road to my tent.

I quickly fell asleep, but at about 11:30pm, I was awakened

by a bright light. For the first time, in nearly four months, my sleep was interrupted by the police. The officer asked what I was doing and I explained that I was on a journey and, that Pastor Lantzy had given me permission to set up there. The officer just said, "OK, it's just unusual to see someone camped out at a church." and he left.


**Thursday-September 17, 2009**

Once again, I was awakened early by lawn equipment. They were mowing at the school across the street. I carried my backpack to the church's parking lot, then moved my tent there, to dry in the sun.

There was a convenience store across the street, so I went to buy something for breakfast, bringing it back to the church parking lot to eat. As I was eating, a lady, who was working with the lawn service, came up and was curious about my tent and backpack. I told her about my journey and suddenly, she reached her hand out with a folded $20 bill in it. I thanked her and she said "God bless you, keep up the good job." then she turned and went back to work. By now the tent was dry so I sprayed it down with waterproofing and waited for that to dry.

Soon, people started arriving at the church and I went to ask about using their washer and dryer. One of the ladies got me set up with the washing machine, then showed me where I could sit and write. When the clothes were dry I packed up, expressed my thanks and headed towards Inglis, FL.

Inglis was only about ten miles and, after walking about one of them, a van made a U-turn and pulled beside me. The couple, whose names were Jeff and Rebecca, offered me a ride to Inglis. Both Jeff and Rebecca seemed to have some knowledge of God, but had little understanding of Him. They asked about my traveling and didn't understand the concept of my Journey of Faith. First they suggested that I try and get a Greyhound bus, then said that I would get more rides if I hitchhiked.

Then Rebecca started telling me about a ministry in Inglis

that would give me food, clothes and possibly put me up for a couple of nights. I tried to explain that I didn't ask for anything; that I allow people to listen to God's voice, and took only what was offered to me. They still didn't understand. We arrived in Inglis and Jeff pulled into a convenience store. I thanked them and gave them a gospel tract that had my name and website on it, asking them to read it.

At the convenience store, I checked my location, deciding what to do next. It was only noon, but the next town was eighteen miles, and, judging by the satellite image, didn't seem to have anything there. After praying about it, I decided to head towards Gulf Hammock and see what God had in store for me. I made sure my water bottles were full, and I had a little to eat before heading out.

After about three hours I saw what looked like an intersection. As I was approaching it, a pickup truck pulled up and sat there; the driver watching me as I got closer.

The intersection turned out to be an entrance for some type of commercial operation. As I passed the truck, the driver offered me a ride. When I told him where I was headed he told me that there wasn't anything there, and said that Chiefland was the first place that had anything. He said that he hadn't planned on going to Chiefland, but decided that he would, and then take a cross highway to his destination.

His name was Richard and he was a fellow believer, so along the way we talked about what the world would be like if everyone claiming to be a Christian would act like Jesus did. Once we arrived in Chiefland he dropped me off at a small shopping mall, right at the crossroads, where he needed to turn.

There was a restaurant nearby, so I headed for it. I was in line to order a meal and, as I was waiting, an elderly couple commented on my backpack. I told them of my journey and they bought my dinner.

I sat and wrote for several hours; watching people coming and going with their kids and friends and, for the first time during this journey, felt extremely lonely. There had been times when I would have moments of loneliness; but this time it was a dwelling feeling of being alone, the feeling was deepened when, going online to do my update, I found that no one was there.

I had looked online and had seen that the churches in the area were either behind me or a mile or so north. I headed to an area I had noticed, where I thought I might set up. It was behind a business –I made it there, and got set-up, just before it started to rain.

### .Friday-September 18, 2009

Once again, I slept undisturbed. I packed and made my way back to the restaurant, ordering breakfast and setting up at the same table I had used the night before.

At one point, I got up to get a refill on my coffee, and saw a young man, sitting at a booth with a Bible; I noticed that he was not just reading it; he was studying it, highlighting passages. Once I got my refill I stopped and chatted with him and asked what he was studying. He was in Proverbs, and we talked about the wisdom that could be gained there. At that time, I didn't get his name but, as God would have it, I did get to know him better at a later time.

Like the evening before, I sat at the table watching families and friends coming and going, and the feeling of loneliness returned. I fought it off the best I could, but it just got deeper.

Towards evening, a young man, who had been working there the previous afternoon, came in with some of his friends. When he saw me sitting at the table, he came over, shook my hand, saying, "I see you made it back here." Then he proceeded to tell his friends about my journey. That one act, though it seems so small, lifted my spirits. It reminded me that, even something as small as a genuine smile or sincere greeting, can make a difference in someone's life.

### Saturday-September 19, 2009

A night without rain, finally. I awoke, packed and then stopped for a quick breakfast before heading for Cross City, FL.

Cross City was only about 20 miles from Crystal City but,

once again, there was little between the two towns. The distance didn't matter though. I had only walked half a mile, when I saw a pickup truck sitting at an intersection. As I was about to pass in front of it, the driver asked if I would like a ride into town.

His name was Rodney and, other than telling him about my journey, we didn't have much time to talk. He received a phone call, and before long we were in Cross City. I was let out at a small shopping center on the south edge of town and walked to a McDonald's, where I could sit and spent the rest of the day trying to catch up on my journal.

Towards dinner time I asked some of the employees about a place to eat, explaining that I had been living on Dollar menu items and needed a real meal. They told me where there was a family restaurant and then started asking about my journey.

One of the ladies, whose name was Thelma, invited me to attend her church in the morning and, after getting directions, I headed for the restaurant. With dinner done, I located a church and set my tent up behind.

## Sunday-September 20, 2009

I had set my alarm, but woke up before it went off. After packing, I hiked back to the McDonald's, using the restroom to shave before getting breakfast; then headed for the church in plenty of time to find it before service started. I soon come to an area where, to my understanding, I should have been able to see the church. I didn't, so I walked a couple blocks down one street, moving a block over then back to where I started. Just as I started to walk down the next street, Thelma pulled up beside me with her family and took me the rest of the way to the church.

The church was Royal Temple Church of God in Christ and, when I entered, a man greeted me and introduced himself as PJ. I later found out that PJ Was the assistant pastor.

After Sunday school, I heard someone say, "I'm glad you found our church." Turning, I found the young man, that had been studying his Bible, in Chiefland. His name was Steven, and it turned out that he was married to Thelma's cousin.

182

The service started. The pastor was Ella Peterson, an elderly lady that had a love for God and people. Pastor Peterson didn't compromise God's word at all. She let you know that, you either live for God 24/7 or you belong to the devil, there was no in between. The worship was awesome and the sermon was as dynamic and charismatic as the worship had been. When it came time for Communion however, it was equally solemn and respectful. Pastor Peterson insisted that everyone was in the sanctuary, calling for the ushers, who had just taken the offering, to return –then insisted that no one leaves until after communion. This was a time to reflect on what Jesus had been through so that *we* could have salvation.

When it was time to find an evening service, I made my way to the First Baptist Church where, to my surprise, instead of a service, they were serving "breakfast". The church was kicking off their AWANA program, and the youth had made pancakes, sausage and grits. I was invited to join them and, after eating, obtained permission to set up my tent for the night from the pastor, Mike Brown, who suggested that I set up on the playground –as it was the best area; And, indeed it was. It had been prepared to be soft and level and I slept like I was on a firm mattress instead of the ground.

## Monday-September 21, 2009

Today was one of the hardest days so far. I discovered that I had lost a hat somewhere. The only others I had were black and all material; but I figured that I would wear one, when the sun got higher in the sky.

Just outside of Cross City I came to a man that was working, and he commented on my load. I was telling him of my journey and he noticed that I wasn't wearing a hat. I told him that I had lost one, and, once the sun got too hot on my head, I would wear one of the canvas ones. He told me that he had an extra hat and offered it to me.

Other than a couple of churches in the first mile or so, the road was barren. Not only was there nothing around, but it got hotter than I remembered it being during the journey. By noon, my water was hot enough to have made coffee with. There was plenty of traffic, but no one showed any sign of offering a ride.

A pick-up truck went by me, and, as it passed, a beer bottle landed at my feet. The passenger was yelling obscenities and gesturing with his middle finger. I guess I realized how much I had grown during my journey. My thoughts, instead of being of anger, were of compassion, and I wondered how much hurt and pain some people had in them.

As I was walking along, I had my first, and only encounter with a snake. I don't know as I heard anything, but I looked down, and there it was, a cottonmouth, about 2 feet long, its head pointed up at me; its pure white mouth opened, ready to strike.

I jumped as far to the left as I could, spun around, and then jumped as far forward as I could. It was a combination ballet, martial arts, pee-pee dance –which, I'm pretty sure was quite amusing to the people in the vehicle passing me just then. When I landed, I looked behind me, and saw that it was about five feet away, still poised to strike. I firmly believe that, if it had bitten me, it couldn't harm me; but I would rather not test it to find out if my faith was really that strong.

I was starting to get low on water. There was also another storm coming and I wasn't seeing any place to get out of it. Until this journey, I would have welcomed a storm on a hot day, but I had found that, in this area, the storm didn't cool things off, it just made it more humid.

I finally saw a house, and made my way to it; finding a man, in his eighties, sitting in the back yard under the canopy. He invited me under, it just as the rain started, and we talked while it fell. He pointed out a water faucet where I could fill my bottles. After drinking as much as I could and filling my bottles, I thanked him and continued walking.

Five miles later, I came to Tennille, FL, which consisted of an R.V. park, convenience store and a restaurant/bar. I got something to eat, and, by the time I was done, it was dark and I found a place to set up my tent, across the street from the convenience store.

**Tuesday-September 22, 2009**

I started out this morning sore and stiff. Often, when I set up after dark, the area is hard and uneven; but I'm so tired that I don't notice it until after a few hours of sleep. Such was the case last night. I broke camp, went back to the store for a quick breakfast, refilled my bottles and headed out for another long day's journey. I had a good four hours walk before I was where I had planned on being the night before, then a full day's journey to get to that night's destination of Perry, FL.

Not by God's clock though. I had walked four or five miles when a pickup truck went past me, turned around in the median and came back. It was a work truck that was full, but the driver managed to find room for me and my backpack.

His name was Don Parker and, once again, I heard of someone that had felt that they should help me as they came upon me, but went past before giving in to the call of the Holy Spirit. After hearing my story, and learning my destination for the day, Don told me that he would drop me off at his church, and then return after he finished work. He explained that a small group would be meeting there in the evening and, after having a dinner, would split up and do visitations.

Don stopped and bought me a sandwich for lunch, then dropped me off at Cross Point Baptist fellowship, telling me that he would return in a few hours. The church had a large pavilion with picnic tables so I sat there, eating and working on my journal for a while. Then I decided to lie on the bench, and take a nap. I had just dozed off when a door opened and someone commented about me sleeping on the job.

This man's name was Sonny Parker, Don's cousin. After I introduced myself to him, we sat and talked for a while, as he told me about the church, its pastor and some of the members. It was obvious that this church family was dear to him.

Sonny left, and a few minutes later several school kids and a couple of women came out. I introduced myself to the adult

185

ladies, and learned that the church 'home schooled' as many kids as they were legally allowed, without being a licensed school. Two men came over, wondering who I was; understandably they were concerned for the kids. It was obvious however that the kids were able to sense my spirit, or rather the Spirit of God in me. They were coming over, sitting at the table, smiling and making faces, trying to get me to laugh, as the two men questioned me about my journey and purpose.

Finally, one of them asked if it would bother me if they had the police check me out; which of course it didn't –in fact, I was glad that these men didn't take any chances when it came to the safety of the children. They called a member of the church, who happened to be an on- duty police officer, and soon he, and two other patrol cars, were there; running my name through the computer and asking me questions. When all was said and done, I was invited to sit in the Fellowship Hall, where it was air conditioned, while I waited for Don to return.

Don returned and took me to his home, where I showered, and then he started a load of laundry for me. We sat and talked about how God had brought us together that day, and how faithful He was to us. Before we knew it, it was time to head for the church, where some of the women had prepared a full meal.

After eating, we had a short study, not surprisingly, on faith. When the study was over we split into groups for visitation. The people I went with were a lady named Elizabeth Allen and a man named Don Hilton.

Our first stop was to visit an elderly couple, that had missed church due to illness. I was introduced and asked to share about my journey and, before we knew it, we had spent more time there than we had planned. Before leaving, we all joined hands and prayed.

Next, we visited a lady that was suffering from psoriasis; so severe that every inch of skin was covered with it. She commented that she had to have someone come in to do her cooking, because she couldn't stand the heat from the stove.

After visiting for a while we once again joined hands in

prayer before returning to the church; where each team gave a briefing on what they had done; sharing the prayer needs. One team had gone to a jail to visit a prisoner, another had followed up on a family, that had visited the church. Another team had visited other sick people. It was Matthew 25 in action.

When we left the church, Don told me that he was going to put me up in a motel for the night. We returned to his house – where his wife had dried and folded my laundry –and I retrieved my backpack. After getting me set up in a hotel, Don told me that he would be back in the morning and, that he wanted to drive me to Tallahassee, if I didn't mind.

By now it was about 11:00pm and I was exhausted. I climbed into bed and was asleep before my head hit the pillow.

## Wednesday-September 23, 2009

I was awake, showered, dressed, packed and eating breakfast by the time Don arrived. There had been a change of plans. Don had a shipment coming in for his business and had to be there to receive it. So, his mother was going to drive me to Tallahassee instead.

I finished eating and Don took me to his mother's house or, as he put it, "The house his mother built". Her name was Jo Ann, and she had, indeed, built a house. With the exception of the roof, which her family had done, she had *built* the house, including an 8' wide porch that stretched the length of the house. Don and I said our goodbyes then Jo Ann and I headed out.

By noon I was in Tallahassee. Joann dropped me off on U.S. Highway 319, where I needed to begin traveling north. I found a restaurant and spent the afternoon working on my journal –which I was actually catching up on. At this point I was one day ahead of schedule, and was praying about whether to stay in Tallahassee the next day to write or, to continue onto Cairo, GA, which was my next destination.

As it was so early I decided to continue walking until I came to a church and then decide from there whether to continue or stay. I headed north on U.S. Highway 319, walked a few miles and came to Bradfordville First Baptist Church. It was just after 5:00pm, but there were several cars already there. I thought they might be having an early Wednesday night service. It turned out that they were having a dinner to raise money for M.O.P.S. (Mothers of Preschoolers). The dinner was only $4.00 so, I joined them, talking to a few people about my journey.

After dinner I joined the adult Bible study, which started off with half an hour of intercessory prayer and then a study of James, led by Pastor Mark Wilbanks. The way he taught was almost mesmerizing. Pastor Wilbanks didn't use a microphone and he spoke just loud enough to be heard, with a passion and understanding that had you clinging to every word.

After the service I set my tent up behind the church, and settled in for my last night in Florida.

**Thursday-Sept. 24, 2009**

I didn't wake up until 7:00 this morning. The night had been cool, but not cold and it was quiet behind the church. I had considered staying where I was for the day, but felt led to continue on to my next destination of Cairo, Ga.

I traveled northbound on U.S. Highway 319. Again, I hadn't walked more than one mile when a pickup truck pulled beside me. A young African-American woman offered me a ride. Once I was in the truck, she asked me where I was going; I told her that I was heading to Cairo. She told me that was where she was going and would give me a ride the entire way.

I introduced myself and she told me that her name was April. Expressing my appreciation for the ride I got this answer: "When God tells you to do something, you have to do it." I was telling her of my journey and times when others had listened to the voice of God, then I asked her how long she had been a Christian.

Her answer floored me. She responded, "Oh, I'm not saved, my mama's a preacher and my sister's married to a preacher." Of course I asked her why she hadn't committed her life to Christ, and she said that, she wanted to understand God better first. My response was that she couldn't understand God enough to decide to give her life to him. That was what faith was about. I also told her that she couldn't begin to understand God until she committed her life to Him and then, the more you learn about Him, the more you realize you can't really understand Him.

Then I said, "Besides, if you were to die today, your mama and your brother-in- law being preachers aren't going to save you from going to hell." I think this struck a cord with her. I could imagine that she was like the one that answered Jesus' question about the second greatest commandment, and Jesus told him that he was very close to seeing the Kingdom. April knew how to treat her fellow man, but hadn't accepted God as master, nor had she accepted Jesus as the way to God.

By this time we were in Cairo and she was dropping me off at a fast food restaurant. I thanked her again for the ride and asked her to officially give her life to God and then we parted ways. As I went into the restaurant, I was praying for April; and about what God wanted me to do now. Here it was, 10:30 in the morning; I was already at my day's destination, *and* a day ahead of schedule. I went online and posted an update on social networks, ending it "I can't wait to see what God has for me next."

It wasn't long before I found out. The next town was Camilla, GA, which was 26 miles away. It was now 11:00am and I couldn't decide whether to stay where I was or continue on. I figured I'd eat something, then decide. When I went to order, I discovered that this fast food restaurant didn't have a dollar menu. I knew that there would be little to nothing between Cairo and Camilla, so I figured I would have to spend the extra money. I was about to order, when I heard the Holy Spirit tell me that I didn't need to eat, I just needed to leave.

My first thought was that God was saying that I was getting fat, eating all the fast food hamburgers, but then I said, "It's in your hands, Father." I headed northbound on U.S. Highway 84, continued on to State road 112. I only walked about four miles, when I saw a pickup truck pull up to the road, from what looked like a driveway.

It was about a quarter mile away, but it just sat there. I thought they may be headed northbound, waiting to offer me a ride. When I was about 200 yards away, the truck pulled out, drove towards me slowly, and then, pulled across the road behind me and stopped.

I saw that the driver was a Latino man and, once it stopped, a young Latino female got out and walked towards me. She said, "My father would like to know if we could make an offering of a meal?" That explained why the Holy Spirit had told me that I didn't need to eat earlier. I said "That would be very nice." She told me that they had to go into town, but if I waited at the mailboxes, they would be back in a few minutes. I agreed to wait and, before they left, they gave me a me a bottle of Gatorade.

After they left I walked the rest the way to the mailboxes, where I saw a small church with a sign in front of it, and another sign, next to a dirt drive, that read "Iglisia de Cristo Ministerios Elohim". My guess was that the man driving the truck was the pastor of the church.

Within a few minutes the pickup returned and I climbed into the back. From that point on, it was like being in Honduras. The drive was about a quarter mile long and was like many of the roads I had traveled in Honduras. At the end of it was a sheet metal building –which was the church –and the family lived in a small home. Running around were several chickens, a couple cats, two dogs and a goose.

When we stopped, the teenage girl introduced herself as Maria then, introduced her father, Cristabal Jimenez, verifying that he was the pastor and then introduced her mother, Antonia, her cousin, Manuel and a friend, Flavio. I also found out that Maria was supposed to be at school that day, but, her eyes had been red that morning, so she had stayed home. Many would look at this as a coincidence, but God knew that I would be there and, that I would need a translator that day.

Inside the home was just as I had expected it to be. The furnishings were very basic and the decor simple, yet homey.

Maria was the only one there who spoke English, and she translated for me and her father, relaying questions and answers back and forth. I ended up pulling my computer out and was showing pictures of the kids in the orphanage, the kids that lived in the landfill and so forth.

Cristobal asked Maria a question and she translated it "Are you a missionary or something?" It suddenly dawned on me that, in all the conversation, I really hadn't introduced myself other than by name, so I confirmed that I was a minister and we continued to look at photos.

Soon, dinner was ready, and we ate a delicious meal of fresh chicken –that they had raised themselves –rice soup, and tortillas. It was apparent that the soup had been made with me in mind, thinking that I wouldn't be used to hot foods. It was tasty but didn't have any heat to it. Flavio said something about *Chile*, which means either a hot sauce or peppers, and I asked if they had Chile. Antonia chopped up several Jalapeno peppers, which quickly disappeared into the bowls of soup.

I met Maria's three siblings, –Ana, Carolina and Jonathan, when they got home from school . When it came time to leave, it was like leaving family; the kids all gave me hugs, then Manuel and Flavio gave me a ride, some fifteen miles to Camillo, GA.

I received another small blessing that night. My belt buckle broke and I had to buy a new one. You may ask why I look at this as a blessing. I was in a city, where I was able to buy a new belt, and I had money to buy it. There have been many times when I would go days without seeing a store, and many times when I would only have two or three dollars. To me, being able to walk into a store, late at night, and have money to buy what I needed, was a blessing.

## Friday-September 25, 2009

I only slept for about three hours. At about 1:00am I woke up and couldn't get back to sleep. I don't know why, I wasn't anxious about anything and the temperature was comfortable. There have been times when I have been awakened to pray for someone or something; I didn't feel that there was anything specific to pray for, but I spent a couple hours praying.

Somewhere around three o'clock I finally got up and broke camp. I made my way to a Waffle house, ordered an early breakfast and worked on my journal; deciding to head out at about 7:00a.m.

I heading Northbound on U.S. Highway 19, towards Albany, GA. After walking 10 miles or so I came to a store, next to a small sub & sandwich shop. I was strolling through the store, when a young man came up to me. He and his wife had seen me walking and he offered to buy me lunch at the sandwich shop. Accepting the offer, I thanked him, and we went next door, where he had me place an order. We sat there for a few minutes visiting before they needed to leave.

About two hours after I started walking again, I was offered a ride by another young man, whose name was Jeremy, and his wife. They were in a pickup truck so I rode in the back after telling them that I was headed for Albany. When I was dropped off, I gave Jeremy my ministry card. He looked at it and said, "I just had a feeling that you were a preacher or something."

I went online to plot a route for the next day. I found that I was in the southeast part of Albany and, that I needed to make my way through the city, using side streets. I didn't find any churches nearby, but I did see a large area, that was wooded, so I walked there and found a place to set up my tent for the night.

**Saturday-Sept. 26, 2009**

My goal for the day was to get from one side of Albany to the other, find a church to attend on Sunday, and rest for the remainder of the day. I walked west on E. Oglethorpe Boulevard about two and a half miles, and came to Ray Charles Plaza. I stopped there to take a break, snapping a few photos before heading North on N. Washington Street. Turning West on 7th Street, I stopped to get water and chat with a few people before heading North on Jefferson St. to the edge of Albany.

Once I got out of the city, I stopped at a Convenience store for a break. There was a fruit vendor there, and I went to get some fruit for lunch. While I was waiting, a man and a woman started asking about my backpack so, I shared about my journey with them. When it was my turn and I went to pay, the vendor told me it was on him.

Within a few miles I was again at U.S. Highway 19, but, just as I got there it started to rain, so I took refuge in a restaurant and looked for a church online. Finding one a few miles north, I planned on making my way there, spending the night, then attend services the next morning. I wrote the directions on a piece of paper and headed out.

As I was walking, I passed by a storefront church in a small shopping center. There were two people at a van, either loading or unloading chairs. Though I couldn't explain the feeling, it seemed that something here was to be part of my day. But I wasn't feeling led to go there, and, even if I did, there was nowhere for me to set my tent up.

Realize that I had forgotten the name of the street to turn for the church. I reached into my pocket and pulled out the paper, but because I was damp from the rain, it was unreadable. I could only hope that I would remember it when I saw it.

A pickup truck went past me and pulled to the side of the road. When I reached the passenger window, the driver, a young man, asked about giving me a ride. I told him that I was trying to find the Assembly of God Church, and explained that I had forgotten what road I was supposed to turn on.

The young man's name was Matt and, as it turned out, he had been one of the people at the store front church, moving the chairs. He said that he didn't know of an A/G church in the area, but offered to give me a ride, then he called a friend to see it they knew where it was. The friend didn't know either and we drove into Leesburg, GA, without me recognizing any roads as the one I was to turn onto.

Since we couldn't find it, I told Matt that any church would be good, so he took me to the First Baptist church; telling me that it was the church his parents attended. Once Matt had shown me where the church was, he dropped me off at a restaurant near the church. I spent the rest of the evening working on my journal, until 9:00pm, when I went online for my nightly update.

For the fourth night in a row no one showed up for the update. Even with the blessings I had received and the people that God had put in my path in the last few days, this deepened my sense of loneliness.

I found an area nearby, and set up my tent behind a cedar tree, which blocked it from the road. It had been sprinkling when I left the restaurant and the rain was getting heavier as I set up the tent. Sure enough, as soon as I was inside, it started to pour –but this time I was prepared, having sprayed the tent with waterproofing a few days earlier.

### Sunday-Sept. 27, 2009

I woke up about 4:30am, and the rain had stopped. Finding an area that was paved and dry, I carried my backpack and tent to it, then cleaned up using a garden hose I'd spotted. After I changed clothes and broke the tent down.

At 7:30 I made my way to the church, arriving before anyone else was there. It wasn't long before a man arrived. I introduced myself, and he said that his name was Roger and that he worked the sound system at the church. Roger invited me inside and offered me a seat in the sanctuary. The door we had come in was at the back, behind the platform, so I took a seat in the front row.

Roger asked about my journey, how I had been led to do it, and how I had been called into missions. After listening to me he excused himself and went about setting up microphones and such, and I pulled out my journal. As I was writing, others started arriving, many of them coming up and welcoming me.

The worship service started and we sang a few songs, then the pastor got to the pulpit. After an opening prayer, the first thing he said was, "We have a special guest with us today." As he said this, he looked straight at me. Obviously, Roger had told him about me being there.

No Mere Coincidences, a journey of faith

The pastor said "This man over here is on a... 4,000 mile journey? Why don't you come up here and tell them what you're doing?" So, that's what I did. I went up to the pulpit and shared about my journey, then, about the vision God had given me.

After the service, people came up to me, greeting me and giving me their blessings, many slipping me love gifts. One lady came up and introduced herself as Matt's mother. Another man, who had already given me a love gift, came back and gave me a coin, encased in a plastic holder. He said, "No matter where you are in the world, how alone you feel or how bleak things seem, take this out of your pocket and remember, first, what Jesus has done for you and second, that there are people in Leesburg, GA praying for you. Accepting it, I thanked him and put it in my pocket, with all the other love gifts that I had received.

After everyone had greeted me, I went to the Fellowship Hall, got a cup of coffee and officially met Pastor Billy Harrell. I gave him a more in-depth account of how I had been led to do the journey, and shared some of my encounters with him.

The second service began. The first service had been traditional, the second was more contemporary. towards the end, Pastor Harrell recognized me as a guest and encouraged people to visit with me and, if they felt led, to help me financially.

Several people did come up, asking about my journey, offering their prayers and some offering love gifts. My habit, as I received a love gift —which were often given in a handshake —was to discretely put it into my pockets while thanking the person. By the end of the second service my pockets were bulging. The first thing I did when I arrived at restaurant, was to go into the bathroom, locked myself in a stall and started organizing the money. I pulled the bills out of my pockets and, when I got to the bottom of one pocket, there was the encased coin I had given me.

On one side of the coin was the head of Jesus, on the other 'The Last Supper', on the upper half and a hand, reaching down from above, to grasp another hand reaching up from rough waters. To me, it was my hand reaching out of the water. I had been drowning in my sin, being pulled down by the rough waters I had created for myself by running from God. When I finally reached out, God reached down. He had been there the entire time, waiting for me to seek him and to cry out for help.

I considered finding a jeweler to see if the coin was gold and to have it appraised, but decided that it didn't matter what worth the world put on it. It had been given to me as a reminder of God's grace and a reminder that people were praying for me. That was worth more than any amount of money.

As I've said before, I don't usually talk about money amounts, but once again, feel it is appropriate, to understand how God works. I finished organizing the cash, and, to my surprise, there was over $800. I said a prayer, thanking God for his abundance. As I prayed, felt that there was a reason God had supplied so much at one time. The answer was to come a few days later. I set aside enough for Tithes and enough to live on for the week, then put the rest into my backpack.

Just past 5:00pm I headed back to the church and enjoyed the evening service. There was a guest speaker, and the service was fairly short. Afterward, a few people came up and greeted me. A couple gave me love gifts, which I later counted, and found were exactly what I had given as tithes from the morning service.

A man came up, introduced himself as Heath Odom and offered to let me stay at his house for the night. We loaded into his truck with his sons, Gunner and Wyatt, and his daughter SaraGrace. They took me to dinner and then to their home; where Heath and Wyatt endured me showing pictures of the kids, both in Honduras and India, before we retired for the night.

## Monday-Sept. 28, 2009

I woke up at about 4:30 and spent some time reading my Bible and praying. Heath had said that he wanted to drive me a ways before he went to work. When he got up, we headed out, talking about many things along the way and, before I knew it, I was being dropped off in Americus, GA.

I decided to spend the day writing, and was actually caught up to date in my journal for the first time. While I was writing, several people stopped and chatted with me, asking about my backpack, then my journey and I was able to share the Gospel with them.

Later, looking for a place to sleep, I felt led to go behind a building that looked like a manufacturing business. I found that it was wooded on two sides and had a large container on another side. While I was preparing the tent, a patrol car came behind the building. The officer was spotlighting the building, and then drove off. At times, I feel as though God places a veil around me at night. In all the places I have slept, there had only been two times that I had been interrupted at night, once on Siesta Key beach, when a young man was looking for a place to sit and think,- and I ended up counseling him for several minutes-, and again in Crystal River, when I was 10 feet from the road and one block from the police station.

I finished setting the tent up, and, moving it into the shadows, went to sleep.

## Tuesday-Sept. 29, 2009

At some point in the night a cold front came through, and with it came strong winds and rain; which blew up under the tent cover, getting my sleeping bag and blanket wet. When I awoke – before the sun was up –the temperature felt about 50 degrees. I dug my sweatshirt out from the bottom of my backpack and, once I was packed up again, I headed north on Highway 49.

Shortly, a pickup truck pulled to the side of the road, and an older, African-American man, with a younger passenger, offered me a ride. He introduced himself as Sonny, and helped me get arranged in the back of the truck, then we started towards Oglethorpe, GA. The air was still cool which made it a very invigorating ride.

I was dropped off at the main intersection in Oglethorpe, where I was supposed to turn, and found a Laundromat. I put my blanket and sleeping bag in a dryer, and, that done, went across the street to a small, cafeteria style, restaurant –where everyone knew everybody.

Once I finished eating I took State Road 128 through Oglethorpe. People in yards, or sitting on porches all greeting as I passed by. At one point, the only sounds I could hear were a bird singing and a train in the distance. Everything about Oglethorpe reminded me of visiting my grandmother, in a small Illinois town, in the 1960's and 70's. It was like the people there hadn't let time change things.

Once again, I hadn't walked more than a couple of miles when a vehicle, which had pulled up to a stop sign, waited for me. This man's name was Ricky and he was headed to Reynolds, GA to pay a bill, so he offered me a ride. Ricky was another one who had been brought up in a Christian home, turned from God to do his own thing, and now, was realizing that his life was empty without God in it. I couldn't help but think of Proverbs 22:6 *"Train up a child in the way he should go; and when he is old, he will not depart from it."*(MKJV)

I was dropped off at a convenience store in Reynolds and, after getting something to drink, I left there and headed for the First Baptist Church of Reynolds. I found an elderly gentleman there and, introducing myself, asked who I would talk to about setting my tent up there. Together we went in search of the pastor, only to find out that he had left. The secretary was in the office and, between the two of them, they decided that it shouldn't be a problem to sleep there that night.

From there I walked into the small business district, to see what was in this small town. There was a jewelry store called Paris VonRabenau Jewelers. I had been carrying my watch around in my backpack for almost two months; the pin on the band broken, and now, it needed a new battery as well. I decided to see about getting it fixed. The man behind the counter, who turned out to be Paris –the owner –started asking about my journey. I finally got around to asking him about my watch and he said to leave it and return half an hour later. When I returned, the watch was fixed and he didn't charge me for the repairs.

Towards evening, intending to get my tent set up and then get ready for the nightly broadcast, I returned to the church. There was a meeting going on –and an SUV parked beside where I was going to set the tent. A few minutes later, a man came out the back door, where the SUV was parked, and I greeted him, asking if he was the pastor. When he said that he was, I asked if the secretary had let him know that I was pitching a tent there for the night. He said that she had and we began talking about my journey and how I had gotten into the ministry.

His name was Michael Gibson and, he too had been in law enforcement for several years before being called into the ministry. We talked for about 45 minutes, then he offered to put me up in a motel for the night. He took me to a restaurant/motel and got me a room. After I got settled in, I did my nightly update, though a few minutes late, before going to sleep.

**Wednesday-September 30, 2009**

Michael said that he would be there at about 8:15, to drive me up the road. I got up, making good use of the shower before packing and leaving the room. I had been downstairs just long enough to get a cup of coffee, when Michael arrived, so he bought me breakfast before we started the trip.

As we traveled, we shared more of our testimonies, cop stories, events in our lives where God's hand had been evident and even a couple of jokes. Soon, we were in Barnsville, GA, about 40 miles north of Reynolds, and Michael asked where I wanted to be dropped off. I saw a place that had picnic tables outside, and asked to go there. After praying together and saying goodbyes, Michael left. I pulled my computer out, to locate my position –what my next destination was –and plot a route to it.

The name of this place was "Mama's Kitchen". It was a small building where people would walk up, place their order and then either take it with them or sit at one of the picnic tables to eat it. As I plotted my day's travel, a car pulled up to the building and an elderly man went inside.

Soon another vehicle, pulling a large BBQ trailer, pulled in.

This man came up and began talking to me. His name was Thomas Wellbrook. He was a Christian, whose father had started a truck stop ministry. He also had a brother who had started a post-prison ministry in Griffin, GA.

As it was now late morning, and, as there didn't seem to be anything between Barnsville and Griffin, I ordered a sandwich before heading out. When the food was ready, Thomas wouldn't let me pay for it. After eating and thanking Thomas again, I headed northbound towards Griffin, which was 15 miles away.

I stopped an hour later and sat on a guard rail to rest. A car, that looked like a Crown Victoria, started slowing down, then, pulled onto the shoulder. I figured a deputy had decided to check me out, but, as I got nearer I saw that it was a Mercury Marquee, and not a patrol car. The car stopped and an elderly man asked if I would like a ride into Griffin. He said that he had seen me sitting at the side of the road and felt that he should give me a ride. I introduced myself to him, and asked his name. He said it, and I heard "Dall" so I asked "spelled D-a-l-l?" and he said "No, D a l e". I said "Oh yeah, I forgot I'm back in Georgia." and told him about my language lessons on "Bald Peanuts" and "Darl" that I had gotten as I traveled south through eastern Georgia.

Dale was in no hurry and, actually drove about five miles under the speed limit. We got to Griffin, and I was being dropped off at yet another McDonald's.

I went searching for a church, finding one along the route I would take the next day. It was Cornerstone Assembly of God. There were a couple cars in the parking lot, so I went to the door and pulled on it. It was locked, but I figured that it would be open soon. I was about to take my backpack off to wait, when a man came to the door and opened it. He introduced himself as Pastor Tony Kent and I introduced myself, giving him a piece of paper with my name and website on it, apologizing that I had run out of ministry cards.

I told him of my journey and asked about setting my tent up behind the church after the service. After talking for a few minutes, he took me into the office and asked about a design for business cards. He made about 100 cards for me,then we went into the sanctuary and Pastor Kent lead a Bible study on how to know if you are where God wants you.

Afterward told me that he wanted to put me up in a motel for the night. Once again, I slept in a bed.

# OCTOBER

*"Put out into the deep water and let down your nets for a catch'."*

### Thursday-October 1, 2009

I slept in this morning, not getting out of bed until 7:00am. I went to the lobby for the complimentary breakfast, then showered, packed and finally started walking about 8:30. My destination for the evening was only about 17 miles from Griffin, and the weather was just right for walking.

I had contacted Brother Sean Rogers, whom I was going to be meeting in Atlanta, and he had made arrangements with one of his friends, Jeremy Bayless, who lives in McDonough, GA to take me in for the night.

Once again, I had only walked about five miles before I was offered a ride, this time, by a young man named Owen, who dropped me off in Stockbridge, GA at about 11:30. As it was rather early, and Jeremy wasn't expecting me until that evening, I went into a restaurant, got a coke, and then went online. Brother Sean was online. He asked if I had called Jeremy to let him know that I was there. I hadn't and he suggested that I did so, I called Jeremy and, an hour later I was being picked. Later that evening, me, Jeremy, his mother, his friend, Brian, a neighbor and a few others got together at Jeremy's house and made 550 peanut butter and jelly sandwiches, to be delivered to Brother Sean, and passed out to the homeless on Saturday.

**Friday-October 2, 2009**

I woke up at my usual time this morning, and, after spending time reading my Bible and in prayer, I worked on my journal until the others were awake. About noon, we loaded the sandwiches into Jeremy's truck, picked Brian up at his house and headed for Atlanta.

I finally met Brother Sean Rogers. So far, I have traveled four months and about 3,050 miles. I have only met up with six people by prearrangement, and, as with most of these, I knew Brother Sean only from MySpace and Facebook. He had invited me to meet with him once I got to Atlanta, Georgia and, to possibly work with him some.

I wasn't really sure what to expect. I knew only that Sean was a Catholic missionary and the founder of Deep Waters Ministry; an inner city, street ministry to the poor and homeless. I later learned that he got the name of the ministry from the book of Luke, where Jesus is talking: '*when He had finished speaking, He said to Simon, "Put out into the **deep water** and let down your nets for a catch'." (Luke 5:4 NASB).* That's what Brother Sean did. He went into the deep waters of the inner cities, places where most Christians have heard about, but many have never seen, and he cast a net of love down for a catch.

At first glance, Sean he wasn't an 'impressive' person. Not being very big, he had his thinning hair pulled back into a pony tail, and wore a simple pullover shirt, beige pants, and sandals. He also carried a staff, which was almost as tall as he was.

Once we were on the streets, we walked through parks where men and women –young and old –sat or slept, and parking lots of abandoned buildings where homeless gathered. It didn't take long to realize that, although this man wasn't very big, his heart was. His love for God and his fellow man was bigger than any physical body. As he talked with people, you could see the authentic concern for each and every person he had contact with. He knew many of the people by name, and they knew him by name. It also became apparent that his staff was more a trademark, as many people referred to him as Moses.

Many of the people would tell me about things that Brother Sean had done for them and, one lady just plain attributed her purpose for living to Brother Sean.

Her name is Justine, and hers was a story of dying with A.I.D.S. –with no hope and no reason to go on. Brother Sean had found her sleeping behind a trash dumpster, and had let her know that she was loved, that there was more to this life than she knew about and, a hope for life eternal.

One thing I learned from Sean; So many times, people say "God Loves You" or, "You matter to God", but how many people say, "I love you and you matter to me." Part of the basic human need is to be loved and to feel needed, yet so few are willing to say these simple words: "I love you and, you matter to me", and convey them in a way that the receiver knows it's true.

Brother Sean continued to lead the way through the parks, parking lots and streets to the Pine Street Mission, where hundreds of people sat, with nothing to wait for but nightfall. We concluded our day in the inner-city, having touched many lives and letting people know that we would be back the next day with food for them.

After dropping Brother Sean and Brian off, Jeremy and I headed to meet Meagan Jeffries, a friend of Jeremy's, whose grandparents had agreed to take me in for the night. By the time Meagan and I got to the house, it was dinner time, and as we ate, they listened to me go on about my journey, the wonderful things God had done, and some of the situations He had put me in. Before I knew it, it was late and time to go to bed.

**Saturday-October 3, 2009**

For the first time since starting this journey, my alarm went off before I was awake and, even then, I lingered in bed, not wanting to get up. I did finally get out of bed and took a shower. By the time I had everything packed I could smell coffee and, going to the kitchen, I was offered a cup by Meagan's grandma. We sat and talked as we drank our coffee and soon Meagan was up and getting ready. About 7:30, We went back to Jeremy's house, where his mother had made breakfast. About noon we picked Brian up again and headed for Atlanta.

Jeremy had a ministry called Chess on the Streets, and we started the afternoon by setting up tables and chess sets. The area was known as Little Five Points, where there were several shops and sidewalk cafe's; It was an area with a colorful assortment of people. When we arrived, one young man strummed on a ukulele and sang, in hopes of getting a few dollars; when he left, he was quickly replaced by a man with a guitar.

Brother Sean soon arrived; walking around, greeting people and visiting with the homeless, sitting on the sidewalks.

Before long I was saying goodbye to Jeremy and Brian and meeting J.T. and Romeo, two of Brother Sean's friends, who were going to be working with us for the day. We left Little Five Points and headed for Sweet Auburn. Parking at Historic Ebenezer Baptist Church, visited the grave site of Dr. King before heading out with food.

Once again Brother Sean's love and compassion shone. At times we were surrounded by people, wanting something as simple as a sandwich and banana to eat. When we saw someone sitting by themselves, or sleeping in the brush, we went to them; taking time to chat, listen and pray with them.

Brother Sean and I don't agree on everything. One thing we did agree on though. We agree that, no matter what a person looks like, acts like or even smells like, you treat them with the same love that Jesus has shown us. You have no Idea what circumstances brought a person to where they are. They may be there so that *you* can learn from *them* and mature spiritually.

As with everything, I learned from my experience in Atlanta with Brother Sean and Deep Waters Ministry. Through years in law enforcement, I came to profile people. God has been dealing with me on this issue for the last couple years and I know, spiritually, I grew immensely because of my encounter with Brother Sean. It was an experience that will help me be more Christ Like as long as I live.

Sean had arranged for me to stay at the Home of Mary Campbell, and later, we met up with her.

(Note) *A few weeks after finishing my journey, Brother Sean invited me back to Georgia, where he supported me while I wrote the rough draft of this book. I wrote during the day, and we went out, ministering at night. A few month after I left Atlanta, Sean became ill. Brother Sean passed away October 7, 2011.*

**Sunday-October 4, 2009**

Mary lives in Marietta, GA and we attended her church there. It was a good size church which had two morning services –though we had missed the earlier one, we got there for Sunday School. There were about ten people in the class and they warmly welcomed me.

I met Peggy when we got home from church. She works with juveniles, that have been certified as adults, and stays at Mary's house when she isn't on the road. Peggy and I made plans to visit a church for the evening service, and found one online about 1½ miles away. By the time we got there, the worship service was over, and the sermon was about to start. The sermon was on the last Passover that Jesus was on the earth for. We usually call it the Last Supper.

After the sermon we partook in Communion –which is one thing I will not, and cannot, take lightly. I was in a church once where the pastor preached, sat down and Communion was served, without so much as recognizing it as Communion. Any non-believing visitors would have thought it was snack time. It had become nothing more than a ritual. I wanted so much to jump up and make sure everyone knew what they were doing.

There is a reason for this and I feel as though I need to share it with you. I do not do so with great ease. Few have heard what I'm about to write, and fewer know the whole story.

I had suffered with depression much of my life, being on and off anti-depressants most of my adult life. Early in 2000 I went into a depression. By the end of February I was in counseling and on anti-depressants. I couldn't tell you which one as they tried several.

Sometime in May that year, I quit taking the medication. In late July I felt what were like electrical currents in my brain. Then, everything came crashing down on me. I remember feeling dark, my mind filled with ungodly thoughts. The sins of my youth became desirable to me and I was denouncing my faith in God. I moved out of our house, into an apartment, intent on returning to a life of sin, motivated by lust and physical pleasure.

At some point I was put on another medication, though it just seemed to knock me out, instead of making things better. My wife talked me into going to Minnesota to talk to the pastor of the church I had grown up in. Because of the medication, she drove the 500 miles to Minnesota, and we got there on Sunday afternoon. My mom had made arrangements for me to talk to Pastor G. Mark Denyes before the evening service. I sat in his office, denouncing my faith in God. I don't even remember what all I said to him; and, though I know he counseled me for over an hour, the only thing I remember him telling me was "Dennis, you weren't raised that way and you know better. I know because I helped raise you." We went straight from his office into the evening service, and I sat there with my arms crossed, refusing to sing or pray, with hatred burning in my heart.

It happened to be the night Communion was served. Communion was led by the Assistant Pastor and he went into greater detail than most communion services I had been in. I heard how the bread symbolized Jesus' body and the cup his blood. How he was whipped until his back was laid open, how his beard was pulled out and his face repeatedly struck until he wasn't even recognizable. I heard how the crown of thorns was pressed into his head. I heard how he was nailed to the cross and mocked. I was told again how he loved me so much, that he suffered all of this and died, all so that I could be forgiven of my sins and reunited with the Father. Then, I watched the pastor of my youth watching me, I saw the pain on my wife's face and the anguish in my mother's eyes as I passed the Sacraments on, refusing to take any.

So, No! I don't take Communion lightly. I take it with great gratitude and love for my Lord and Savior who, even after all I've done, will still say "I did it for you, because I love you. Now, will you do this in remembrance of me?"

A year later, that I found out that, when you cold-turkey the type of medication I was on, your brain does 'short circuit'. Our marriage never recuperated from the experience. Things that I had said to my wife during that time never healed.

**Tuesday-October 6, 2009**

Mary had offered to let me stay as long as I like; so I took Monday off, working on my journal and relaxing. I needed to take care of some ministry business at the bank and found a branch in Marietta, which Mary said she would drive me to. When we arrived, Mary and I said our goodbyes, and she left.

After I was done with my business at the bank, I found a place to plan my next move. While I was online, Bobby in India was contacting me, wanting to know if I had heard of the flooding there. I told him that I hadn't, and he let me know that several people had died, and many had lost their homes. He said their church wanted to help the flood victims and wondered if I could help. I thought of the money that I had received in Leesburg. I had felt that God had provided it for a reason, and told Bobby that I would pray about it and get back with him.

I found that I was only about 13 miles from my day's destination. I plotted a route to Acworth, GA, –which only consisted of two turns –and headed on my way. The first part of the trip was through an industrial area, then, to my surprise, it turned into an almost country setting. I knew from the satellite image that I was surrounded by housing developments almost the entire way to Acworth. The road I was on was apparently only accessed the streets that entered the neighborhoods.

I reached Acworth just before sundown and found a convenience store, buying a 'snack' meal. I did find out that there was a retail area, which included a fast-food restaurants, about a mile towards the interstate.

It was too late for my update, so I found an isolated area to set my tent up in and was soon asleep.

## Wednesday-October 7, 2009

I awoke at first light, spent time in prayer and then headed for the interstate. I had already decided to spend the day in Acworth, as my back was sore and had stiffened during the night.

Once I got to a restaurant, I went online. Doing a search for flooding in India, and learning that over 400 people had died and 2.5 million had lost their homes in the flooding. I had been praying and was certain that God had intended the money, that I had received a week and a half earlier, was meant for India. I located a Western Union and sent the majority of the money to Bobby.

Towards evening I set out to find a church in Acworth to worship in, and sleep at; and came to the First Baptist Church of Acworth. I met the pastor, Dr. David Joyner, and, after introducing myself, I asked about setting my tent up there for the night. He recommended that I sleep inside the church and took me to a room where I could put my backpack; then showed me to a restroom where I could wash up in private. As I was finishing he came back and told me that he had decided that, after the service, he would put me in a hotel for the night.

The Bible study began and Pastor Joyner introduced me as his new found friend. He then led the group in an outstanding study on the gifts of the Holy Spirit, after which several of the members came up to me, giving me their blessings and a couple of small love gifts to help me along the way.

The hotel Pastor Joyner took me to was about three miles off U.S. Highway 41, but he said that he would pick me up in the morning and get me back on route.

## Thursday-October 8, 2009

I had done some stretching the night before and my back was feeling much better. At about 7:00am, I called Pastor Joyner, who picked me up a few minutes later. Asking what my destination was for the day, I told him that it was Adairsville, GA; and he told me that it wasn't that far by interstate. Indeed, in half an hour we were sitting in a parking lot, in Adairsville, praying, before parting ways.

Pastor Joyner left, and I headed northbound on U.S. Highway 41. I had only walked a mile or so, when a vehicle, coming from the opposite direction stopped. The driver asked if I would like a ride and I accepted. The occupants of this vehicle were a young couple; the driver's name was Nila and her husband Stanley. I was told that Stanley had been out of work for a while, and they were headed to pawn their computer in the next town.

They began asking me where I was headed and why. As I was telling about my journey, Stanley looked like he was on the verge of tears. I asked him if he was alright, and he began telling me that he had been close to God as a youth, and how he felt God had called him to be an evangelist. He had gotten caught up in the things of this world and, though they were back in church, Stanley was still struggling with problems that his pastor was counseling him on. He said that he didn't think that he could be an evangelist now, because he had a wife and kids to support.

I told him that if God has called him, it was never too late. God doesn't change his mind and, if he got back in God's will for his life, God would provide his every need. I shared how God had been providing for me, to the point that I was able to support kids in India each month, while living on faith.

Before we knew it, we were just south of Dalton, GA; several miles further than Stanley and Nila had planned on taking me. After we pulled into a truck stop, we sat there for another 15 minutes talking. It was times like these that I knew why God had me at certain places at a certain time.

While we were sitting there talking, a bus was loading. I noticed an older Latino man, with a plastic bag of clothes and a large, bulky comforter, just folded up under his arm. The bus driver seemed to be motioning that the comforter had to be tied before it could go under the bus. Excusing myself, I dug a couple of extra straps out of my backpack and took them to the man, who thanked me, and began rolling his comforter up like a sleeping bag. Then I went back to Stanley and Nila and, after praying together, I pulled my backpack out of the van, and we parted ways.

Inside the truck stop I found a table where I could get my computer out to check where I was, and where I needed to go. As soon as I was online, I was being contacted by Bobby, who was excited about the money I had sent. He told me that they had purchased quite a bit of food, and his church was planning on passing it out the next day.

From there I headed toward Dalton. About two hours later I came to a convenience store, where I filled my bottles. Across the street was a church and, I felt led to go there and ask about setting up for the night. There was a sign which gave the pastor's name, and I noticed that the pastor was a female. I approached a man outside of the parsonage, whom I figured was the pastor's husband, and introduced myself. His name was Robert Daniels, and he verified that he was the pastor's husband, but said his wife wasn't home. So I told him about my journey and asked about setting up my tent for the night. He gave me permission and was interested in hearing more about my journey, so we talked for a while and he asked if I would stay until Sunday, adding that they were having a BBQ on Saturday. I didn't feel led one way or the other so I decided to pray about it. We talked a bit longer and he showed me where I could set up.

**Friday-October 9, 2009**

I woke up with a certainty that I was supposed to spend a couple days in Dalton. I got up, rolled my sleeping bag, moved everything to a picnic shelter and, as my tent was wet from the dew, left it up to dry. I had run down the battery on my computer the night before, so I plugged it in where Robert had shown me; between the parsonage and its garage. Once that was done, I spend some time reading my Bible before starting to write in my journal.

It wasn't long before a van pulled to the back of the church and an older man got out and walked over to me. I introduced myself, reaching my hand out, but, he just pointed to the tent and said, 'What's this about?' I told him that I was on a journey of faith and that the pastor's husband had given me permission to set up there and had invited me to spend the weekend. His only response was 'Huh!' and he walked away.

I had to laugh. This man, whom I discovered later was Hoyt Gazaway, reminded me of a First Sergeant I had in the military. Often my team would be working on a project, using unorthodox means. He would walk up, watch us for a minute and then grunt and move on. Being a combat veteran, he cared about the end results not making sure it was done by the book.

I met the pastor when she got home. She introduced herself as Leslie and we talked for a few minutes. I learned that she was a nurse, and, worked nights, so I let her go to get some rest. I also decided that it was time to get something to eat besides the sweet roll I had eaten a few hours earlier.

The only place I knew of, besides the convenience store, was a Wendy's, about 2 miles back the way I had come the night before. Not wanting to carry my backpack around with me, I took my camera bag and computer out of it and put the backpack out of sight, next to the church, then headed out.

The girl that took my order at Wendy's commented on seeing me walking the previous day, so I shared about my journey with her and another employee. After eating I had, what I call, a "possible angel experience".

I had looked on Google map and had seen that Dun Gap Road was on the east side of Wendy's, but there were no roads between the Wendy's and Interstate 75. Even so, when I left Wendy's, I felt led to walk towards the interstate anyway. I walked past a building that had once been a home decor store. As I passed it, I noticed that it was empty, had a cracked window and, there was a small, empty cardboard box in front of it. Past that, there was only a motel before the interstate and so, I turned around. When I did, I saw a man sitting in front of the store I had just passed. He wasn't a small man either. He was about 6'3" tall and wider than me, built like a football player. Beside him were two bags, one was a large plastic bag with a comforter stuffed into it and the other, a smaller bag, with a few clothes in it.

After twenty years in police work, investigating serious crimes as well as patrolling at night; in my mind, if he had been there when I first passed, I would have noticed him. Unless he had been following right behind me, I don't see how he could have gotten there in the time I had passed and turned around. In my pondering, I actually walked back past him, but then I thought, "What am I doing? God has put someone in my path and I just about ignored him."

I turned back around and walked up to him, asking how he was doing. He said that he was OK and I asked his name, getting 'Richard' as a response. I talked to Richard for a few minutes and then asked if he had eaten that day. Learning that he hadn't, I took him back to Wendy's, had him order a meal, and added a gift card to the order. The same girl took his order that had taken mine. She and her co-worker knew I was living on faith and I could see in her eyes that she understood what I was doing. I prayed that God would kindle a desire in her to know *Him*.

I gave the gift card to Richard so he could get another meal or two, and then spent some more time talking to him, making sure that he knew it was because of my faith in God, and God's blessings on me, that I was able to do anything.

Being out and about without my backpack I didn't have a witnessing tract, nor Bible to share with Richard and I decided then that, should I leave my backpack somewhere again, I would make sure to at least have some tracts on me to give out.

### Saturday-October 10, 2009

I set my alarm to get up early. I had been told that the men of the church would be there to get ready for the BBQ and I wanted to be cleaned up and packed before they arrived. After cleaning up, I packed everything, then went to the convenience store to use the restroom and get a cup of coffee. When I got back to the picnic shelter, a man came out of the church and headed straight for me.

Before he reached me, I was up, reaching out my hand towards him, introducing myself. He told me his name was Bruce and I began telling him about my journey, some of the things God had been doing in my life and, the love I had been shown along the way by God's people. After a few minutes he said that he had an errand to run and started to walk away. Then he stopped and asked if I would like a breakfast sandwich from Hardee's. He returned a few minutes later with the sandwich and we went into the church to help prepare for the BBQ.

Inside, I was introduced to several people, one of which was a young man named Trace. I racked my brain to think of a name that would sound like Trace in the south, like Dall that was spelled Dale or Darl, spelled Darrel. I couldn't think of any so I finally asked how he spelled his name. He said "T r a c e". He got me on that one. His name was Trace spelled Trace.

Pastor Leslie and Robert stopped by and later, Robert asked if I was staying for the Sunday service. The day came to an end and, as I was doing my update online, Robert came out with a heavy sleeping bag, offering it to me, telling me that it was going to get cold that night.

### Sunday-October 11, 2009

I was up and packed before anyone arrived for church. When the church was opened I went in and shaved, then joined a Sunday School class. After Sunday School the choir director invited me to sing with the choir and I accepted. Pastor Leslie also came up to me and asked if I had ever read a book called "The Way of The Pilgrim", I hadn't, and she gave me a copy of it.

After service a few people came up, asked a few questions about my journey, giving me their blessings and well wishes. I thanked Pastor Leslie. Robert had already taken the kids to the house, so I asked her to thank him.

As I was about to leave the parking lot, one of the men from the church asked if I was going into Dalton and, learning that I was, offered me a ride. He dropped me off at a shopping center on U.S. Highway 41 in the northwest part of town.

The nights were getting colder, and, though I had a small blanket, it was not big enough to cover me; I went into a store and, finding fleece in the fabric dept., bought a six and a half foot piece. Once I had that in my backpack I started walking on U.S. Highway 41 towards Ringgold, GA.

About three miles later a vehicle passed me and then turned around. The driver said that he was headed to Chattanooga and asked if I would like a ride. I told him that I would love one and we headed out. As we drove we talked about my journey. He said that, he wished I could meet his pastor, and I asked where his church was. He told me that it was in Ringgold and I kind of chuckled, telling him that Ringgold was actually where I had planned on stopping for the night. He asked if I would like to meet his pastor. I told him that I would and, we turned around and headed back towards Ringgold.

The church was Grace Church of Catoosa County, and, was a good mile out of the city. I was introduced to Pastor Steve Sullivan, a man who was zealous for the word of God. We talked for some time about the Bible and beliefs. Then it was time for the evening's activities to begin.

They had a youth service and a parenting class, led by the pastor, which I joined in on. It was excellent. Pastor Sullivan used many personal experiences as illustrations, but mostly, correlations on how God parents us. It would have been good, just as a Bible study, for anyone.

After the class everyone gathered in the sanctuary for a time of praise and worship. Afterward, people came up to me, greeting me, giving me their well wishes and blessings and a few love gifts.

I got my tent set up, and, as I got into it, it started to sprinkle; and the sky looked like it could drop a lot more rain.

### Monday-October 12, 2009

It rained most of the night. I got up about 6:30, carried my gear to the church, which had a wraparound overhang, then went back for the tent. As I carried the tent, I heard a loud "Crack" and figured that one of the poles was splintering again. When I got to the overhang I examined the poles, and found that the center pole was broken in two pieces, with no hope of repair. Without the center pole, there was no way to set the tent up to sleep in, since it was the one that enabled the tent to spread out tight. I couldn't complain. That type of tent is made to use a few times a year, and, to be dry when put away. I had used that tent nearly every night for four months, often rolled up wet.

I spread the tent over a few chairs to let some of the water drip from it before rolling it up and spent time reading the Bible and praying, while the rain poured down. After two hours, the rain still didn't let up. I packed everything, covered up with my poncho and started walking the mile into Ringgold.

I finally made it to a restaurant, where I spent the rest of the morning and part of the afternoon waiting for the rain to stop. Finally, about 2:00pm, the rain let up and I left, connecting to State road 2; and walked about seven miles before I got to Fort Oglethorpe, GA, where I found a church, and a shopping center.

The church really didn't have a place to set up; I asked about another church nearby and was told that it was about two miles further. I had just come down a hill that had a great view of the mountains, and, I had noticed a flat area. I decided that, after getting new poles for the tent and eating, I would go back there to set up for the night.

I went into the Wal-Mart, to see about replacing the broken tent pole, only to find that the replacement poles were for a different brand of tent, and wouldn't work. The smallest tent on the shelves was a six man tent. I asked the associate if they had any 3 man tents in stock; explaining that I was on a journey, and had only enough for that tent. He called his manager and, after hearing my dilemma, gave me an employee discount on the larger tent. This left me with enough money for a pair of shoes and a couple of meals.

From there I went to get something to eat. There were three teenage boys, about 15 or so, at a table. I felt that they found me quite amusing; often glancing at me, whispering to each other, and then snickering. They were joined by a middle aged man, who brought their meals. I considered engaging in conversation with them, I guess, so they would see that you can't judge a book by its cover; but, what happened next said more to the boys, than anything I could have said.

While they were eating, the man began choking on his food. First, he gave the universal sign of choking; holding his hands to his throat, then started indicating to the teens to hit him on the back. One of the boys kind of patted him on the back; with the type of pat on the back you would give someone you were comforting. I got up, gave the man three hard blows, and pulled his chair out from the table, ready to perform the Heimlich maneuver if needed. The strikes on the back did the trick, and the man thanked me. After making sure he was alright, I told the boys that, when someone was choking, they had to hit hard enough to dislodge whatever was in the esophagus. I asked if they knew the Heimlich maneuver, which they didn't, and I told them that they should take a CPR class. They looked at me with different eyes than they had been, and said "Yes sir".

After I finished eating, I walked up the hill to set up my tent. The new tent was much bigger than what I needed, but still rolled up small enough to attach to the backpack. Setting up the new style of tents is easy-- as long as you know how it goes up. Setting up a six man tent, in the dark, not knowing how it assembles was a challenge for me. But I did finally get it, and climbed in it to get some sleep.

**Tuesday-October 13, 2009**

I had set my alarm to get up before sunrise, but I didn't need it. The ground that I was on was wet and muddy, and was sucking the heat from my body. The morning, however, was beautiful. The air was clear, with fog drifting up from the mountains. I spent close to an hour taking photos of the mountains in different lighting as the sun rose.

Following Battlefield Parkway into Tennessee, I came to

Lookout Mountain. By now it was already late afternoon, but, not being as far as I had wanted to be, I decided to cross the mountain before stopping for the night.

The road going up was winding and there wasn't much room to walk. When I reached the top there was an area where I was able to get off the road and take a break before heading down the other side. By the time I reached the bottom it was dark. I had only covered about 15 miles that day, which kind of disappointed me, but I figured that God had a purpose for it.

The only place I could find to eat was a family owned Mexican restaurant and, as it had been a long, hard day, a good Mexican meal sounded better than another cheeseburger or hot dog anyway. I saw a sign for a Church of the Nazarene on the same the corner the restaurant was on and decided that I would go there after I ate.

When I got to the church it was late, but there were lights on and a pickup parked near a door. I went to the door, and, finding it locked, knocked. A minute later a man answered and I introduced myself to him. He introduced himself as Pastor Joshua, or Josh. He gave me permission to set my tent up for the night, inviting me inside to talk for a while. He was very interested in my journey, and asked several questions about it. After talking for close to an hour, we headed outside and he showed me where I could set up. We talked as I set-up and, by the time the tent was up, it started to sprinkle. I thanked him, he left and I went into the tent.

## Wednesday-October 14, 2009

It was not one of my better nights. The sprinkling quickly turned to a heavy rain. When I bought the tent, I didn't buy silicon spray for it –not that it would have had time to dry if I had sprayed it on –and worse, there was also a section of the tent that was made for storage, that I hadn't had room to set up. Instead of water running off of it, it pooled there and seeped into the tent. In short, I woke up soaked, laying in a puddle of water, with more water dripping down on me. There was no indication that the rain would let up anytime soon either.

The best I could do was to tuck the storage area under the tent floor, and soak up as much water as possible. Then, I found an area that water wasn't dripping in, and spent the rest of the night wrapped in my other blanket, sleeping on my knees.

The rain finally stopped about 6:00am and I started pulling stuff out of the tent. After wringing about five gallons of water from my pillow, sleeping bag and blanket, I folded the tent up so the water would flow towards the door, rolled it as tight as I could, pushing as much water out as possible. The wet items added several pounds to my backpack.

I walked about three quarters of a mile to the intersection where I would turn and stopped to get something to eat. While I ate, a pool of water drained from my tent, but the pack was still extremely heavy. As I left, I prayed that, not only would I have the strength to carry it, but also that my worn pack didn't break under the strain.

I had only walked a few yards when an old pickup truck pulled over, and I was offered a ride for about five miles. The driver went by "Pappy" and was the owner of a small restaurant with the same name. When we arrived, he offered me breakfast and, when I told him that I had already eaten, he insisted that I at least accepted a cup of coffee. I stayed for a good hour, talking to Pappy, his employees and customers that came in. While I was inside, more water had run out of the tent and bedroll, reducing the load a little more.

I had seen on the map that the road I would be walking paralleled the interstate, and, it was a country road, which meant that the only traffic would be the few people that lived on it. I headed out, not sure how far I would make it that day; trusting that, wherever I ended up, would be where God wanted me. I walked for about five hours, taking breaks wherever possible to take the load off my back and legs. I finally ate some crackers and peanut butter for lunch at an area where I had a great view of the hills, with their changing leaf colors.

An hour later I came to an intersection, where I could see a

convenience store about a mile away. I sat on a guard rail to rest
and decide if I wanted to travel a mile off route to the store, or
continue on to the next town, still miles away. I was pondering
which I wanted to do, when a car pulled up, and the driver asked
if I wanted a ride to Jasper.

There have been few times when I was more thankful for a
ride than this one, as it was already three o'clock in the afternoon.
The car was loud and we traveled with the windows down, so I
didn't get the man's name and there wasn't much conversation.
When we got into Jasper he asked where I wanted let out. I told
him that a Laundromat would be nice.

Laundry, which included my sleeping bag, blankets and
pillow, took the next couple hours. I also checked for churches in
Jasper and saw that there was a Baptist church a couple blocks
away. I decided to go there for the Wednesday evening service.

Laundry dried and packed, I walked to the church, with my
now lighter load, and found one vehicle in the parking lot. I went
inside and was greeted by the youth pastor. He said that someone
would be there later that could give me permission to set-up for
the night. I asked if it was alright for me to leave my backpack
there, while I went to get something to eat, and he said that it
was; so I went to a drive-in, got a sandwich and ate it.

Headed back to the church, I was walking past a building
and, glancing in through the glass door, saw what looked like a
Prayer Shawl. I walked closer to the window and, sure enough, it
was a shawl, spread out on a small table, with a Temple Menorah
and a small Shofar on top of it. I looked closer, and saw lettering
on it, proclaiming the building as House of the Risen Savior.

The door was open so I went inside and was greeted by
Pastor Don. He invited me to join the service and I apologized,
telling him that I had already made arrangements to worship at
another church and had already left my things there. I then told
him that I was interested in the beliefs and teachings of the
church. I talked to Pastor Don for a while, and he introduced me
to the members of his church, who were there waiting for the
study to begin. Then he asked me to tell them more about my

journey and ministry and I did.

It came time for me to head back to the Baptist Church, and Pastor Don followed me outside. Before I left, he prayed for me and then reached into his wallet and gave me a love gift to help me on my way.

When I returned to the church, I learned that the pastor was on vacation, and there was a short business meeting scheduled for the church members. After the meeting I talked to one of the elders and obtained permission to spend the night on the grounds. Then, some of the church members, who were curious about my journey, came up to greet me.

Everyone left and I went to the back of the church to set up my tent, and discovered that there was a covered area at the back door, and a couple of wooden platforms leaned against the wall. It had been cool enough at night that there wouldn't be insects out, so, I decided to sleep on one of the platforms.

### Thursday-October 15, 2009

I was awake at first light. The air was cool and damp and it was foggy. My legs and back ached from carrying the extra weight the day before, and I really didn't feel like traveling; preferring to stay there and rest for the day. But knew that I needed to press on. I rolled my sleeping gear, then spent some time praying and reading my Bible before leaving.

Once I started down the road it began to drizzle. I got to an intersection where U.S. Highway 41 turned northwest, towards Manchester, TN and, when I made the turn, saw the outline of a mountain through the drizzle. I silently prayed, "Lord, if at all possible, move that mountain out about my way; or at least, give me the strength to climb it." Within two minutes God showed me his sense of humor.

The first vehicle that passed me that morning was a large, black, dully pickup truck. It pulled into the first driveway ahead of me and sat there, half way up the drive. As I got closer I could see that there was lettering on the side of the truck that read, *"Mission Possible Ministries"*.

# No Mere Coincidences, a journey of faith

I was so stunned that, when a lady got out of the truck, and asked if there was anything she could do for me, all I could say was, "like what?" She said, 'food, clothes, a dry place..." I told her that, about the only thing I needed right then was a way to the other side of that mountain. She asked me where I was going and I told her that I was supposed to be in Murfreesboro in a couple days and, was hoping to get to Manchester by night fall.

It suddenly dawned on me that I hadn't introduced myself and gave her a card and started telling her about my journey. She told me that her name was Tanya and explained that she had some errands to run that morning. Tanya said that she would take me over the mountain when her errands were done, adding that Highway 41 was too dangerous to walk, especially in the rain.

I loaded my backpack into her truck and, as we drove back into Jasper, she told me that she had just dropped her kids off at school and had seen me walking. I told her about the prayer I had just prayed and she laughed, going on to tell me that Mission Possible Ministries was a local ministry, that took donations of food, clothing and any other items, and distributed them to those in need, or to people who had suffered loss due to house fires.

She took me to her home, where I checked email while she got ready for the day, and then we went into the downtown area where she took care of some business. When she was done, she told me that it would take about the same time to drive to Murfreesboro, on the interstate, as it would to drive U.S. 41 Highway over the mountain to Manchester. So, we headed towards the interstate instead of the mountain road.

As we traveled we talked about what had brought Tanya to where she was, without income and working with a ministry and I soon realized that God had us both on the same path. Neither of us was lacking anything that we needed, and, spent our days ministering to people, though in different ways.

Before long we were in Murfreesboro –a couple days earlier than I had planned. Tanya dropped me off at a shopping center on Franklin Road. I worked on my journal, then, later, visited a Christian bookstore.

I was to meet Jesse and Casey Campbell in Murfreesboro, spend a night and then attend their church on Sunday. I had waited until late to call Jesse, as he worked nights, and I figured he would be sleeping in the afternoon. Also, as I was early, I didn't want him to feel obligated to put me up earlier than he had expected. When he found out that I was just a few miles away though, he insisted on picking me up and taking me to his home. A few minutes later I finally met Jesse after being 'online friends' for over a year.

Jesse had to go to work, but had a friend come to spend the night, and, later, I met Jesse's wife, Cassey, who had been at a church function.

### Friday-October 16, 2009

Jesse got home from work and went to bed, then Cassey left for work. I spent the morning working on my journal and relaxing. When he woke up, Jesse, having heared about the tent problem I had encountered, took me to a sporting goods store and bought me a new backpacking tent, in exchange for the Family tent I had. He also bought enough waterproofing spray for both tents. When we got back to the house I set up both tents in the garage, the small one to spray and the family tent to dry out.

Cassey was home by then, and, as they had planned on spending the night visiting Cassey's parents, Jesse quickly packed and they left. I was left alone and, though I was behind on my journal again, just felt like resting, so I went through a large pile of DVDs and picked out two that I hadn't seen; "The End of the Spear" and "Invisible Children".

### Sunday-October 18, 2009

We had to leave for church early today, as the drive was an hour long. We attended "Jesus is the Answer" church, which is a Charismatic, Multicultural congregation in the small town of Watertown, TN.

After the service, Jesse took me to Nashville, where I spent a good portion of the afternoon in a fast food restuarant. As I sat and watched, I saw several people that seemed to be homeless; and, one couple in particular, that God laid on my heart to help. Jesse and Cassey had given me a nice sized love gift and, although I already had plans to send most of it to India, I decided to at least get this couple a meal each.

I went online and found a church along my route. Then I went and bought a gift card for from the restaurant. I gave the couple my last English witnessing Bible and a gospel tract, along with the gift card, before heading down the road.

About 100 yards further, I came to a man, with a cane, digging through a trash can. I did an about face and went back to get this man a gift card too. While I was in line, the Holy Spirit laid it on my heart to get four more cards. I figured that I could use money, which I had in the ministry account, toward India; so I bought four more cards. As I passed the man, I gave him one of the cards, and made my way to the church.

Within the mile or so to the First Church of the Nazarene of Nashville, I came upon two more homeless men, giving each of them a card, letting them know that it was God who had provided me the money for the card.

I arrived at the church and enjoyed a wonderful service, after which the pastor gave me permission to set my tent up on the church grounds; though he expressed his concern about the type neighborhood around the church. I assured him that God would make sure I was safe.

### Monday-October 19, 2009

I awoke early this morning, intent on finding a Western Union to send money to India. I also needed to transfer money from the ministry account.

I found a restaurant to get breakfast, and while eating, checked my email. I was shocked at one of the emails; without going into details, I'll just leave it at saying that, the money wasn't in the account anymore. I prayed about what I should do. It was time to send money for food for the kids, and I had already committed to send extra so they could buy sweaters too.

I was led to send as much as I could. I walked until I came to a grocery store that had a Western Union, and sent all I had but $3.00. I figured that I would have the $3.00 and the gift card to eat a few meals on, and could stretch it a couple days if needed.

One thing I have learned on this journey is: Never assume God is going to let me keep anything. I headed down the road towards Gallatin, TN, and guess what I came across? A man, walking towards me, clothing tattered and carrying a small plastic bag, with a few more clothes in it. I greeted him with a "Good morning" and had walked about twenty feet.

I joke that the Holy Spirit kicked me in the rear, but actually, He gently whispered, "Don't you have another gift card in your pocket?" I thought "Yeah, but..." and the voice said, "After all we've been through, don't you trust me?"

What was I to say? What was I to do? I turned around and quickly caught up with the man, calling out, "Excuse me, have you eaten today?" He stopped, and turning, answered that he had not. I handed him the card, telling him that I loved him and he mattered to me. As I did, I could see that he was about to cry. He said "Thank you", and I told him not to thank me, but my Father, God in heaven. He was the reason I had the card to give in the first place. After talking to him for a few minutes we parted, and soon afterward, I spent my last $3.00 on lunch.

As I ate and worked on my journal a thought came to me, and I wrote it on the top of the page. **"Never underestimate the power of God!"**

I now had less than one dollar of change in my pocket. I headed out of the Nashville metro area and towards Gallatin. It wasn't the first time I had nearly been out of money –but it had been a long time, and, for some reason it bothered me somewhat. Satan used it to try and bring me down once again, trying to make me doubt that God would provide. But, as I walked along, I started singing a song we used to sing; 'Jehovah Jira, My provider, his grace is sufficient for me, for me, for me...'
The Bible says that God "inhabits the praises of his people" so if

you are in a state of praise, Satan doesn't stand a chance.

I walked on for a few hours. The traffic from people headed home from work had all but ceased, and, I was about to give up on anyone offering me a ride.

It was getting dark, and I needed a place to set up for the night, which I figured it would most likely be in a field alongside the road. I started looking for someplace that would be safe and comfortable. About the time I saw a place that might work, a pickup pulled up beside me and I was offered a ride.

The drivers' name was Mike and, as we drove towards Gallatin, I shared my journey and the vision God had given me with him. I'm not sure if I was further from Gallatin than I thought, or if Mike was driving slow to make the trip last longer, but it took a good 15 minutes to get there.

Mike took me to a church in downtown Gallitan, and, as I was getting my backpack out of the truck, he told me that he needed to tell me something. Continuing, Mike shared that he hadn't been intending on driving that road. He confessed that he had been upset, and had gotten into his truck to drive off his anger.

Even in his turmoil, or maybe because of his turmoil, he felt that he should offer me a ride when he saw me. Then he told me that, listening to the stories about my journey and hearing my dreams and visions, had totally turned his attitude around. Mike thanked me for being such a blessing to him and, as we said goodbye and shook hands, he pulled some money out of his pocket. He told me that he didn't know how much was there –it had been given to him as a tip, and he had put it in his pocket. I thanked him and prayed for him, asking God's blessings on him, and he was on his way. When I looked at the love gift, It turned out to be enough for a couple days of meals.

The church that Mike had dropped me off at was what I call a parking-lot-church, meaning there was the building, surrounded by parking lot, and no grass at all. I headed towards the main street, hoping to find someplace to eat, as well as a chance to find a suitable church to spend the night at. I found a small Mexican store/restaurant and ate there.

As I left, it dawned on me that I hadn't looked for a church online. Then I saw, across the street--at an intersection, a man holding two signs; one said "Jesus Saves" and the other said "Repent". I decided that this man might know where I could find a church so, I crossed the street to talk to him.

Although the noise from the traffic was loud, I believe he said his name was James. He directed me to a church that was about half a mile away, not too far off the route I would be taking the next day.

The church was Zion Upper Room Apostolic Church, and there were people there. I was greeted by a lady that introduced herself as Sister Julie. I asked if the pastor was there, telling her about my journey and my desire to put my tent up there. Sister Julie made a phone call, then told me that it was too dangerous to sleep outside in that neighborhood, but that she was sure the church would help me in some way. Once again, I assured that God would keep me safe. Soon a man appeared and listened to my story and petition then, we were off to see the Bishop.

Bishop Isaac Williams was a man that I could tell had a zeal for the things of God. As I told him of my quest and the vision God had given me, I could see a spark in his eyes; as though he wished he was on the journey with me.

I was shown where I could set my tent up, which was a field across the street, which the church was preparing to expand onto. Soon I was asleep, but awoke twice during the night to someone talking a short distance away. Once, I heard 'back there, behind the bushes', which was where I had set up; then later, 'he's sleeping in a tent back there'. I just told God, "I'm in your hands Father." and went back to sleep.

## Tuesday-October 20, 2009

I awoke to cold, heavy dew. While I was in the process of rolling up my sleeping bag, James appeared at the door of the tent. He had walked through the tall, dew laden grass to bring me a bag with some fruit and granola bars for breakfast, as well as some flavored instant coffee packets. He asked me if there was anything else I needed, and I told him that I only accept what God lays on people's hearts to do.

He said he needed to get to work and he prayed with me, asking God to bless me and keep me safe on my journey. I thanked him for all he had done and he left, only to reappear a few seconds later with a love gift of cash.

I felt so ashamed about questioning God the day before. After everything he has done for me, especially during this journey, I worried about possibly missing a couple of meals and, in less than 20 hours he had more than tripled what I had been reluctant to give up.

Done with packing, I ate before leaving Gallitan, heading towards Westmoreland, TN. The mornings were cooler now and, today especially, the walk was easy. I had gone only a few miles on U.S. Highway 31E when I was offered a ride by an elderly man. I rode in the back of a pickup, to Westmoreland, TN and was dropped me off at a gas station/restaurant on State Road 52.

It was still early, and the next town was an eight hour walk away. After eating an early lunch and filling my water bottles, I headed out towards Scottsville, KY.

The afternoon was as close to perfect that I could have asked for. The humidity was low; the temperature just right, the road fairly level and, the leaves seemed to be in full color. I walked on until mid-afternoon, when I came to a car parked at the side of the road and, half a mile later, a middle aged man, picking up cans from the side of the road.

I began a conversation with him, asking how much further it was to Scottsville. He said that it was about five more miles and, telling me that he was about to head back there, offered me a ride. Half an hour later he was back with his car and, once I got my backpack in the car, we were headed to town.

The man's name was Rick and we talked about the economy. He was unemployed and was living by collecting and selling aluminum cans and doing a few odd jobs. He dropped me off at a restaurant and we prayed together before he left.

I went in and got dinner, went online, plotted the next day's journey, then looked for a church online. I found one on Bowling Green Road and walked there, but as the church was built on the side of a hill, it didn't have any ground suitable to set a tent up on. Just up the hill from it was another church. I walked up the hill and what I found was an excellent spot, secluded from the neighboring area by a thicket of trees on two sides, overlooking the hillside across the highway.

The driveway for the church went out to a road that intersected Bowling Green Road. I walked to the entrance and saw a sign showing that the church was the Powerhouse Pentecostal Worship Center.

As I was setting up my tent, noticed that the sun was setting, and the clouds were reflecting spectacular colors. I spent the next half hour or so getting pictures of the church steeple and various cloud formations during the sunset.

### Wednesday-October 21, 2009

When the sun rose, it was almost as beautiful as the night before. The church on the lower road had a colorful, wooded hill for a backdrop and the sun was shining bright.

Before I was packed, one of the men from the church was there. I went up and introduced myself, letting him know that I had spent the night there. He said that it was fine and added that, if I was around that evening, I was more than welcome to attend their service, but I told him that I would be headed out as soon as I got my tent rolled up. He went into the church, and returned a few minutes later with a couple containers of juice and some snack foods. I thanked him and ate some before leaving.

Walking, I traveled a few miles on U.S. Highway 31E. I came to a bridge that crossed a clear, clean looking creek. I was standing there, considering going under the bridge to bathe in the creek, when a car stopped in the middle of the road. The driver, an upper-middle aged woman, offered me a ride for a few miles.

I accepted and, once in the car, introduced myself to her. She said that her name was Lynn and she asked where I was headed. When I told her about my journey of faith, she asked if I had eaten breakfast. I told her that I had eaten a sweet roll a couple hours earlier, and she offered to take me home, and fix me a meal. She also offered to let me shower and wash my clothes.

People like Lynn were such a God sent blessing to me throughout the journey. When we got to her house I showered, then Lynn put my dirty clothes in the washing machine and fixed me a large, country style breakfast, even though it was getting close to noon.

Once the clothes were dry, we left again. I thought Lynn was just going to take me back to the main highway, but she said that she was going to take me to Glasgow, which was about 20 miles away. She said that she had some shopping she needed to do and might visit her husband, who drove a dump truck for a company there.

The area offered several fast food restaurants, so I entered one, went online, plotted the next step of the journey and then, found a church online that I figured would have an evening service. Around 6:30pm, I headed out to a church that was a few blocks away.

Though it wasn't the church I was headed to, I found a small Baptist church, and felt led to go there. As expected, I was warmly welcomed, and I asked the pastor permission to set my tent up in the church's yard, which he granted.

During the service, it became apparent that the small church was full of prayer warriors. They not only prayed for church members, but family, neighbors, co-workers, friends of co-workers and anyone else they knew of in need.

The pastor mentioned that I was there, and had me tell a little about my journey. After the service, most of the members came up and greeted me, and one elderly gentleman slipped me a love gift. Once most of the people had left, the pastor offered to put me up in a motel. So, he and his wife took me and got me a room, and once again I had a bed to sleep in.

**Thursday-October 22, 2009**

I made use of the shower before packing and leaving the motel, and, after stopping for breakfast, headed northwest on State Road 90. Once again, travel was as close to perfect as I could ask for. The weather was cool but not cold, the sky was clear and the road level.

I had walked about four or five miles, when a Blue Cadillac pulled up to an intersection some 200 yards ahead of me. Having stopped for the stop sign, the car continued to sit there. The wheels of the car were pointed towards me, so I didn't think they were waiting to offer me a ride.

When I made it to the intersection, the driver, who was an elderly lady, said something that I wasn't able to hear. Walking closer, I apologized and asked her what she had said. She said "I should be walking like that." and I told her that the backpack gets kind of heavy after a while.

I introduced myself and she told me that her name was Charlcie. She asked where I was headed and where I had started. I told her about my journey and, after a few minutes, Charlcie told me that her husband was a retired minister. Then, with a tear in her eye, she said, "I have to tell you something. I'm headed to a lady's house that had just lost a loved one. This morning I prayed that God would send someone to encourage me. When I saw you, I had to wait, because you looked like an Angel of God walking towards me." My only thought was, "Lord, let your light shine through me like that always."

Charlcie and I prayed for each other before parting ways and I continued to walk north, as she headed south. I had only walked about ten minutes when a pickup pulled over in front of me. This time the driver was a young lady, whose name was Chrissie. She had been to Glasgow to pick up supplies for her husband's siding business and, seeing me walking, felt led to offer me a ride. I loaded my backpack on top of the siding and climbed in.

Chrissie had a small child with her who kept looking at me, smiling and giggling. It was like he knew something about me and found it funny. It wasn't the first time this had happened.

No Mere Coincidences, a journey of faith

There had been times when I would be in a restaurant and kids would be waving or giggling at me and the parents would be embarrassed or upset and would try to stop them. I have been told by a few different people that the kids, being more innocent and open to spiritual things than adults, could sense God in me and recognized the love of Christ. I hope that this is more the case than I just look funny.

Chrissie gave me a ride to the outskirts of Cave City, KY and dropped me off at a convenience store on U.S. Highway 31W. It wasn't lunch time, but not knowing what lay ahead, I bought a pizza pocket and ate it before heading out for Horse Cave, KY. I walked though Cave City and, was only a couple miles outside of town, when a car stopped and a young man offered me a ride.

His name was Joe and he said that he was headed for work in Horse Cave. Joe told me that he was a new Christian and was engaged in learning about, and living his life, the way that Jesus taught. I told him that he was on a good start and we talked about the ways of Jesus as we traveled.

When we got into town, Joe turned towards the downtown area, dropping me off. As it was just after noon, I headed out towards Munfordville, KY. I walked for the next five hours, making my way through Munfordville to a restaurant next to Interstate 65 before stopping. It was early enough that I wasn't ready to eat and, late enough that I felt that I had gone my distance for the day, so I just got a coke and went online to see where the churches in the area were.

I saw that there was a church about a mile ahead, and another about three miles. I was praying about what I should do when, for the first time during the journey, I felt led to stand at the entrance ramp to the interstate. I won't say that this was the first time I had thought about it, but this time, I felt led to stand there. I loaded everything up and walked the short distance to the northbound entrance ramp to I-65.

I stood under the sign announcing that pedestrians were prohibited to go any further. I couldn't stick my thumb out or hold a sign, as that would be asking for a ride. So, I just stood there, my backpack on and my hands folded in front of me, watching people watching me as they drove by.

To be honest, I felt a bit foolish. But, God is wiser than I am and, after standing there for about twenty minutes, a van pulled to the side of the road. A young man in a long black, western style overcoat and hat got out. He looked like something out of the old west. I thought it was a little odd, considering that it was rather warm out, but later learned that he suffered from a sunlight allergy.

He helped me get my backpack into the back of the van and then climbed into the back seat, giving me the passenger seat. As we started onto the interstate, he introduced me to his wife, who was also in the back seat, and then to the driver, a young woman, about the same age, as his third mother.

I remember thinking, "That's an odd way of introduction." Like I said, she was about the same age as the other two. I had, of course, seen instances where a man marries a woman the same age as his kids, but they would normally introduce them as their 'Step-mom' not their third mother. As we talked, I discovered the reason for it. His father was a polygamist.

The young man's mother had been his first wife, His father's second wife, he called "mom" and this one he called "Mother". He was the oldest of 16 kids, all being from the first two wives. I'm not mentioning their names as they are from a small community and I don't want the kids stigmatized because of their parents' beliefs.

They were headed for Elizabethtown, KY for dinner, and they wanted to hear about my journey along the way. When we got to Elizabethtown they invited me to join them for dinner at a Chinese buffet. During dinner we talked about the Bible, God, Jesus and salvation. After dinner, as we parted ways, I prayed that seeds planted would be watered.

I found a place to get online in order to locate a church, finding one that didn't seem to be too far away. I headed to where I thought the church would be. Instead of being there in ten minutes, like I thought I would; I spent an hour walking through the countryside, making a loop around the shopping center that I had been in. It was well after 10:00pm when I came to an area that was a bean-field, surrounded by a wooded area and decided to pitch my tent there.

### Friday-October 23, 2009

Despite the strong winds and lightning throughout the night, it didn't rain, for which I was thankful. I was awake before sunrise and ready to go at first light. Within ten minutes I was back at the shopping area that I had spent an hour walking around the night before. I went to a restaurant, got breakfast and went online to plan the day's journey.

I had been turned around the night before and had gone left instead of right. This time, when I left, I passed the church I had intended on going to the night before within minutes.

I continued walking out of town and soon came to a road that the map had shown would cut a couple of miles off of my walk. I debated taking that one or, staying on the main highway. Once again, I was reminded of the narrow path, the path less traveled and often harder to walk. I turned onto the less traveled road. I have found that, even though it is symbolic, I have been more blessed when I take the "Narrow path"; and, once again I was rewarded. I had walked less than a quarter mile when a car stopped and an elderly man offered me a ride. He had made an early trip to Elizabethtown to pick up a prescription and, was headed back home, to Lebanon Junction, KY.

As with many elderly people, this conversation turned to the lack of youth in churches, and the evidence, in the declining morals in our country. We have gone from "One nation Under God" to taking God out of the schools, then the workplace, then out of the public eye and now to a generation that is trying to take God out of the *churches*. A generation that wants to sing uplifting songs and get a motivational sermon to make them feel good about where they are, instead of motivating them to draw closer to God.

I was dropped off at a gas station on the edge of Lebanon Junction. I went online to figure out where I was, and, how to get where I was going. Right after I got online Jeremy Caverley sent me a message that Kristin was wondering where I was and, let me know that he had given her my phone number to call me. Kristin and her husband, Keith, live just south of Louisville, KY, and wanted to host me for a day or two while I was in that area.

No sooner had I read the message, the phone rang and it was Kristin. When she found out where I was, she told me to stay there, she would pick me up shortly. Twenty-five minutes later she and her daughter, Brooke arrived.

The rest of the day was full. We went to the fire station where Keith volunteers and I met him, along with some of the other firemen, then went to lunch and then to meet some of Kristin's friends. We got to Kristin and Keith's house in time to eat dinner and go to bed.

### Sunday-October 25, 2009

Everyone was up early this morning as Keith had to be at the fire station. I attended a small church, whose pastor was charismatic and energetic. After service he announced that I was there and told the congregation about the journey. Several of the members surrounded me and prayed over me before leaving.

I made my way to a restaurant for lunch and prayed about what I should do. I wasn't sure if I should stay there, work on my journal and find a church there for an evening service or, to make my way towards Louisville. I decided to stay and find a church there. So I spent the afternoon working on my journal until about 4:00; then I headed towards State Highway 61, which would be the road I would take in the morning.

About an hour later I came to Little Lamb Ministries, a good sized Baptist church/Christian school. It was still well before the service started when I got there, but I chatted with the man at the information desk for a while, and then took advantage of the quietness to spend some time reading my Bible.

When Pastor Rodney Alexander arrived, the man from the

information desk introduced us and I asked about setting up my tent. He gave his approval and we went into the service. After the service a few people came up to greet me and ask me about my journey.

One man in particular was interested in the journey and, offered to pick me up for breakfast in the morning, and then take me to Louisville afterward.

## Monday-October 26, 2009

I was picked up right on time this morning and taken to the Cracker Barrel for breakfast. All through breakfast my host sat and listened to my stories of the kids in Honduras, my vision and my journey. Then, we headed on out on Interstate 65, towards Louisville. He took me a good 10 miles towards Louisville, to 31E near I-265, dropping me off at a White Castle. I got a cup of coffee and plotted a route.

The map had me going into Louisville a little bit and then, turning north; but, as I left the restaurant, I suddenly felt that I should go back towards the interstate. As I approached the northbound entrance ramp, I was, once again, led to stand on a ramp to the interstate, and once again, I stood just under the sign announcing that pedestrians aren't allowed.

I watched as vehicles went past and people looked as they passed me. I had come to the realization that, sometimes, God places me in people's paths to give them the opportunity to do what is Godly, just as He has put people in my path for the same reason. Over the next half hour there were four people who, if I am correct, God was leading to stop for me. As soon as the 4th one went by I felt that I was to go get something to drink.

I walked to a restaurant, got a drink and worked on my journal for about 2 hours before, suddenly, feeling that it was time to leave again. This time, knowing that I was to stand on the ramp, I headed back and stood in the same place I was in before.

The first vehicle went past. The driver had a curious look

on his face, but not the look as though he were debating whether or not to stop. The second vehicle, a loud, older pickup truck went by. The young man driving had that look, but went past and disappeared behind the rock that the ramp was cut out of. Before another vehicle had pasted by me, I heard an engine behind me and turned to find that the pickup had backed down around the ramp to pick me up.

The young man's name was Matt. He had just come from a funeral and, had a plant and flowers in the cab of the truck. Once they were moved to the bed of the truck we were on our way, north on I-265 and then east on I-64 towards Georgetown, KY. This wasn't the route I had planned on taking but, it would put me due South of Cincinnati, and, as I had learned over and over during this trip, God had a purpose in it. I believe, this time, it was at least a twofold purpose.

Matt, like me, had been raised in a church, attending twice on Sunday, Wednesday evening and, any and all youth events. That is, until two months earlier. Matt had gotten a job miles away from home and, like so many of us, when he got away from home, he stopped going to church.

I told Matt my testimony; how I too had been raised in a church and attended as many services and functions as I could. In my case, it was the military. I stopped attending church, started going out with my new friends and, instead of influencing them, for God, let them influence me. First it was going to the clubs with them and having a beer, then a pitcher of beer, then... You get the picture. Before I knew it, I was drunk whenever I wasn't working, smoking several packs of cigarettes a day and always seemed to have someone to sleep with. I didn't plead with Matt to get back into church or try and convict him for not being in church. I let him know what kind of a mess *I* had been, when I forgot that God wanted me to live for him and I lived for me.

Then I shared the vision that God had given me, how much I desired to serve God in any way he wanted. I shared the need of workers in the harvest. I prayed that something I said touched him. Matt dropped me off in Georgetown and gave me a love gift as I got my backpack out of the truck.

I went into a restaurant and got a late lunch, then recalculated my route from there. I also needed to find a church for the night. It wasn't that late yet, but I had made good distance and felt that I could find a church, then work on my journal.

I headed out, planning to follow my new route. However, when I got to where I was to turn, the Holy Spirit told me to keep going. I could see that I was not that far from where I had been, and wondered why I hadn't noticed an easier way to get there when I left the restaurant to start with.

God's timing is perfect. I got to the ramp of northbound I-75 and, the Holy Spirit told me to stand there. I did, and, the first vehicle that came down the ramp was a van, which pulled over; the driver, a young African-American man, asked where I was headed. I told him Cincinnati and he said to get in.

His name was Adam. He had left from somewhere in Florida the night before and had driven straight through, headed for Cincinnati. I was almost afraid to talk to him much –I know my voice is mono-tone, and I was afraid I would put him to sleep. I did manage to let him know how great God is and, how much he had blessed me on this journey. Maybe it was just enough to plant or water a seed.

I kept as much activity in the van as I could by singing and keeping beat with the radio and by about 7:00 we were in Cincinnati, still awake and alive.

After I got some dinner, I walked a few blocks to where I had seen a church online, contacting the pastor at the parsonage and receiving permission to set up for the night.

### Tuesday-October 27, 2009

I had a long walk through Cincinnati today.
The original plan was to spend a day or two with David Mock again. However, since David had moved, I made arrangements to go back to Chillicothe, OH to see Jeremy and Miranda again.

The map showed that I had a 12 mile walk on the same road the church was on, which would get me most of the way through the city. I headed out, not sure what the area would be like. It could have been all residential or business.

I walked east on West Galbraith Road until it turned into East Galbraith Road. Then, about two miles further, a pickup, that had passed me, came back around and picked me up. The driver's name was Randy Morgan. He was headed to pick up his son, but felt that he should give me a ride.

We talked about God, and making Him a priority in your life. How God wanted a relationship with us, not just a people satisfied with sitting in a church once a week. God wanted to be a part of our everyday life, to be remembered in the good times and not just someone to call on when things aren't going well. Randy drove me the rest of the way thought the city as we talked and left me in Mulberry, OH.

I sat at a restaurant and looked for a church nearby, then I ate an early dinner as I didn't figure I would be near anyplace to eat once I headed out for a church. There was a church a block away, but I wasn't led to go there. I planned on going to one about a mile away. I had barely started walking, when a van pulled beside me and I was offered a ride. When I told the driver that I was looking for a church, he said he knew of one, and took me to the Heartland Christian Church in Goshen, OH.

There were people at a house type building on the grounds, and I met Robert and Jenny, who were there to operate the food pantry. Robert was the director of outreach, and gave me permission to set my tent up for the night.

I sat and talked to them for quite a while, and Robert invited me to a bible study he and the pastor were having in the morning. I accepted and, after making sure I was set for the night, they left.

## Wednesday-October 28, 2009

I was up and packed before Robert and the pastor made it in. Robert brought donuts and coffee, and I met Pastor Bill Ponchot. He asked me about my journey and, while I was talking, I mentioned how, so many times during the journey, I had thought about the book, Pilgrim's Progress by John Bunyan. Pastor Bill got up and walked to his bookshelves, pulled out a book, handed it to me and said "Here, you can have this one." It was an antique copy of The Pilgrim's Progress.

We finally got to the Bible study; the first three chapters of Ephesians. When we finished reading and discussing the passages, we prayed before I left.

I headed east on State Highway 28 and, an hour later a car pulled up beside me. After a second look, I realized it was Robert. It turned out that his wife had the car for an appointment that morning, and, as soon as she was done, he came to find me.

We stopped in a small town, where Robert bought us lunch, and then we drove on to Highland, OH. After praying and saying goodbyes, Robert headed home and I headed towards Leesburg, OH, covering the distance in about two hours.

Here, I took a break at a convenience store then headed back down the road towards Greenfield, OH. I hadn't walked more than a couple miles out of Leesburg when an elderly man, named Alvin, picked me up and took me into Greenfield, dropping me off on the east edge of town.

It was still fairly early and, I didn't feel as though this was where I was to spend the night so, following the lead of the Holy Spirit, I continued east, on Highway 28, towards Chillicothe. As always, when I go with what the Holy Spirit is leading, something happens. I had only walked about a mile when a pickup truck pulled over, and I was offered a ride.

This man's name was Mike. It was Mike's birthday and he had been celebrating; In fact, he was headed to buy more beer to *continue* celebrating. As I talked to him, I realized that he knew the Bible better than many people in churches did. I asked him about it and, it turned out, he had been raised in a church but had strayed from God. He had lived a rough life and had been arrested, from the sounds of it, several times.

Then he started in about how hard this was and how hard that was, and, if he ever got his life straightened out, he would be able to live for God. I have become a fairly compassionate person, but I had to ask Mike when he was going to stop making excuses. So many people look at Christianity in one of two false ways. One way is "I have to make myself perfect before God will accept me", and the other is "God loves me just the way I am, so I don't have to change." --Both of these beliefs are false.

Yes, God loves you, even in your sin. However, when you come to God and seek forgiveness, there is repentance; a turning away from your sin, a growing in Holiness and a desire to be like Jesus Christ. The Bible tells us we are a new creation, given a new heart. We should have a love for the things that God loves and a hatred for the things God hates. We get baptized to symbolize the dying of the old man and resurrection into a new life with Christ. Will we fall once in a while? Of course, Solomon tells us in Ecclesiastes 7:20 *'Indeed, there is not a righteous man on earth who continually does good and who never sins.'* But, when we do, we accept our responsibility and don't try to blame it on others.

Mike was one who had tried to make himself perfect in order to begin being a Christian and, since he found it too hard to be perfect, just decided not to try. OK, I can't say that he didn't try. He did say that he had confessed his sins at one point (a jail house conversion) and, when he got out of jail, attended church for about six months, but seeing imperfect Christians in the church and giving into sin himself, decided to quit trying.

Mike decided to take me to his cousin's house, as he felt that she may either let me set my tent up there for the night, or possibly help me get up the road further. When we got there Mike introduced me to Stacy, once he made sure that she knew who he was. (Apparently they hadn't seen each other for years).

Stacy said that she and her husband were headed into Chillicothe as soon as he got home from work, and would be glad to give me a ride. Mike and I stayed outside and talked so Stacy could get ready. I asked him about family and he said that he had a wife and children at home. I told him that I couldn't understand why he would choose to be out drinking, instead of spending his birthday with his kids and wife. He really didn't have a reason for his choice, other than he had made alcohol more important than even his own kids.

Stacy's husband, Curt, got home and Mike decided that he should leave. I asked if I could pray for him before he left and asked God to open his eyes and heart. I also prayed that I had made some type of difference in his life. I may never know. That is what is so frustrating sometimes. I pour my heart out and try to guide people towards God and, sometimes, I just feel like it is in vain because I don't see any results. I just pray that one day, someone will come up to me and say, "Do you remember me? You set me on the narrow path. Thanks." To hear those words would be so rewarding.

Once Mike had left and everyone was ready, we headed towards Chillicothe. They dropped me off a few blocks from Steven and Leona's house, and I made my way there. As I walked up the yard Chris, Leona's son, saw me and greeted me. Steven was inside and I spent a few minutes catching him up on where I had been since I had left there in July.

After a much needed shower and shave, I headed out to see if I could find a church with a Wednesday night service. I found the First Baptist Church of Chillicothe, OH. The front door was locked, but I saw people around the back and so went around and asked an elderly African-American lady if there was a service that night. She said there was a Study in the Fellowship Hall.

I was surprised that everyone was African American. Though church's have finally become more integrated, and –as it was pointed out in South Carolina –it is more of a preference of worship styles that segregate many rather than race, traditionally a church named First Baptist, or First Assembly of God, or any other "First", is predominantly White –in general.

In any event, the Bible study was conducted by Rev. Michael Alston and, was the beginning of a thorough, comprehensive study of their Covenant. We barely even got into the first paragraph in the study. One part that really struck me was what the pastor called 'Unintended consequences'. We seek God and, in doing that, the 'unintended consequence' is that we suddenly have brothers and sisters in Christ. And, just like biological siblings, we're stuck with them whether we like them or not. We are responsible for their spiritual walk, we are to keep them accountable for what they do, and we ask them to keep us accountable for what we do. When we see a brother or sister faltering, we should go to them, in love, not judgment, and help them through it with prayer, encouragement and love.

After the study I was invited to attend the Sunday morning service, which I agreed to do.

# NOVEMBER

### Sunday-November 1, 2009

After a few days of resting and visiting, I returned to the first Baptist Church on Sunday morning for service; Once again being warmly welcomed. The sermon was on the importance of prayer and not only praying but listening to the voice of God.

I also discovered the reasoning behind the name of the church. The Church's original name was, The First Regular African Baptist Church of Christ of Chillicothe. It had been formed in 1824 by David Nickens with the help of two other pastors. Later that year, David Nickens became the first African American to be ordained in Ohio. In the 1830s its name was changed to the First AntiSlavery Baptist Church of Chillicothe, with members that operated in the Underground Railroad. The Church had a rich history in bringing about changes in this country.

Later that day Jeremy and I headed out, traveling on U.S. Highway 35. When we turned off of the highway we were in Xenia, OH. Just down a street were two churches. Both had vehicles in the parking lot indicating that there were Sunday evening activities. Both of us felt led to go to the First Church of Christ, so we headed there. We were greeted by a man named Dave and, as it turned out, it wasn't actually an evening service; they were having a multi-church youth activity.

I spoke to him about my journey and obtained permission

to set my tent up for the night. Dave invited us to attend the youth event, which would consist of worship and games. After a few songs, we began playing Dodge Ball. We had played several games, changing the rules for variety; the latest was one where we had to use our "weak arm" to throw the ball. I ran up to the line and threw the ball I had, when one of the other team started running towards me. I was running backward hoping to either catch the ball or dodge it when he threw it. Unfortunately, I'm not as agile as I used to be. As I tried to dodge the ball, I fell backward, striking my head.

Have you ever hit your head and seen a bright light? That's your brain hitting the inside of your skull. It means you've hit hard enough that it pushes the fluids, cushioning the brain, out of the way. When I hit, I saw the light. I remember the bright flash and sitting up. I thought my arms were straight out, and yet I could see my hands up against my chest. I couldn't feel or move them or, my legs. People were asking if I was OK, and, in my head, I was telling them to give me a minute, but it wasn't coming out my mouth.

My only thought was, God, I don't believe you brought me here to cripple me, so I rebuke this in Jesus name. After, what I thought was a few seconds, I got feeling back in my body and started speaking, but Jeremy later told me that it was several minutes. Once I got up, someone said something about getting the blood washed off my head. I didn't realize that it was bleeding. Jeremy and a lady took me into a room and cleaned me up and, within a few minutes I was fine, other than a headache.

We rejoined the group as they were finishing the night's activities. As they closed, the youth surrounded me, with as many laying hands on me as possible, and with the others connected to each other, they all prayed over me.

Dave let me know that they wanted to get me a room for the night, so Jeremy and I followed him to a hotel. Jeremy stayed for an hour or so, worried about me, but I had no worries. I had already given it over to God.

He stayed until I had done with my online update, then left

and I had a good night's sleep.

**Monday-November 2, 2009**

I didn't rush out this morning. I did have a bit of a headache, so I kind of took it easy and worked on my journal, played a game on my computer–and just rested. At checkout time I headed out and walked back to the highway.

I hadn't realized it the day before, but U.S. Highway 35 had become limited access, and pedestrians were not allowed on it at that point. I stood there, debating if I should walk back to town or, dig my computer out there, at the side of the road, to plot a route.

God provided a solution immediately. The first car that came by me stopped, backed up, and the driver asked if I would like a ride. As I was getting into the car, he said "I don't normally pick people up, but a little voice said I should offer you a ride." I said, "A little voice or, the Holy Spirit?" He almost sighed and said, "Thank you." He was thanking me for acknowledging that it was the Holy Spirit speaking to him. The driver's name was Doug and his passenger was Dallace. As we traveled we talked about how Christians seemed to be afraid to admit that God speaks to them. As in this case, Doug preferred to say "A little voice" instead of saying "God" or "the Holy Spirit". What a far cry from the apostles who, after being beaten for preaching the gospel, would go right back on the streets and preach again. And, in total defiance, told the religious leaders that they had to continue spreading the gospel.

Nowadays, too many are afraid to even admit that they believe in God, at risk of ridicule. This is what Jesus meant when he was talking about being ashamed of him. Many will confess Jesus as Lord of their life, as long as they are among believers, but don't mention him among non-believers. These people think they are safe. But, it is when you can stand and be run down for your belief, that you are blessed. As Jesus says in Matthew 5:10-12 *"Blessed are those who have been persecuted for the sake of righteousness, for theirs is the kingdom of heaven. Blessed are*

*you when people insult you and persecute you, and falsely say all
kinds of evil against you because of Me. Rejoice and be glad, for
your reward in heaven is great; for in the same way they
persecuted the prophets who were before you.* (NASB)

Doug drove me to Beaver Creek, OH, and dropped me off
at an intersection with a few businesses. He left, hopefully with a
new courage to speak out about his belief in God, and I found a
convenience store with some booths. I sat there for a while,
drinking a Coke and plotting my route.

When I was done it was still only about 3:30 PM, and I had
only actually walked a mile so for the day. Although there were
a couple churches nearby I didn't want to stop yet. The route
towards Dayton, OH was a hiking/bike trail that ran along U.S.
35 Highway. It would be about 6 miles before I started walking
on roads again; I headed towards the trail and began my hike.

As my head still hurt, I wasn't walking fast, and before I
knew it daylight was already slipping away. I met an elderly
couple, out for a walk, and engaged in conversation with them.
They told me that there was a church at an intersection of the trail
where I might set up for the night, but, less than a mile past that,
was another intersection that would have restaurants near it.

As it was a nice evening and I didn't have the threat of not
being seen by motorists on the trail, I continued on until I came to
Spinning Road. I could see signs from fast food restaurants on an
adjoining road. As I was getting off the trail, I saw a spot that
would be an excellent place to set my tent up for the night. I had,
pretty much, decided to come back after I ate, figuring that it
would have me on the trail the next morning, ready to go.

Continuing to the nearest restaurant I ate, then headed back
to the spot I had noticed at the trail. I was just about to turn,
when I looked ahead and saw a sign for East Dayton Baptist
Church. I thought about going there, instead of back to the trail,
and debated which to do. I felt led to go to the church. After
praying for a minute, and still feeling led to go to the church, I
walked the extra distance to the church. The church was built
back off of the road quite a ways, with the entrance to the parking

lot on the street to the west side. There was one pickup truck in the parking lot, but no lights in front were on, and all the front doors were locked.

I walked around to the back and, as I rounded the corner of the building, two cars were leaving the parking lot. There was one car still there, so I figured that there must have been a board meeting or something. I went to the door closest to the car and, sure enough, it was unlocked. As I entered the building I was calling out "hello?", as I didn't want to startle anyone or have them think I was up to no good when they found me wandering around inside the church.

My calls were soon answered and I followed a voice to a hallway where I was met by a man wearing a yarmulke. He introduced himself as Rabbi Tzion and added that he was a Messianic Jew, which I had already assumed.

Rabbi Tzion led a small group of Messianic Jews, who met in the Baptist church. The church had given them their own room for study and worship and it was nicely decorated. He and I started talking and I asked about what one Jewish lady had said to me while we were discussing Yeshua being the Messiah. She said that he hadn't fulfilled all the prophecies, wasn't supposed to be a deity, and, that he wasn't going to be given a second chance (which is what we consider the second coming).

Rabbi Tzion explained that it was what the more modern writers (post-first century) had written to discredit Jesus, and this had deceived many. He explained that, most of the rabbinical studies are from writers from the third century on. He said if you get into the older writing, they talk about the deity of the Messiah.

Rabbi Tzion and I talked for close to three hours. He taught me about the significance of praying prostrate, how it symbolizes offering your life to the King, about the incense and other Jewish traditions; a gleam in his eyes showing his great passion for the Father *and* the Son.

We talked so late that the church phone started ringing and, it was his wife, worried about him. Rabbi Tzion made a couple phone calls to make sure that, at least someone from the church was aware that I would be spending the night on the grounds, then came out with me to the tent to make sure I had everything I needed, praying together before he left.

## Tuesday-November 3, 2009

It was another wet night. No rain, just enough dew to make everything as wet as if it had rained. After eating the apple pies I had bought the night before, I headed down the road, making my way through Dayton, OH.

The route I took was through an older section of town, first through an old industrial area then, an old residential area and, finally an old business area. I stopped for lunch at a Mexican restaurant and then headed into the downtown area of Dayton, OH, finally making it to the west side.

I walked until about 4:00pm, when I came to what looked like the edge of the Metro area. After getting something to eat, I walked through Drexel, then in to New Lebanon, stopping to look for a place to set up my tent for the night.

I found the New Lebanon Assembly of God. It had a parsonage and, although I felt bad about knocking on the door of the parsonage as it was getting late, it was the last church in town. I considered just setting up, but I didn't want them to wake up, surprised to find me in their back yard in the morning. I received permission from the pastor to use the grounds and went around back to find a place to set-up my tent.

It was already cold by the time I got set up and into my blanket and sleeping bag. I was grateful for the sleeping mat Jeremy had bought me a few days earlier as it put a nice insulator between me and the ground.

## Wednesday-November 4, 2009

Cold and wet! Once again, no rain just heavy dew, and, once again, I didn't want to get out of the sleeping bag. I hurried to get dressed, ate some of my crackers with some peanut butter and headed East on Highway 35. I had walked for about three miles when I came to a Farm Market named Tükens Orchard.

I was more than ready for a break, so I walked up to the store door, only to find that it wasn't open. There was a pickup truck in the parking lot that didn't have a tailgate so, I set my backpack in the bed of it and dug out one of the meals that I had been given in Florida.

As I was standing there, eating a cookie from the meal, a man came out of the back door of the house and asked if he could help me. I introduced myself to him and explained what I was doing. He said his name was Frank. He was the owner of the farm and told me that the store wasn't open today as he had to run some errands. I told him that I had been hoping to use the restroom and buy a couple of apples from the store. Frank let me into the store to use the restroom and, while I was in there, he assembled a bag with about 3 pounds of apples, some cookies and a small loaf of apple bread from the store.

I could tell that Frank had a heavy heart, and as we talked, I mentioned it. Frank told me that he had some ducks that had been hit and killed on the road that morning and, that the driver didn't even stop. I didn't feel that was the reason for the heavy heart, but, I could tell it may have triggered something deep inside of him to cause the heaviness. We continued talking and he opened up, sharing that he had lost his daughter earlier in the spring –and of course it had put a strain on him.

I just let Frank talk. He told me about her, things they had done together, and how he missed her. Then I prayed with Frank; I prayed that God would send peace, comfort and healing.

As has happened many times during this journey, God had appointed a meeting with someone and, once the appointment is over, God provides transportation. I had only walked about half a mile from the Farm Market, and decided to sit on a guardrail for a minute. While I sat there, eating some of the apple bread Frank had given me, a pickup pulled to the side of the road and I was offered a ride into West Alexandria, OH.

I never did get the man's name. He had his three young kids, all strapped in car seats and booster seats, in the truck and I rode in the back end, but he took me to the west edge West Alexandria and dropped me off. I made my way to Eaton, OH, which was about five miles away.

This was another town that seemed as though time had forgotten it. To walk down the street just seemed as though you were in a different, simpler time. As I walked down U.S. 35, which was lined with shops, I decided to go into one called Crosswalk Coffee. I hadn't had any coffee yet and I hoped that I had enough for a regular cup.

The Coffeehouse was a small, relaxed shop, with easy listening music playing. There was a man and a woman working there who, I later found out, were the husband/wife team of Nevi and Sheryl. I asked how much a cup was and then counted up what change I had, which was just enough. As I was handing the change over the counter, Nevi asked if that was all that I had, and when I told him that it was, he told me to keep it. Giving him my thanks, I sat at a table, pulling out my notebook.

Sheryl was beginning to decorate the coffee shop for Christmas, but took some time to talk to me and ask about my backpack. After I told her about my journey, she asked if I would like something to eat. At first I declined, but then, at her insistence, accepted a bowl of soup and sat there for a good hour, enjoying the atmosphere. When I felt it was time to leave, I thanked Nevi and Sheryl one more time and, moved on down the road.

This time I was just barely outside of Eaton when a vehicle pulled in front of me and, an elderly man offered me a ride. The vehicle was loud and the seals on the doors were worn out so there wasn't any talking. He dropped me off just east of Richmond, IN, on U.S. Highway 40, and I walked into town; finding a place to go online, and figure out exactly where I was. Left, hoping to find a church on the main street going into town.

Just a few hundred yards later, I passed a pickup truck, that was waiting to exit a parking lot. The driver called out and asked if I would like a ride somewhere. It was rare that I get offered a ride inside a city and, this was only the second time that I had been offered a ride after dark. I told the driver that I was looking for a church that might have a Wednesday evening service and he said that he would help me find one.

This young man's name was Jeremy. As he drove me around to a couple churches that he knew, he was telling me about himself. Jeremy was a disable veteran, having served in Iraq and Afghanistan. He told me how he had been shot 6 times in Iraq and, how every shot had hit his vest. Then, during a tour in Afghanistan, his Humvee was hit by an IED. He nearly died, but for the grace of God. Since coming through that had renewed his walk with God. He talked about how, so many of the people he knew were having emotional problems dealing with Iraq and Afghanistan but, while he had nightmares and memories of it, he had a peace that he knew was only through his walk with God.

Jeremy asked about me spending the cold nights outside and I had to admit to him that my sleeping bag was inadequate for the colder weather and that, even though I had a fleece blanket as well, it was still getting cool enough to be uncomfortable some nights. He told me about the new sleeping bags that the military used and how the ultra-thin bag was good to freezing temperatures.

Eventually, we were at Victory Baptist Church, and he went inside with me, telling the people there about me, and what an inspiration I was. I told him that *he* was the inspiration and should be going around, telling *his* testimony. I told Jeremy that I didn't feel that God let him live just so he could live longer. God wanted him to use his testimony as a witness, to minister to others. I could see him going from place to place, sharing his story and encouraging others to commit their lives to God, or deepen their commitment to God.

The church was without a pastor, so when one of the leaders of the church arrived, I asked about setting my tent up on the lawn for the night. One of the ladies recommended that I be allowed to sleep inside the church where it would be warmer. It was agreed upon that this would be better, and we proceeded to have Wednesday service.

When it was over, we went to the back door, where I had left my backpack, and there, on top of it, was a new style, military sleeping bag. At some point during the service, Jeremy had returned and left his sleeping bag for me.

As I prayed that night I asked for an extra blessing on not only Jeremy, but on all the men and women that sacrifice every-day for our freedom.


**Thursday-November 5, 2009**

There are some days when God's hand is so evident that, even the biggest skeptic has to see it. This was one of those days. I awoke at about 6:00am, but, as the sun was rising later and later, decided to take time to shave and wash up before heading out.

I finally got on the road about 8:00am, walked two blocks to U.S. Highway 40 and a block to Centerville Road, where I was to turn. The first car I saw this morning, pulled through the intersection, stopped, and the driver asked where I was going. The driver, a lady named Kim, offered to take me to Hagarstown, IN, which was about 15 miles.

Once again, I was told about how, "I never pick people up along the road, But..." Kim told me that, just the night before, she and one of her friends were talking about how they would like to hike around a country, but thought that would be safer to do in England.

She took me into Hagarstown and, actually went further into town than she had intended, as to drop me off near the west side of town. I continued walking west on State Road 38, and had only walked about 1 mile outside of town, when a Pickup truck, coming towards me, made a U-turn, pulled over to the side of the road, and the driver offered me a ride.

As it turned out, he wasn't planning on going as far as he did either. He took me to New Castle, IN and dropped me off in a parking lot, near a small shopping center, giving me enough money to buy lunch.

There was a KFC next door and I decided, as I hadn't had breakfast, to get an early lunch. It was about 15 minutes before they opened and, as I waited, two vehicles pulled up. One was a van, there to pick up a donation for a woman's shelter. In conversation with the driver, talking about my journey and mission, I mentioned that I was going to try and make it to Pendleton by evening. The other man there was Danny Walters, who, in overhearing our conversation, said "Well, if you can wait until I get a bucket of Chicken, I'm going to Pendleton."

Danny took me to Pendleton and I went online and plot my next move. By 1:00pm I had traveled about forty-eight miles – and had walked only one. Seeing that I was only about twelve miles to Noblesville and, that there were churches along the way, I decided to continue along State Road 38.

I don't know how I did it. I was sure that I was on Road 38 leaving Pendleton. But I was apparently on State Road 9/67 and, after an hour of walking and not coming to the interstate that I had seen on the map, I began wondering if I was going the right way. Finally, I came to the interstate where there was a truck stop and asked about my location. It turned out that I was North of where I wanted to be. After checking online, I decided that I would have to spend the night in Anderson, IN.

I found a place to get supper, and located a church, where I figured I would be able spend the night.

**Friday-November 6, 2009**

It's definitely getting closer to winter. The ground had a heavy frost on it this morning and it was all I could do to get out of the sleeping bag. I was so thankful for the military sleeping bag that Jeremy had given me just a few days before. As I'm nearing the end of my journey, the nights and mornings are reminding me of the beginning of the journey. Even though I was on the edge of town, I walked two blocks to a convenience store for a large cup of hot coffee to drink as I broke camp.

I had been walking about 4 hours when a car pulled to the side of the road in front of me. The driver, a man who was maybe 38 or so, asked where I was headed. I said I was headed to Noblesville, and he said he would get me there. Once in the car, he introduced himself as Frank. Frank was unemployed, but believed that if he helped others out, God would take care of him; And, according to Frank, God had done just that. I agreed with Frank and we talked about reaping what you sow

As I told him about my journey and talked about my intent to have been at Noblesville the previous day, I suddenly realized that this, like so many others, was a meeting ordained by God. Had I not made the wrong turn the day before, I wouldn't have been on the road that Frank had picked me up on.

Frank asked where I needed to go in Noblesville and answered that I intended to head out of Noblesville on State road 38 towards Sheridan. Frank made a phone call and told the party on the other end that he would be late, as he was going to drive to Sheridan. Sure enough, when we arrived at the intersection in Noblesville where 38 headed northwest, Frank turned. I was able to minister to and pray with Frank about his job before we parted ways in Sheridan.

The next town, with any real population, was Thorntown, IN, which was about eighteen miles away. It was just noon and, not feeling led to stay where I was, I headed west on State Highway 47. As it was starting to get dark, I came to Elizaville, Indiana. I pitched my tent at one of the two churches there, and after eating part of a ration pack for dinner, I retired for the night.

## Saturday-November 7, 2009

The night was just opposite of the previous night. The air was warm and dry, and it was a very pleasant morning. I broke camp and was ready to go at sunrise.

Less than half a mile of walking down Highway 47, I saw a pickup truck, going the opposite direction, and felt like that was my ride; watching as it went up the road and turned into a driveway. Ten minutes later the same truck went passed me and pulled into a parking lot just ahead of me. As I was about to pass in front of it, the driver asked where I was headed. I told him that

I was trying to get to the intersection of Road 47 and U.S. 52 Highway. He offered me a ride and we were off, westbound.

He introduced himself as Nathan, and asked about my presence there, so I shared about my journey with him. I told him that I had actually gone through Thorntown earlier in the summer and, mentioned that I had second cousins that were the directors of the Teen Challenge in Lebanon, Indiana. Nathan said that his parents were big into working at Teen Challenge and asked what my cousins' names were. I told him Dawn and Dave Rose and he asked if I was kidding. As it turned out, he had gone to school with one of my third cousins and Dave had been a substitute teacher on occasion.

The rest of the way to Thorntown, Nathan and I talked about the way God lines things up in our lives. When we reached the intersection of State Highway 47 and U.S. Highway 52 Nathan turned towards Lebanon and kept going. I mentioned that I needed to be headed the other direction, he acknowledged that he was aware of that, but had decided to take me to get something to eat first.

He bought me breakfast in Lebanon and then returned me to Thorntown, dropping me off at the intersection of the two highways, where I turned to the north, retracing the steps I had taken months earlier. This was the only stretch of road I would be on twice during the journey.

I hadn't walked a full mile when a Police Officer, southbound on 52 Highway, pulled into a turn-a-round and parked. He exited his patrol car and, as he was walking towards me, asked how everything was going. My response was that it was going well, and he began asking me typical questions, where I was going etc. After he verified that I wasn't wanted anywhere, he loaded me up into his patrol car and drove me about 10 miles, to the County Line.

I thanked him and started back up the road –but before I had gone another 100 yards, a van pulled beside me. It was occupied by a woman driver and a younger passenger. The driver called across the van and asked me where I was headed. I told her Lafayette and she offered me a ride.

They were Laniya and her son, Royce. I was telling them about my journey and she, finding it exciting, was asking all kinds of questions. She asked what denomination I was and I told her that I was Pentecostal, and Laniya took me to the First Assembly of God Church, in Lafayette. It was only about 10:00 in the morning, but the church was abuzz with activity. As it turned out, they were doing extensive remodeling of an area of the building.

I asked about the pastor and was directed to Robbie Wilson, the Children's Pastor. Arrangements were made for me to pitch my tent on the church grounds. My questions about a place to wash up and a Laundromat nearby got the reply from Robbie that they had both a shower and laundry facilities at the church, so after showering, I spent the rest of the day working on my journal and washing my clothes.

## Sunday-November 8, 2009

Pastor Robbie had told me that someone would be there to open the church about an hour before the first service and so I was up and had eaten breakfast early –ready to wash up and change clothes when it was opened.

The church was finishing its mission's week and the service was nothing less than inspirational. Pastor Hackett talked about the early days of the Assemblies of God and how its early missionaries would get a boat ticket to a country, not knowing how or where they would live; and say goodbye to families, not knowing if they would ever return to see them again.

The afternoon was spent writing, reading and praying and, when it was time, I returned to the church. The guest speaker was a former addict, and Teen Challenge graduate, who had started an inner-city ministry. He had not only succeeded in that outreach, but had planted several inner-city churches. What intrigued me the most was that he had done it totally on faith; leaving the life that he knew, he had gotten off the bus at an inner-city stop, asking God what to do next.

More and more, I am feeling that this is what God wants me to do, serve people, totally relying on him for everything.

### Monday-November 9, 2009

I had looked at the map of Lafayette the night before, and realized that it was a bigger city than I had thought. The nearest town west of it was Pine Village, IN; about 22 miles from where I was. I stopped to get breakfast –with a quick online check for email, which led to being caught up in chat for a while, so I didn't get started walking until after 9:00am. Then, I had to walk through city traffic, stopping at nearly every intersection, waiting at the crosswalks, so I was still in Lafayette at 1:00, and stopped for lunch.

As the sun started to go down, the air was starting to get chilly. There didn't seem to be anything around but farm land, but I finally came to an area which, at first glance, I thought was a park in the middle of nowhere. It turned out to be a wildlife area for Purdue University. I found a caretaker's house just up the road, and obtained permission to set up for the night.

### Tuesday-November 10, 2009

Today started a sequence of events that, even after all I've been through with God, just left me in awe.

I knew I still had a good 10 miles to go before I was in Pine Village and, I had finished the last of my food the night before. That translated into nearly 5 hours of walking with the 80 lbs. backpack before I would be eating anything. I was up and ready to go at first light, and started walking on State Highway 26. I had just reached the next farm when a car went past me, stopped, and backed up.

The driver was a young Hispanic man named Fernando. He asked where I was headed and, when I told him, he said that, while he wasn't going the entire way there, he could get me several miles closer, apologizing for not being able to take me all the way into Pine Village.

Fernando worked two jobs, one at a McDonald's in

Lafayette, and another on a farm. He was running late getting to the farm, but even so, he knew that he needed to stop and help me as much as he could. He dropped me off about eight miles closer to Pine Village, leaving me only a couple miles to walk into Pine Village, which I made in less than an hour.

On the main street of Pine Village I found a small cafe and went inside to get breakfast. There were few customers there. The waitress, whose name I think was Darlene –it sounded like everyone just called her darling –asked me about my backpack and I told her about my journey.

Before long, more people started coming in, and soon there were a good fifteen people there. Each time new customers arrived, they were told about me as they were having their orders taken. Some asked me questions and listened as I told them about my adventures. At one point, a man, whom I later learned was Charles Coffman –and that he was 84 years young –came up and asked 'if the offering plate was out' as he gave me a love gift.

As I was thinking of heading on down the road, Charles came back to me and said that he was going to be driving about 40 miles up the road in the early afternoon, if I was interested in waiting for a ride. I told him that I would appreciate that, and that I would spend the morning working on my journal and be there when he was ready to leave.

I had already paid for my meal, but as I had planned on walking that day, I hadn't ordered coffee with my breakfast. Now, since I wouldn't be walking until afternoon, I went ahead and ordered some. People came and went throughout the morning, and one lady who had been told about me, told Darlene that she wanted to pay for my meal. She seemed disappointed that my coffee was all there was to pay for.

A few minutes after noon, Charles and Barbara (his wife) returned for lunch, which they had with their Sunday School group and, after they were finished, Charles and I headed west on State Road 26, talking about spiritual maturity and so many things of God during the ride that I couldn't begin to account them all.

We drove west for about 20 miles and then we turned... southbound. I knew that Indiana 26 would turn into Illinois 9, which would take me straight into Bloomington IL. I considered having Charles drop me off but, after a moment of thinking and praying, I decided to let the wind of the Holy Spirit take me where I was to go.

Before long, Charles let me off at a truck stop at U.S. 136 and Lynch Road, on the outskirts of Danville, IL. After praying with him and expressing my thanks, I went into the truck stop and got online to ascertain my location and obtain directions. As it was still only about 3:00pm, I decided that I could easily get through Danville before dark, and I headed out on Highway 136 towards Highway 150.

I was in downtown Danville when I saw a man, walking the opposite direction, on the other side of the street, cross over and walk towards me. As he got within speaking distance he said, "If I were you, I'd keep walking until I was out of this _ _ _ _ _ _ _ town." and he kept walking.

This kind of took me back for a second, but then my thought was "Huh, Satan doesn't want me here for some reason." So, of course, I began to walk slower, taking my time as I traveled, until I'd made it through the Downtown area and into the residential. As the afternoon progressed, I passed different restaurants and churches, not feeling led to stop at any of them to eat or stay for the night. I continued walking into the darkness, passing a few more restaurants and churches until I was finally led to stop at a restaurant on the edge of Danville.

It was The Little Nugget, a steak house, which would cost more than I would normally spend, but it is where I was led to stop, as well as seeming to be the last place for miles. I went in and found a seat, and before long, a waitress was there to take my order. She was curious about my backpack and I told her about my adventure and then ordered –only a hamburger, as I was watching my funds. The waitress, Linda, asked if that was all I wanted. I told her that I was living on faith and that was all I could afford at the moment. A few minutes later, she returned with the hamburger, and an order of homemade potato chips, saying that the chips were on the house.

As I ate, I looked for churches online, finding one that was just a few blocks away; Hillery Assembly of God. Done, I paid for my meal, and went to hand her a tip, but she said "don't you dare leave me a tip. I'm trying to bless you." Giving her my thanks again, I left and headed to the church.

Knowing that it was far too late to find anyone there, I set my tent up. I wonder what it was that Satan had tried to keep me from. I didn't feel as though anything had happened to that point, but from experience, know that it wasn't always right away. God's timing would have me where I needed to be at the right time, as long as I sought his will.

After thanking God for the day and, spending some time just listening for His voice, I turned in for the night.

## Wednesday-November 11, 2009

It was yet another cold night. The humidity wasn't too bad though, so at least the tent was dry and ready to roll up once I got myself out of the sleeping bag. As I was doing this I heard a voice asking if I had spent the night there. I turned and saw a man walking across the church lawn towards me. I told him that I had, explaining that I had gotten there late the night before and hadn't found anyone around to ask permission from.

The man assured me that it wasn't a problem and asked if I would like a cup of coffee. I accepted and he pointed to a house directly in back of the church, telling me to come over as soon as I had everything packed up. When I got there a few minutes later, and officially introduced myself to him, he told me his name was Ron and introduced his son, Drew.

We enjoyed a cup of coffee while Ron told me how they had come to start attending the church and then, all of a sudden, as though someone had told him "IT'S TIME", Ron said "You know we have a gospel track print shop here, don't you?" I responded that didn't know that. Ron grabbed his hat and said,

"Come on," and walked out the door. I followed him to the street in front of the house and, about half a block away, we came to a small building. Once inside, it was evident that this was a print shop and I was introduced to the owner who started giving me a tour. It was now that it was revealed to me why Satan didn't want me there.

As I was getting the tour, I saw a group of three come into the shop. Two were an elderly, white couple. The third was a younger man, about 30, and my first impression was "he's from India." He was neatly dressed in a leisure suit –in contrast to my worn shoes, faded T-shirt, thread bare jeans and old vinyl jacket, not to mention my lack of shaving for two days.

What happened next so surprised me, that it almost left me speechless. This man, eyes set straight on me, walked up to me like I was supposed to be in charge, reached out his hand and said "I am Christudas Earla, I am from India!" I know that is all he verbally said, but, what I heard in the Spirit was "God has brought us together. How may I serve you?"

Even though I was taken aback, I immediately asked, "What part of India?" and he responded 'Andhra Pradesh.' "What part of the Andhra Pradesh?" I questioned. He answered, 'The Krishna District.' and I asked "Do you know where Hanuman junction is?" He responded "Yes, it is not very far from my village." I asked "Do you happen to speak Telugu?" His eyes lit up as he said "Why yes, that is my native language!"

I proceeded to tell him about Village Gospel Team, and about Bobby, trying to care for the kids from the street after his father, Pastor Job, passed away and how Pastor Job had helped train people to take the Gospel out and helped plant churches.

I told him how Bobby had told me just a few days earlier that the pastors, with no one to guide them, were starting to go their own ways. Then Christudas exclaimed "That is part of my ministry, to train and empower pastors!" We talked several more minutes. I gave him the information to contact Bobby and he said he would see how he might assist him in the ministry.

Christudas gave me a pamphlet on GAP Ministries, which

had his information as well. As I read it later it didn't surprise me that his name meant "Christ's Servant".

Soon Ron, Drew and I headed back to the house and, after praying for them, I gathered my things and headed on down the road. It was already 10:30am and I had only coffee in my stomach. I knew from checking the map that it was about 5 miles to the next town and I would be there in about two and a half hours, so I didn't want a lot to eat.

There was a convenience store on the corner of U.S.150, so I decided that I would get something there to tide me over until I was where I could get food. I went to the store, leaving my backpack outside, got some milk and a toaster pastry. The man behind the counter rang it up and, as I was getting the money out of my wallet, he suddenly says, "Wait a minute.", hits the clear key and says, "You're an evangelist, you don't have to pay!"

What I was thinking was, "Shoot, I should have gone for the sandwich." But I kind of chuckled and said, "And, what made you come to this conclusion?" Without batting an eye he said, "God just told me." His name was William and he was apparently the manager or owner of the store. We spent a good half hour talking about the things of God, with customers coming and going, some stopping for a moment to listen in or to give some input. By the time we were done it was close to 11:15, and I headed up Highway 150 with the knowledge that, unless God provided a ride for me, I wasn't going to get far before nightfall.

I did however make good time covering the miles to Oakwood, IL, and was sitting in a restaurant by 1:30 or so. As I almost always do, I found a spot out of the way, took my backpack off and pushed it as far back as I could, then went up to the counter and ordered a meal. Upon returning to my table I took my netbook out and started checking email and such.

I was sitting there when a group of women sat at a booth and began talking. They talked about their kids and grand kids; one of them started talking about needing to change clothes before church that night, then, I heard something that blew me away.

One of them started talking about how she had passed a man, carrying a backpack, that morning. Even though I pick up many conversations, this one really grabbed my attention. It soon became apparent from the location and the description, that I was the man she had passed. In the short time that it had been since she could have passed me, I had become an ex-con, probably just released from the prison in Danville and, bent on finding an unsuspecting victim in a small town along the roadway to rob, rape or murder, otherwise, 'why would he have been on the back road instead of the interstate?' It really amazed me that in one breath, the conversation had gone from what to wear to church, to judging someone walking down the road, to the extent of practically accusing them of murder.

I was ready to leave, but being who I am and, not really feeling led to actually *say* something to these self-righteous women, I decided to say it without many words. I stood up, packed my computer away, and then with as much show as possible, pulled my backpack away from the wall and hoisted it up onto the table, where I could get it on easier.

You could have heard a pin drop as the women realized that it was me they had been talking about. I slid the backpack on and, as I walked passed them, I said, "You ladies have a good afternoon, and May God bless you!" Sometimes the best thing we can do is show God's love and give people something to reflect on.

I knew I had spent too much time on lunch, and was also sure that I wasn't going to get much further but, it was too early to stop for the day. The map had shown that there was a town about 10 miles further. As the days were getting shorter all the time, I was in doubt that I would make it before sundown without God providing a ride. I walked until past dark, coming to the small town of Fithian Illinois, population: 200.

About the time I thought I would be missing a meal, I saw a sign in the small business district that said, Main Street Cafe. I should have known. God had never let me down yet and would not have left me without. I went inside and was greeted by a man who seemed surprised to see me –I would imagine that the clientele was pretty regular there.

As expected, the owner of the restaurant was curious about my adventure and, after taking my order, sat and listened to my stories while the cook prepared my food. I asked him about a church that might have a Wednesday evening service, and he said that the only church in town was the United Methodist. He also said he believed that it had some function on Wednesday as the couple that lived across from the cafe walked there each week.

Soon, his wife and kids came in and he was occupied with them. I finished eating, and he came over to ask if he could get me anything else. When I told him that I was good and just needed the check, he told me that the meal was taken care of and wished me a good night. I thanked him and his wife and headed towards the church.

It only took a minute to walk to the church and I found it open. Going inside, I could hear music and came to the conclusion that the Worship team or choir were practicing. I was greeted shortly by a young man, who introduced himself as Josh. I asked if the pastor was there, and he told me that she would be arriving shortly. When I asked if there was a service that evening, he said that there wasn't, but that the pastor shepherded three churches and, the leaders in the churches would be having a study. He said he was sure I would be able to sit in on it.

Within minutes Pastor Kim Dancey arrived and I shared my journey with her, making my petition of a place to set my tent up. Without a second thought, she showed me the only space there was to set a tent. It wasn't much room, but I figured the tent would fit.

We talked for a few minutes about some of my experiences during my journey, and then she asked if I needed a shower, which I did, so she drove me the block to the parsonage. As she showed me where the shower was, she began apologizing that I couldn't sleep in the house, as her husband was out of town and, it just wouldn't be right for me to be in the house at night. I let her know that I fully understood and assured her that I would be fine in my tent. She goes; "OH, no, no, you don't have to do that, you can sleep in the church, just not in the house."

After showing me where things were, and offering up anything in the refrigerator, she left to return to the church while I shaved and showered.

I arrived back at the church just as the leaders were about to start their study. There were about 9 or 10 of us there and, after opening with prayer, Pastor Kim asked if I would share about my journey with the others. I did, answering numerous questions about it before we started into the study.

We read in Nehemiah where Ezra read the books of Moses to the people and how the people worshiped. Then Pastor Kim started a discussion on how to worship, based on the scriptures. The study went on for about an hour, after which Pastor Kim wanted to know if they could pray for me, which of course, was fine by me. The group gathered around me and laid hands on me and, taking turns, several of them prayed over my safety, health, ministry and such. Afterward, a few of them slipped me love gifts to help me on my way. One, whose name was Bob, said that he worked in Champaign and wondered if I would like a ride in the morning, and another one, Jean, suggested that we stop at her house for breakfast with her and her husband before we left.

Arrangements were made and people started leaving. Bob and Pastor Kim showed me where the kitchen was and let me know that I was welcome to anything there-- most of which was for the youth group-- then left me to bed down for the night.

After eating some ice cream, potato chips and drinking a bottle of Coke, I set my alarm and turned in for the night.

**Thursday-November 12, 2009**

Bob showed up just as I was finishing packing, and we headed to Jean's house to have breakfast. Our dining companions were wonderful, not to mention the delicious, home cooked meal.

Bob and I headed to Champaign and he dropped me off in Champaign, IL. I went to a doughnut shop and, after getting a cup of coffee, went online to plan the day's travel. It was about a five mile walk through town and there were only a couple turns. Something I should be able to do in a couple of hours. Yet I didn't feel rushed. I actually felt like I was supposed to take my time getting out of town.

I played around on Facebook for a while, checked email, wrote in my journal, and then, at about 11:00am, headed out, walking into Champaign. I got to the north part of town about 1:00pm. I wasn't really hungry yet, but found a place to get some french fries, spending the time resting and writing. It wasn't until about 4:00 that I felt it was time to leave, and I headed out to finish my last couple miles in town, thinking that maybe there was a church I was supposed to be at for the night or something.

It was beginning to get dark out, and I was sure that, unless I was wrong with how I had interpreted the feeling of not needing to rush out of town, God had something for me in sight. The business area ended, leaving Interstate 74 on my right, and a residential area on my left. Over the next mile I passed the Garden Hill Baptist Church, which looked like an ideal place to spend the night, but felt nothing leading me to go there. Then I was out of town. There were a few scattered industrial buildings here and there and farm land. Though it was dark now, I kept walking, wondering what it was that God was leading me into.

It is times like this that Satan likes to attack. He likes to convince you that God isn't really leading you. He throws darts with thoughts like, "If God was leading you, why would he bring you into the wilderness." Many believers are swayed by this. They feel that God wants them to do something detrimental or, that God had led them somewhere for punishment or, that God isn't really leading them at all. By this time in my journey, if I let Satan deceive me like that, I would deserve what I get. I knew that, if God led me here, he had a purpose in it. Even if it wasn't evident right away, I would trust in God's timing.

As if on cue, like God was just waiting for me to express my faith in him, a small car pulled to the side of the road ahead of me. As I approached it, a middle aged woman called out, asking where I was headed. I told her that I was just trying to get to the next town, and she said that she was going to Mansfield, which was about 12 miles. I told her that would be great and loaded my backpack into her car.

As I got into the car I told her my name, and she said her name was Donna. I thanked her for the ride and let her know how unusual it was to be offered a ride after sundown. Donna just bluntly said, "I saw you and God told me that you were His servant on a journey. There was never a question of whether or not to pick you up." I was thinking "Whoa, cool, I like it when God tells people that."

I told Donna about my journey and she in turn told me her testimony. She had been addicted to drugs and on a one-way suicidal path to destruction when God pulled her out of it, delivered her from drugs and put her in a Godly relationship with a wonderful man.

After talking for a while she asked if it would be Okay to take me further than Mansfield. I said that it would be, and Donna called her husband to let him know. After explaining the situation to Michael (his name), she handed me the phone and asked that I tell him about my journey. Michael and I talked for about 5 minutes about the journey and the greatness of God. It was like talking to an old friend.

We went on to Farmer City, where Donna stopped at a truck stop, saying repeatedly that she felt so guilty just dropping me off there. I assured her that I was fine and that if she hadn't picked me up, I would have found a place at the side of the road. Before she left, we prayed for each other, and she gave me a small love gift to get a meal with. I thanked her and once she left, went into the store where I figured out my location and searched for a place to spend the night.

I found that there were several churches in the town, and chose one which wouldn't be too far and that was close to Highway 150. It was the First Baptist Church, which I came to after walking a short distance. I discovered that it was actually what seemed to be a group of buildings. The older building seemed to be attached to a house, where the lights were on, so I went to the door and knocked. A moment later it was answered by a young child, and I asked if it was the parsonage.

The pastor's wife came to the door and I explained myself and asked about setting my tent up for the night. She said that the pastor was at the church, and sent one of the kids running out the back door to let him know I was there, then told me how to get to where he was.

I found the pastor, Pastor Michael Jenkins, as was coming out of the back door of the church. Once more I explained my journey and made my petition to set my tent up for the night. He had no problem with it and showed me a nice flat, grassy area to set up on. As we talked, he decided to leave the door of the church open so I could use the restroom. He also showed me where the kitchen was, giving me permission to eat whatever was there and to make coffee in the morning.

### Friday-November 13, 2009

On this supposedly 'unlucky' day, I slept until about 7:00, got up, went into a nice, warm church to start a pot of coffee. After I washed up, I packed up my tent, then sat in the kitchen for a couple of hours reading my Bible and drinking coffee. I don't know if it was just that I knew I was ahead of schedule or the Holy Spirit just telling me to relax, but I was in no hurry to leave.

When I was finally ready, I walked out the door just as an elderly couple were about to come in. Their names were Richard and Jeannie, and they were interested in knowing about my backpack and my situation. I spent a few minutes telling them about my journey, mentioning that Pastor Michael had allowed me to set up there, with access to the building. We talked for another several minutes before I headed on down the road. It was already late morning, but I only had a ten mile walk to the next town.

I really didn't expect to get a ride here. Like it had been since Danville, the towns were connected by the Interstate and the highway was basically used by farmers, traveling in farm equipment, in between towns. I was wrong! I walked through

267

Farmer City and, once I was out of town, hadn't walked half a mile when a pickup pulled over in front of me and a young man offered me a ride.

His name was Wes and he was headed to Le Roy, IL on an errand. We didn't engage in any deep theological discussion, rather, Wes just talked about the area, how you could see for miles when there were no crops in the way, about how good God had been to them during the growing season. It seems that, in this area at least, the bounty was bigger than the storage and the grain elevators couldn't get the grain out fast enough. Many of the crops were still in the fields.

Wes dropped me off in Le Roy and I went inside a fast food restaurant, and, after getting something to eat, retreated to a booth in the back corner. I ate and then just spent some more time praying and reading. I was ahead of schedule and felt no leading to press on any further for the day. I spent part of the afternoon there, and then went to find a Western Union to send some money to take care of the kids in India.

The Le Roy Christian Church was across from the truck stop and I stopped in there, finding one person in the office, and got permission to set up my tent for the night.

## Saturday-November 14, 2009

It was a beautiful sunrise! I was able to capture it with my camera before heading back to the truck stop to use the facilities and get breakfast. In the restaurant was one of the workers that had been there the day before. She bought me breakfast and then took several minutes to listen about my journey and about my faith in God.

I plotted my route out for the day and, by about 8:30am, was headed through Le Roy, making my way up 150 Highway towards Bloomington IL, which was only about fifteen miles away. I'm not sure how far I walked that day. It was an extremely nice day and I could have easily walked the entire distance but, I was picked up by a man who was headed to Bloomington and I was there by noon, eating lunch.

I wrote for a while and then headed for a church that I found online, called Vale Community Church. Finding the doors open, I went inside and talked to the people at the information desk, explaining my journey to them. They located Pastor Ken Graham, who, after hearing my story, took me to the church's food pantry and started loading me up with food before showing me where I could set my tent up.

I asked if he knew where there were any Laundromats. A quick check of his phone book found that there were none close by, and he said that he would take my clothes home and have them washed. He also showed me to a men's room where I would have some privacy to wash up.

Once I was done, I gathered my clothes and gave them to him, then I spent the rest of the day writing until it was time to do the update.

**Sunday-November 15, 2009**

It started raining during the night, at some points quite heavily. The weather made a total turnaround from the previous day. I was awake by about 6:00 and the rain had slowed to a drizzle, so I made my way through the drizzle to a convenience store to get a cup of hot coffee.

When the first people arrived at the church, I went back to the restroom that Pastor Ken had shown me the previous afternoon and shaved. About the time I was done one of the maintenance men came in and told me that the pastor's wife was outside the back door, wanting to see me. She had my clothes, freshly washed and ready for me.

Once I was ready for the day I was told that the church served coffee and was shown where to get some. Several people came by, greeted me and listened to my adventures as we enjoyed fellowship before the service. I attended both morning services that day and, afterward, heading out to get across town so I would be close to the west side of Bloomington for the morning.

It was still drizzling and the temperature hadn't risen much from what it had been in the morning. As I walked on, I was totally surprised when I came to an intersection and, coming from the opposite direction, were several people, young and old, running in the cold drizzle. Some of them were so 'Hard core' that they weren't even wearing shirts. I don't know what they were running for, whether it was for a cause or just for fun, but I said a silent prayer for their health.

Turning west at that intersection, I soon came to a sandwich shop, where I went in, warmed up and got a late lunch/early dinner. While eating, I checked the map and thought I saw where I needed to go and, when I was done, headed north on Main Street. It was further than I thought it should be to find Highway 9, and I knew for sure that I was in the wrong place when I discovered that I was in Normal, IL.

I found a place to go online to see where I had messed up. Apparently, when I came out onto Main Street, I was further north than I thought. I was actually only a couple blocks south of Highway 9. It was about 4:30pm; I debated whether to backtrack or re plot my route. Feeling led to go back, I headed southbound, hoping to find a church that had an evening service.

I pressed on, finding the highway without coming to a suitable church and walked another half mile or so to a convenience store. I asked about any churches in the area, and was told that they were a couple blocks north and several blocks back to the east. As a rule, I don't backtrack, and with the area I was in, could have probably found a place to set up for the night, behind a building or something, but still feeling led, I went back north, then east.

I came to Harvest Family Worship Center. Their sign said they had a service that started at 7:00 but, as close as it was to 7:00, there were only two cars there. I went to the door near the cars and it was open, so I went inside, calling out so as not to startle anyone. I was rewarded with an answer, letting me know that they were downstairs. I walked down the stairs and into a room, where a small group of about six people, and, the one that seemed to be in charge was in a full sized wheelchair, obviously paralyzed from the neck down.

No Mere Coincidences, a journey of faith

I introduced myself, telling them that I was on a journey and asked if there was an evening service. I was told that there wasn't one, but I was welcome to join in on the baptism class they were having; accepting, I sat down.

The man in the chair said that he would like to hear more about the journey I was on, so, I shared with the small group, and they seemed intrigued by the accounts of my travels. As their leader asked more questions, it occurred to me that he wasn't just the leader of the class; he was the pastor of the church.

As the lesson continued, I was included as though I had been a member of the church for months, and when it was at an end, a couple ladies asked me more questions. They soon left and I was alone with the man and the woman I believed was his wife.

It's odd how, sometimes you can spend a few minutes with someone, feel that you know them, and not never even get their names. I asked and was told that they were Dale and Tammy Miller and they were co-pastors of the church.

They began asking me more about the Missionary Convention that I was heading to, and I told them that I had been praying for the funds to get some cards and fliers printed for it. Pastor Dale asked if I had something in mind and I told him that I had a design on my computer. Pastor Tammy made a phone call and asked if I could email the design to an address. I did and they arranged to have several cards and fliers made for me.

I had noticed that Pastor Dale's chair was pneumatic, operated by air pressure, delivered by a mouth tube. As we waited I asked about his situation. Pastor Dale had a remarkable story. He had been the pastor of the church for years, supplementing his pastor's income by painting houses. When he had a big job, he would hire his deacons to help him out.

He was bidding on a house, when the Holy Spirit told him that it would be the last house he painted. His thought was, there was going to be a financial breakthrough, making it possible for him to quit the painting for extra income.

One morning, as they were beginning to work, the Holy

Spirit told him that there would be a fall. Pastor Dale said that he prayed that God wouldn't let anything happen to his Deacons. Just moments later, the scaffolding *he* was on gave out, sending him to the ground. The account of events that followed was anything but coincidence. The list of people that were where they wouldn't normally be amazed even me. And, the support the Millers received from their congregation is nothing short of the epitome of love.

I don't know how long we talked that night, but it was long enough for several sheets of cards and fliers to be printed. Pastor Tammy cut them on a paper cutter. As everything was winding down, Pastor Dale told his wife to check with a hotel to put me in for the night. This sounded so wonderful to me; I was still damp from the day and hadn't been looking forward to waking up cold.

The hotel I was put up in was right on the edge of town, giving me a straight shot out of town in the morning. After taking a long, hot shower, I climbed into a nice warm bed, thinking, once again, about how we never realize how good we have it, until we don't have it for a while.

## Monday-November 16, 2009

I was in no hurry to leave the hotel. It was still cold and rainy outside, and nice, warm and comfortable inside. Besides, it was only about forty miles to my destination, and I had three days to get there. I took my time in eating the complimentary breakfast and was just kind of lazily getting my things gathered when the phone rang.

It was one of the ladies that had been at the church the night before. She had contacted the pastor and, discovering that I had been put in the motel, she wanted to know if she and her sister could take me to Peoria. Not looking forward to walking in the cold drizzle, I readily accepted the invitation.

Arrangements were made and, after getting packed and ready, I waited in the lobby until they arrived. As we traveled the distance I got to hear their testimonies of deliverance and reconciliation.

No Mere Coincidences, a journey of faith

Looking for a church, we found the Riverside Community Church, just blocks from the Convention Center, and we headed there. It was a large building which, as it turned out, was actually several different ministries. I introduced myself to a lady at an information desk and she contacted a man. When he arrived and I explained my situation. I asked him about a place to set up for the week. I was asked if I wouldn't prefer to be inside a building. I let him know that I would but, as my journey was not over until after the convention, I could only ask for a place to set my tent.

We headed off to locate the Peoria Recovery Mission, which is a men's shelter. After explaining my situation to the director, arrangements were made for me to spend the majority of the week there. I was, of course, expected to follow all the rules, but exceptions would be made on the curfew during the time of the missionary convention.

I found a place where I could get online, and posted that I had reached my destination of Peoria. Within minutes I had a message from a Facebook friend, who wanted to meet with me the next day. Arrangements were made and I spent the rest of the afternoon writing in my journal until it was time to go to the shelter.

The Peoria Recovery Mission was the most organized and well-run mission I had seen. Curfew was before dinner and everyone had to shower first. After dinner was a mandatory service in the chapel and lights-out was at 8:00pm. Wake up was at 5:00am and, if you wanted to eat lunch there, you had to attend the service at 11:00am.

**Tuesday-November 17, 2009**

Being in Peoria early gave me an opportunity to minister to some of the men at the mission for a couple days. One was of particular interest; his name was Steven –a middle aged man whom, I had been told, was Hindu.

I saw an opportunity to begin a dialog with him at lunch, where we were served Pizza. Plates were set out on the tables and each person got an assortment. I noticed that Steven's pizza was mostly sausage and pepperoni, where mine was mostly cheese. Knowing that he was Hindu, I offered to exchange my cheese pizza for his with the meat on them. He thanked me and we exchanged pieces.

I began the conversation by asking him his name and where he was from. Then I shared that I was on a journey of faith, and talked about my faith in God and Jesus Christ. To my surprise, Steven started asking me about things like, Abraham and Sarah, Josiah, Jesus and other people and situations in the Bible. I answered his questions, and asked some of my own on his understanding of the Bible.

As it turned out, he had studied many religions, including Islam, Judaism, Buddhism, as well as Christianity. Unfortunately, he had come to the conclusion that, whatever you believed, you had to believe and practice it in whole and, that it was your way to whatever end you chose.

Steven seemed to know how to live a Christian life better than many people I meet that claim to be Christian. He, however, being raised Hindu, had chosen to remain Hindu. I asked him how a Hindu achieved the state that they strove for. His response was that you have to live 1,700 lives and, at the end, you will reach your goal or become a god or something. I have to admit, he kind of lost me with the living so many lives.

I asked him if he wouldn't rather believe in One, omnipotent God, commit your life to Him, learn to love and serve like his son, Jesus, taught us to and then, after one life on this earth, live an eternity in God's presence? I don't know about him, but I don't think I could appease 330,000,000 gods in 1,700 life times.

Did I make a difference? I may not know until the end, but the last time I saw Steven, he was reading a New Testament.

Later that afternoon I met Dennis James, a Facebook friend and fellow Christian. Dennis has a ministry called Quantum Pork, which is an apologetic ministry for young people, who may be leaving the support of family and church to go to college, where their beliefs may, and probably will, be challenged.

We spent a couple of hours talking and he asked where I was going from there. I let him know that I would be headed back to Minnesota. With the journey God had laid on my heart done, I would be able to hitchhike and ask for rides. He surprised me by offering to buy a bus ticket for me. He made a phone call and everything was set up. On Saturday evening I would be on a bus, going home.

## Wednesday-November 18 – Saturday-November 21

Wednesday was the day ministries were allowed in the convention center to set up. It was, of course, a learning experience, as it was my first convention. I knew right away that this was bigger than I had expected. Some of the ministries had entire stores or living areas set up. I found a lady in charge of the booths and she set me up with a table at no charge.

The next few days I visited with the men in the shelter during breakfast, ministering and sharing my faith in God with them. Then spent the rest of the day meeting people, and attending training functions that were offered.

The main speaker was Jay Henry, a friend of mine, who is the president of Mid-India Ministries in Hyderabad, India, so I got a chance to catch up with him. He reiterated an invitation to host me when I get a chance to visit India.

I was preparing to leave the convention on Saturday afternoon. When I went to put my computer into its case, I discovered that someone had slipped a $50.00 bill into it, apparently during a time that I was out, walking around, saying goodbyes to some of the other ministries I had befriended. It was as though God was saying, "I'll take care of you to the very end."

As I was headed for the bus station, a wave of sadness overcame me. I was excited about seeing my family again, yet, at the same time, I was sad to have the journey end. I had met so many fellow believers, many inspiring me and, hopefully inspiring them to have a closer walk with God, and perhaps planting seeds in fertile ground.

I have come to realize, however, that this was not the end

of my journey, but the beginning.

# Epilogue

Since the end of the journey in November, 2009, I've traveled to Atlanta, GA to work with Brother Sean and Deep Waters Ministry, made a journey from Atlanta to Waverly GA, where I spent a week with Miss Lauren and Miss Harriett, gone to the Pine Ridge Indian Reservation in South Dakota, working with Wings as Eagles ministries and, again, journeyed back to Atlanta, where Brother Sean had offered to put me up in a room, doing work with the poor and homeless while I wrote the rough draft of this book. Each journey I have been on, God has taken care of me, through His children.

I have spent the last four years taking care of my mother, who has Alzheimer's, full time.

As a new season seems to be approaching I am planning a 5,500 mile bicycle ministry journey, ending at a YWAM school in Colorado.

I don't know all that that God has in his will for me, but I will continue to trust him. I know that, whatever it is, as long as I stay in God's will, He will provide.

No Mere Coincidences, a journey of faith

No Mere Coincidences, a journey of faith

Made in the USA
Columbia, SC
07 June 2017